The Politics of

THE POLITICS OF

PLACE

**Contentious
Urban
Redevelopment
in Pittsburgh**

Gregory J. Crowley

UNIVERSITY OF PITTSBURGH PRESS

Published by the University of Pittsburgh Press, Pittsburgh, Pa., 15260
Copyright © 2005, University of Pittsburgh Press
All rights reserved
Manufactured in the United States of America
Printed on acid-free paper
10 9 8 7 6 5 4 3 2 1

Library of Congress Cataloging-in-Publication Data

Crowley, Gregory J.
    The politics of place : contentious urban redevelopment in Pittsburgh /
Gregory J. Crowley.
        p. cm.
    Includes bibliographical references and index.
    ISBN 0-8229-5890-2 (pbk. : alk. paper)
    1. Urban renewal—Pennsylvania—Pittsburgh—Case studies. 2.
Community development—Pennsylvania—Pittsburgh—Case studies. 3.
Neighborhood government—Pennsylvania—Pittsburgh—Case studies. 4.
Political participation—Pennsylvania—Pittsburgh—Case studies. I. Title.
    HT177.P5C76 2005
    307.3'416'0974886—dc22
                                            2005014901

To James F. and Patricia A. Crowley

"Consensual democracy resolves conflict by defining it out of the political picture from the outset. Strong democracy is different. . . . It develops a politics that can transform conflict into cooperation through citizen participation, public deliberation, and civic education."

Benjamin Barber

Contents

Acknowledgments   ix

Abbreviations   xi

Introduction   1

1. Contentious Urban Redevelopment:
   A Research Perspective   7

2. Urban Restructuring and the Formation
   of an Urban Growth Coalition, 1920–1947   31

3. Contentious Politics of Neighborhood
   Redevelopment, 1949–1960   58

4. Another Wave of Urban Restructuring
   and Governing Realignments, 1970–1997   90

5. Contentious Politics of Downtown
   Revitalization, 1997–2000   112

6. Contentious Urban Redevelopment
   and Strong Democracy   140

Appendix   157

Notes   163

Bibliography   181

Index   195

Acknowledgments

Many people contibuted to this project. First, I would like to thank my academic mentor, Thomas Fararo, for his clarity, insight, and exceptional patience in support of my research. My interviews with civic leaders and officials would not have been possible without the assistance of Morton Coleman. Vijai Singh and Burkart Holzner provided encouragement for this project without sparing honest criticism that led to a much better final product. Thanks are due to many at the University of Pittsburgh, especially Carol Choma, Joshua Gregson, Akiko Hashimoto, Nancy Kasper, Tony Lack, John Marx, Eva Riecanska, Veronica Szabo, Amos Tevelow, Kimberly Whitaker, and Chris Wienke. The Andrew W. Mellon Foundation provided generous financial support.

I thank the community leaders whom I interviewed for the project: Mulugetta Birru, Pat Clark, James Murray Coleman, Harry Finnegan, Jake Haulk, Steven Leeper, Bernie Lynch, Patty Maloney, Cathy McCollom, James McGrath, Harold Miller, John Murdoch, Timothy Parks, John Rahaim, Mark Schneider, and Richard Stafford. I also thank staff members of the Archives of Industrial Society at the University of Pittsburgh, the Pennsylvania Department at the Carnegie Library of Pittsburgh, the Archives of the Historical Society of Western Pennsylvania, and the archives for Pittsburgh City Council.

The manuscript was greatly improved through the generous written comments of Amber Barnato, Joseph Coohill, Thomas Fararo, Kevin Fox Gotham, John Markoff, Kathy Newman, Joel Tarr, Jim Williams, and the anonymous reviewers of the University of Pittsburgh Press. Kendra Boileau Stokes of the Press deserves special thanks for supporting this project and encouraging me to finish it sooner rather than later. I also thank Kathy Meyer for her expert editorial work. I owe a great debt to my colleagues and students in the Sociology Department at Oberlin College. Daphne John, William Norris, Veljko Vujacic, James Walsh, Clovis White, and many excellent students supported my research and challenged me to become a better teacher.

Special thanks go to Amber Barnato. Her support, inspiration, and love have advanced this project in more ways than I can say. Lastly, I thank James F. and Patricia A. Crowley. Although they will never read this book, I have written it for them.

Abbreviations

CDBG	community development block grants
CDC	community development corporation
CED	Committee for Economic Development
CPP	Community Planning Program
CTAC	Community Technical Assistance Center
FHA	Federal Housing Act of 1949
HHFA	Housing and Home Finance Agency
LISC	Local Initiatives Support Corporation
MCC	Manchester Citizens Corporation
MDC	Mayor's Development Council
NRPB	National Resources Planning Board
NSPC	North Side Protest Committee
OBRA	Omnibus Budget Reconciliation Act of 1981
OPDC	Oakland Planning and Development Corporation
PAT	Pittsburgh Area Transit
PDF	Pittsburgh Development Fund
PEL	Western Division of the Pennsylvania Economy League
PHDC	Pittsburgh Housing Development Corporation
PHLF	Pittsburgh History and Landmarks Foundation
POTPC	Property Owners and Tenants Protective Committee
PPND	Pittsburgh Partnership for Neighborhood Development
PPWPC	Pennsylvania Post-War Planning Commission
PRPA	Pittsburgh Regional Planning Association
RIDC	Regional Industrial Development Corporation
SIF	Strategic Investment Fund
TIF	tax increment financing
UDAG	Urban Development Action Grant program
URA	Urban Redevelopment Authority of Pittsburgh

The Politics of Place

Introduction

■ In October 1999 Mayor Tom Murphy presented a bold new plan to remake Pittsburgh's distressed retail district. His "Market Place at Fifth and Forbes" plan proposed a $480 million redevelopment of downtown that would have demolished 62 properties and replaced 125 local businesses with upscale retailers and restaurants. Critics compared Market Place to the demolition and rebuilding projects of the renowned Pittsburgh renaissance, which cleared a total of one thousand acres of city territory in the twenty years following World War II. For over a year before the announcement, historic preservationists, neighborhood leaders, architects and planners, taxpayer advocates, eminent domain opponents, and people calling themselves "young professionals" openly challenged the mayor's plan. They held dozens of open meetings and demonstrations, circulated leaflets, protested at public hearings, and initiated an alternative planning process about the future of downtown that eventually superseded Market Place at Fifth and Forbes.

The Fifth and Forbes redevelopment controversy combined, in one episode, two seemingly incongruous forms of democratic participation. On the one hand, Murphy's challengers expressed their right and power to join together in "contentious collective action."[1] They interrupted, obstructed, and rendered uncertain his agenda, and they did so under the belief that it was the best way to get their voice heard in city hall. Political theorist Jane

Mansbridge calls contention a form of "adversary" democracy, where participants have conflicting interests and they maximize power to get those interests represented in a decision process. On the other hand, the mayor's challengers did more than force him to reconsider his commitment to Market Place. They created opportunities for themselves and others to participate face-to-face in a consensus-based, alternative planning process. Mansbridge refers to the consensual form as "unitary" democracy because participants share a priority and agree to reach a solution by talking and listening face-to-face.[2]

Face-to-face participation creates opportunities for "strong democratic talk,"[3] a process of mutual speaking and listening aimed at the discovery of common interests and the achievement of collective goals. In *The Rebirth of Urban Democracy*, Jeffrey Berry and colleagues argue that strong democracy requires institutions that ensure a sufficient "breadth" and "depth" of political participation. Breadth of participation refers to the extent to which each member of a community is given an opportunity to participate at every stage of the policy process, while depth ensures that those choosing to participate "have the opportunity to determine the final policy outcome by means of the participation process."[4] Following a long tradition of political thought dating back to Plato, Berry and colleagues emphasize that the best conditions for strong participation are found at the local level, where citizens can make political decisions in person. These scholars find strong democracy in cities like Birmingham, Dayton, Portland, St. Paul, and San Antonio, where norms and laws have been institutionalized that require direct neighborhood involvement in planning, redevelopment, and other policy areas. By mandating formal citizen involvement, neighborhood participation systems are said to be the most effective way to bring government within reach of ordinary people.[5]

But what about the many other American cities, such as Pittsburgh, that lack a comprehensive, citywide system for citizen participation? Can face-to-face decision making in a context of equal respect and mutual interest occur in places like this? I believe the

Fifth and Forbes process shows that it can, and my goal in this book is to explain how. How did contentious collective action in Pittsburgh between 1997 and 2000 create the conditions for strong democratic participation? I approached this problem from the tradition of comparative social science, which enables the investigator to explore complex patterns of similarity and difference among cases of roughly equivalent phenomena. Following the critics who compared Fifth and Forbes to early postwar approaches to urban regeneration, I selected four cases from 1949 to 1960 in which neighborhoods fought unwanted redevelopment agendas but failed to create the conditions for strong democratic participation. The four "negative" cases provided a basis for comparing what was characteristic of the "positive" Fifth and Forbes case.

The comparative analysis was based on research conducted in Pittsburgh from 1998 to 2002. In addition to dozens of scholarly articles and roughly five hundred newspaper articles, primary sources of data include municipal records, organizational documents (including letters, internal memos, and e-mail transcripts), and thirty interviews with local officials, civic leaders, and community activists. A detailed methodological summary is included in the appendix.

In chapter 1 I present the elements of contentious urban redevelopment, my framework for comparing the five cases and for explaining instances of political confrontation over the built environment in general. The framework is a result of integrating research perspectives from urban politics, urban sociology, and social movements. In order to answer my main research question—How do some instances of political contention in urban redevelopment unleash processes of strong democratic participation while others do not?—three related questions confronted in the urban politics and sociology traditions must be investigated: Who participates in urban redevelopment? What interests do participants bring to the redevelopment process? What are the structures that shape routine interactions among urban stakeholders? Scholars have found that in most places, except for those with functioning citizen participation systems, elites in government and business are prime movers of redevelopment projects. But neighborhood residents and other land-use stakeholders often challenge elite attempts to control land-use decisions, with mixed success. At issue in discovering the interests of participants is the importance of land use to the welfare of American communities. By identifying the stakes involved in land-use decisions, we can better make sense of why local officials often find themselves embroiled in controversial redevelopment projects. Finally, discovering the structures of urban governance sheds light on how elites in business and government manage to exclude other stakeholders from important land-use decisions—a situation that often leads to contentious politics.

Urban politics and sociology have less to say about how challengers of governing elites exert power through contentious or "noninstitutional" forms of participation. We need a vocabulary for analyzing urban contention if we are to explain why and how some contentious episodes generate strong forms of citizen participation while others do not. I have found such a vocabulary in the social movement tradition, where scholars have sought to explain the dynamic aspects of collective political struggle.[6]

In chapter 2, I set the context for the first four cases of contentious urban redevelopment in the urban restructuring of early postwar Pittsburgh. Against the background of a fading industrial economy, population dispersal, and severe environmental degradation, the stakes in land-use politics were indeed high. Future prosperity and a high quality of life in Pittsburgh depended on local policy solutions to the city's badly deteriorated commercial and residential properties. In 1946 Democratic Mayor David Lawrence and financier Richard King Mellon assembled an urban growth coalition that set in motion a renaissance vaunted for its far-reaching improvements to both the natural and built environments. Neighborhood politics in Pittsburgh during this period were shaped by two fundamental conditions. First, the "structure of political opportunities" was not favorable for people harmed by redevelopment who wished to challenge the corporate and government elite that gathered around Lawrence and Mellon. Second, challengers did not have the benefit of strong "mobilizing structures" for mounting and sustaining confrontations with elites.[7]

These structural disadvantages did not prevent leaders in affected neighborhoods from confronting the Lawrence-Mellon governing coalition. In chapter 3 I present my first four cases of contentious urban redevelopment in the order of their occurrence, between 1949 and 1960. Unfortunately for challengers, none of these episodes generated participation in the strong democratic mode. Three of the four movements collapsed with little to show for their efforts, and one led to concessions from the governing coalition.

Chapter 4 sets the context for my fifth case, using the same mode of analysis established in chapter 2. The region's economic crisis continued until the end of the century, with recession in the 1970s, the collapse of steel in the 1980s, and a "brain drain" in the 1990s. In 1994 the urban growth coalition was reformed, with government in a lead position. The built environment was again at the center of the urban revitalization strategy. Efforts focused on restoring the city's historic role as a regional capital and diversifying its economic base. Neighborhoods were now organized into redevelopment politics through community development corporations. The incorporation of neighborhoods did not eliminate the potential for conflict between governing elites and community leaders; nor did it guarantee the latter a strong voice in shaping the redevelopment agenda. Compared to their counterparts in the 1940s and 1950s, however, challengers in the 1990s benefited from a more open structure of political opportunities and more robust mobilizing structures in the form of nonprofit organizations that drew more support from broad social movements than from the local governing coalitions.

In chapter 5 I illustrate how the autonomous mobilizing structures and open political system affected the dynamics of contentious urban redevelopment on Fifth and Forbes. How did autonomous mobilizing structures in combination with a relatively open political system actually produce the transition from contentious collective action to strong democratic participation in the Fifth and Forbes case?

In chapter 6 I return to the literature on social movements and strong democracy to discuss what can be learned from comparing the five cases. By searching the qualitative data for patterns of political interaction that produced the outcomes in each case, distinctive features of Fifth and Forbes were brought into sharp relief. The nonprofit organizations that were prime movers of Fifth and Forbes fostered strong democratic participation by shaping the timing, sequences, and combinations of events across the approximately three-year episode of contention that began early in 1998. The chapter specifies crucial ways in which the pattern of events in Fifth and Forbes differed from the earlier cases and it describes a pathway from urban contention to strong democracy.

Some recent scholarship on civic engagement in the United States has tended to be critical of today's nonprofit organizations for undermining rather than facilitating community involvement in politics. Centrally managed, staff-driven organizations often do good things for the community, the argument goes, but they do less to connect citizens to one another and involve them directly in public policymaking.[8] If future research generalizes the findings of this study to other cases, the view that nonprofits undermine rather than facilitate civic engagement will require some rethinking.

1

Contentious
Urban Redevelopment:
A Research Perspective

■ Most research in the sociology and politics of urban redevelopment is aimed at explaining patterns of decision making with regard to land use and investment in the built environment.[1] Who usually defines alternative plans for deteriorated neighborhoods or tracts of vacant land? Who typically decides which among the alternatives gets the required government support? These are questions about the "structures"—the laws, norms, or cultural assumptions—that shape common forms of local decision making. My goals are different. I seek to explain how political and economic structures are disrupted in episodes of public, collective struggle. Similarly, I seek to locate the processes within such episodes that constitute or produce their varying outcomes.

In my first case, community leaders challenged a redevelopment agenda in the East End neighborhood of Highland Park. After a long battle in the summer of 1949, the city conceded by accepting a land gift from the neighborhood in exchange for a promise not to locate a Civic Light Opera amphitheater in Highland Park. In the second case, which began a few months after the resolution in Highland Park, merchants and property owners in the Lower Triangle challenged a proposal to clear seventy parcels of mixed-use buildings in order to erect the Gateway Center office and apartment tower. The city moved ahead in spite of opposition and by summer 1950 demolition of the Lower Triangle was underway. Also in the summer of 1950, the third case began, with residents of St. Clair and Spring Hill–City View protesting a proposal to locate public housing projects in their working-class community. But the city, as well as the courts, dismissed the residents' claims, opening the door for public housing construction in St. Clair and Spring Hill–City View. Case 4, the final episode from the early postwar era, began in the Lower Hill District in 1958 when a group of parishioners challenged the imminent demolition of the St. Peter's Church. The church was one of the few structures remaining in a project that ultimately cleared 1,324 buildings from the Lower Hill. Protesters met with no success in preventing its demolition and by 1960 construction in the neighborhood was underway for an 18,000-seat civic arena. In case 5, neighborhood leaders and historical preservationists prompted a struggle that later included a wide array of claim makers against the demolition of 60 buildings and removal of 125 businesses. The outcome, to reiterate, was strikingly different from the previous four in terms of opportunities for challengers and other stakeholders to participate face-to-face in the planning of alternatives to the mayor's proposal.

The first step toward explaining each of the three outcomes— concessions from the governing coalition (case 1), collapse of the movement (cases 2–4), and strong democratic participation (case 5)—is to locate the actors in contentious urban redevelopment and to define the interests underlying their participation. The next step is to account for why redevelopment grows contentious, which depends upon a clear understanding of the structures and processes of routine urban decision making that tend to marginalize some stakeholders and thereby incite contentious forms of political participation. The final step in the study of urban contention is to discover the combinations and sequences of interaction that produce varying outcomes across contentious episodes.

Locating Actors in Urban Redevelopment

Sociologist Floyd Hunter was among the first and most cele-
brated researchers to attempt to identify participants in urban redevelopment and other local policy areas. In his study of decision
makers in 1950s Atlanta, Hunter introduced the controversial
term "power structure" to describe a network of top financiers
and corporate executives capable of controlling the local policy
agenda.[2] Hunter's main method of conceptualizing power structure was to ask a panel of fourteen highly knowledgeable people
in community affairs to select the top ten leaders from each of
four lists of leaders in business, government, the nonprofit sector,
and social circles. Hunter found a remarkably high level of agreement on the panel as to who the top leaders were in the four
fields, which strengthened the validity of the resulting list of forty
community leaders.

Combining his "reputational" method with in-depth interviews of top leaders in the group of forty, Hunter was able to
identify important aspects of local decision making in several policy areas. In the area of urban redevelopment he revealed a
"closed" group of top leaders, mostly from the corporate business sector, which he called the "policymaking structure." Informally and in private, the policy-making structure moved many
important issues onto the public agenda. The group then established committees of lower-level leaders to carry out the policies.
For example, Hunter found that regarding Atlanta's controversial urban renewal program, nine top business leaders and four
government and other professionals had "laid the groundwork
for the program and determined its major outlines" before
assembling a somewhat broader "official committee" for implementing it.[3]

Hunter's followers applied his methods to power studies of
communities across the United States, most drawing conclusions
similar to his about the politics of urban redevelopment.[4]
Whether the issue was to initiate a federal urban renewal pro-

gram, finance a bond campaign for road construction, or create a district for business improvement, corporate business executives usually set the agenda, even if they organized leaders outside of business to carry out their plans. The "elite" view of community power advanced by Hunter and his followers presented a rather cynical image of urban democracy in the United States. Critics, however, rejected the methods of the elite theorists and their cynical portrait of democracy. Political scientist Nelson Polsby was perhaps the most persistent critic. He focused on problems related to Hunter's reputational method, arguing that it is impossible to determine who actually exercises influence over specific decisions by asking people who they believe has power. Just because business elites have reputations for power does not mean they will be united on all redevelopment issues or even have the time to examine them in sufficient depth to take a position.[5]

Polsby advocated the decision-making method developed by Edward Banfield and Robert Dahl in their studies of 1950s Chicago and New Haven, Connecticut, respectively.[6] Banfield and Dahl sought to measure actual rather than potential control over specific public issues by observing who initiated policy proposals that were ultimately implemented and who succeeded in vetoing proposals initiated by others. Decision-making studies, however, tended to complement the substantive claims of reputational scholars that important decisions in urban redevelopment were usually made by elites. Banfield depicted corporate business elites as prime movers in his case study of the hundred-acre Fort Dearborn urban renewal project, and Dahl showed that important decisions in New Haven's urban renewal were made by a unified group of professionals in government. Although redevelopment elites in New Haven were elected officials and political appointees, according to Dahl they behaved no differently than Hunter's corporate "power structure." The mayor, the development administrator, and the redevelopment authority director created an urban renewal proposal "in secrecy" and then "tested it for feasibility and acceptability" in the business community.[7] After securing corporate business support they created a half dozen citizen action committees to carry out different aspects of the plan—a central business district, harbor development, housing, and the like.

What makes the decision-making method distinctive is its emphasis upon the limitations of elite power imposed by underlying community divisions. Dahl, Banfield, and their followers observed multiple political factions, rival coalitions, and other "lines of cleavage" in local communities.[8] Through systematic observation of actual decision-making events, these scholars sought to understand how elites attempted to control community decisions. In New Haven, for example, Mayor Lee and his staff created their "bold and daring" renewal plan in secret because it gave them time to generate support from business leaders before releasing it to the public. They viewed business support as a crucial condition for earning the trust of other community stakeholders, thereby minimizing the likelihood of community conflict. Elites in New Haven could not simply have their way in matters of redevelopment. They were limited by the "attitudes and interests of various elements in the community" within which elites had to shape their proposals or risk a political backlash.[9] Similarly, Banfield painted a picture of elite power as quite limited in Chicago. By documenting decisions for and against Fort Dearborn, he observed that business elites who set the agenda had to expend personal "political capital" to get other elites, who stood to gain little from the demolition of downtown, to go along with their project. Implementation, Banfield concluded, is a different process from agenda setting and can easily be compromised by limitations in the stocks of political capital held by different elites.

With its emphasis on the problem of how elites attempt to control decisions and how others might contest such control, decision making is an essential method of research in contentious politics, and I used it to locate actors in the five cases. For each case I sorted through an array of qualitative data, including interviews, municipal records, organizational documents, and media accounts in order to identify who originated select public proposals and how other stakeholders defined themselves and their grievances in relation to the proposals.

While I adopt the decision-making approach, my emphasis is

somewhat different from the community power scholars. None of the decision-making studies systematically observed contentious politics—that is, the making of claims in episodes of public collective struggle. Contention is collective in that participation occurs through the coordinated activity of large numbers of people, as in a strike or protest, which distinguishes it from voting and other individual forms of participation. Contention is public in that the success of a participatory effort often depends on capturing the attention of a wide audience, as occurs in open meetings, public hearings, demonstrations, petitions, and marches. Contention is a distinct form of political participation that has been overlooked or obscured in the decision-making studies of community power.

As McFarland points out, the omission of contentious politics from community power research is partly a result of the pluralist theory that informed most decision-making studies.[10] Pluralism assumes that power on important issues is dispersed under the control of many persons and groups, as illustrated in the studies of Dahl and Banfield. Yet pluralists tend to overlook the structural imbalance in organizational capacity between elites who set agendas and other stakeholders wishing to challenge those agendas. This criticism of pluralism is implicit in Mancur Olson's theory of the "logic of collective action," which states that widely shared political interests will often fail to organize effectively because constituents have a rational incentive to "free ride" on the efforts of others.[11] On the other hand, small groups of elites do not suffer the same organizational problems and will therefore generally defeat their many, less well-organized opponents.

Political contention is one antidote to the collective action problem suffered by large groups. Constituted as it is in collective symbols and rituals, contentious politics both exploits and reinforces social solidarities that can motivate individuals to act politically even when it is not in their rational self-interest to do so.[12] People do not join in protests and demonstrations, participate in open meetings, or sign petitions out of rational self-interest. Such acts of contention express solidarity and commitment and demonstrate political efficacy to others, thereby creating potential for the diffusion of contention from more- to less-organized social groups.[13]

Political contention occurs when stakeholders who are excluded from elite decisions openly and collectively challenge those decisions. The four cases presented in chapter 3 preceded the fifth case (chapter 5) by half a century, yet all followed the same pattern of business and government elites making decisions and neighborhood activists challenging those decisions through contentious collective action. What interests underlie the involvement of each of these actors in urban redevelopment? Although interests are not always sufficient to motivate political participation, understanding the dynamics of contentious urban redevelopment requires that we know why public officials often risk political capital to promote controversial redevelopment projects, and what is at stake for neighborhood residents of redevelopment areas.

Interests and Urban Redevelopment

The most obvious stakeholders in land-use decisions are property investors, developers, and real estate financiers. Each has the potential to gain wealth from practices that intensify the use of properties and increase their market value. As any homeowner knows, the distinctive character of land as a commodity is that its value hinges on aggregate land uses of a larger area. For this reason, those who own, invest in, or develop properties for a living will have a great deal of interest in broader patterns of land use and investment in the city or region as a whole. It is no surprise that landed interests are found to be key players in the urban growth coalitions of many American cities.[14]

Less obvious stakeholders in the business sector are local media and utility companies that often advocate redevelopment projects they believe will help to grow the regional economy and its population. Population growth means greater circulation for newspapers and more users of utilities. Unions can also be major players since they benefit from the demolition and construction jobs created by large-scale redevelopment. Even nonprofit cultural organizations such as museums, symphonies, and operas are stakeholders in urban growth because they also benefit from a growing population. Many cities have "cultural districts," which are nonprofit real estate companies specializing in developing and managing cultural institutions.[15] Though not business organizations in the strict sense, these nonprofit organizations depend upon foundation grants and other sources of flexible financing that require them to operate like regular businesses. Generally, any group benefiting from economic investments that are captured within a municipality, region, or other territory is a potential player in an urban growth coalition.

Growth coalitions depend upon cooperation with local government officials to meet their land-use objectives. Local public policies shape the environment in which economic growth and redevelopment occur. Businesses in search of investment locations look for high-quality services at relatively low rates of taxation. Cities that levy taxes at significantly higher rates than competitors will be less attractive to investors. Growth coalition members can often be found advocating for a "good business climate" and will support politicians who share their policy goals. In their capacity to shape the policy context of economic growth and redevelopment, local governments play a role similar to state and national governments in the larger economy.

Yet local officials can be found doing much more than shaping the policy environment for redevelopment. Like New Haven's Mayor Lee, they often take a direct role in setting and implementing local land-use agendas.[16] Officials work closely with urban redevelopment agencies to acquire and clear specific properties located in areas targeted for redevelopment. Local governments also use low-interest loans, grants, and tax abatements to finance new construction and rehabilitation in targeted areas. But why should this be the case? Why should local governments in a commercial republic—where economic assets are privately owned and controlled—be involved in the controversial arena of real estate development?

Political scientist Paul Peterson has offered perhaps the most widely accepted account of the interests of local government in urban redevelopment.[17] Writing from the public choice tradition, Peterson views elected officials as rational actors competing in the market for votes, much like buyers and sellers compete in other commodity markets. In modern democracies, local officials win votes on the promise of improving their city's economic standing in relation to competing locales for capital investment. New investment increases demand for commercial real estate, which is reflected in rising land values and new construction or rehabilitation of buildings for office, manufacturing, and retail use. Residential real estate is stimulated in turn as business growth increases demand for labor, bringing new workers into the region's rental and homeowner markets. Capital investment, therefore, directly benefits the city as a whole. It increases the amount of tax revenue a municipality can generate at specific tax rates and thereby improves the benefit/cost ratio to taxpayers who finance municipal services. The more battles a city can win in the competition for mobile capital, according to Peterson, the more it can improve the benefit/tax ratio of its residents.

Peterson drew important conclusions about the politics of redevelopment in American cities from the rather obvious fact that American local government is quite limited when compared with the federal government. Unlike the federal government, municipalities can do little to control flows of capital and labor across their borders. Cities must focus on manipulating the use of land, the only factor of production they can regulate directly. They can use zoning and eminent domain authority to control the size and functions of land parcels within their boundaries. They can pursue large-scale real estate projects—stadiums, convention centers, retail developments—to make the city a more attractive place for firms and their employees. Or they can offer tax abatements, low-interest loans, and other flexible financing arrangements to firms that invest within their jurisdiction. Given the severe limitations on the scope of municipal power as well as the overwhelming importance of real estate development to the economic well-being of cities, it is easy to understand why, for Peterson, "urban politics is above all the politics of land use."[18]

All U.S. cities are the same, Peterson tells us, in their need to facilitate conditions for local economic prosperity. And all are limited to land-use intervention strategies for meeting the economic imperative. Yet if all cities must submit to the discipline of market competition, then each must formulate a land-use strategy reflecting the advantages and disadvantages conferred by its unique location within that market.[19] Global and national socioeconomic trends affect different cities in different ways. Scholars of the urban restructuring tradition argue that wide variations exist in the economic opportunities and constraints facing different cities at different times in history.[20] American cities in the past century, for example, have struggled much more than their European counterparts with problems related to the movement of businesses and residents away from the urban core. Deconcentration in the United States has transformed many central cities into "jobless ghettos," with intense racial and economic segregation.[21] Significant variations also exist among different cities and regions within national boundaries. In places like Boston and San Francisco, corporate service economies specializing in law, finance, and accounting created much higher-paying jobs than economies more dependent on manufacturing, such as Milwaukee, Detroit, and Pittsburgh.[22] Variation in the relative prosperity of regional economies is reflected directly in the value of taxable real estate in these regions and their central cities.

The perspective of urban restructuring emphasizes how changes in economic and demographic environments influence a city's governing arrangements, offering insight into a central question raised in the following chapters: why do local officials in Pittsburgh and other declining cities risk political capital by taking the lead on controversial land-use projects? Where central city real estate markets remain weak over long periods of time, politicians feel the effects perhaps more than anyone in their inability to finance high-quality services. Mayors in cities with rapidly growing corporate service economies may be able to choose a laissez-faire approach toward real estate development while their counterparts in declining industrial areas may not have that luxury. Mayors of declining cities who take the lead on projects that change the landscape or skyline often believe that such improvements will enhance the image of their city in the minds of investors and citizens. The symbolic politics of image building are frequently seen as more important to city leaders than the strict economic benefits and costs of alternative growth policies.[23]

Neighborhoods often challenge the city building projects of public officials, and they are the main challengers in the cases of urban contention considered in this book.[24] Neighborhood residents can participate in redevelopment decisions in various ways, depending upon the structure of local political opportunities. Contentious collective action is an alternative mode of participation for areas lacking regular access to government officials. Neighborhood leaders frequently make claims in the name of the "special-use values" of place. Sociologists John Logan and Harvey Molotch invented this term to indicate the additional benefits created and appropriated by a person who uses a particular place.[25] If urban growth coalitions are interested in the commodity or "exchange" value of places, neighborhood residents and many businesses value them for the practical benefits they provide in daily use. The existence of special-use values implies that places are unique, that one place is not interchangeable with another. Living in a particular place might locate a person near family who can help care for children; working in a certain area might help a person to realize the additional health benefits of walking to the office each day. And worshiping at a neighborhood church might create the additional benefit of maintaining close ties to one's ethnic community.

Because people realize additional benefits from using places, a great deal is at stake when places are exchanged and redeveloped. Redevelopment can change how places are used and who benefits from their use, and it is the fundamental condition of the politics of place in its contentious form, whereby stakeholders who lack regular access to government "resort to all sorts of 'extramarket' mechanisms to fight for their right to keep locational relations intact."[26] Why do neighborhoods and other stakeholders get excluded from redevelopment? Robert Dahl hints at an an-

swer to this question by emphasizing that effective coalition building requires public officials to carefully choose when, if at all, it is
appropriate to bring different stakeholders into the planning
process. Urban regime theory, the prevailing view on leadership
in urban politics today, explores the implications of Dahl's basic
insight.

Urban Governance and Contentious Politics

Urban regime theory is founded on the premise that political
power in U.S. cities is divided into separate spheres, with crucial
productive assets under private control and public authority
under the control of government officials. The formal powers of
government alone are insufficient to carry out important policy
agendas, so officials must seek informal ties with business leaders
who can enhance their "capacity to govern." When leaders from
business and government blend their resources for a common
purpose, an urban governing coalition is formed.[27]

Governing capacity that is sustained over the long term creates a regime, which leading regime theorist Clarence Stone defines as the "informal arrangements by which public bodies and
private interests function together in order to be able to make
and carry out governing decisions." "Governance through informal arrangements," Stone explains, "is about how some forms of
coordination of effort prevail over others."[28] Prevailing coalitions
usually include business elites but also, less often, other stakeholders because once business and government achieve a coalition
with governing capacity, they tend to exclude other stakeholders
whose resources are not required to carry out their policy agenda. Stone calls this "preemptive power," which conveys the idea
that elites exercise power in order to produce specific results in
an efficient manner rather than—as classic elite theory implies—
to control the behavior of others.[29] Residents, low-income housing advocates, and others defending neighborhood use values
often have few resources that officials perceive as useful to their
governing agendas. Officials must calculate whether the resource
contributions of marginal actors to a governing agenda exceed

the costs of including them in the coalition. With each additional member, a coalition bears higher costs in terms of managing conflict among potentially competing interests and goals. For this reason, nonbusiness stakeholders are often excluded by urban growth coalitions.[30]

In the U.S. political economy, businesses control investment decisions that create wealth and employment, which politicians depend upon for their electoral success.[31] This relationship of dependency expresses the "systemic power" of business.[32] Their privileged economic position places business interests at the center of governing coalitions, and they join with the government to preempt important policy agendas, in the process excluding other stakeholders perceived as unnecessary and inefficient complications to the process of agenda building. The potential for conflict originating in the marginalization of neighborhoods and other stakeholders from governing coalitions points to a third form of community power, that of social control.

Social control refers to an actor's capacity to overcome resistance to his or her desired agenda or to prevent the agenda of another. Marginalized stakeholders initiate a contest of social control when they collectively and publicly oppose redevelopment plans defined and advocated by urban growth elites. Yet regime theory overlooks the dynamic aspects of such conflicts. What happens after contentious situations arise? What determines their outcomes? With its emphasis on how power is created through systemic advantages and preemptive actions, regime theory gives only casual attention to processes and outcomes of urban contention. There is no denying regime theory's crucial insight into the question of how democratic incorporation occurs in U.S. cities: to gain a voice, stakeholders must match their demands with resources commensurate with the kind of agenda they wish to create. Resources such as land, capital, and professional skills, not the voices of opposition, gain the sympathy and respect of urban governing coalitions. But is it not possible for resources to be generated, and elites compelled to recognize them as valuable, by the processes of collective struggle? The results of two of my case studies suggest that it is.

Structures of Contention in Urban Redevelopment

Research in contentious politics explores how social processes unleashed in collective, public struggle produce varying outcomes in the presence of different structures. A structure is a type of scientific variable that is stable for individual cases but subject to variation from one case to the next. A main premise of process theories of contention is that outcomes of episodes are not determined by, and therefore cannot be deduced from, structural conditions. Structures enable some forms of social interaction and constrain others, but they do not determine their actual trajectories and outcomes. It is still necessary, however, to locate the structures that condition contentious episodes if a complete explanation of their outcomes is desired; therefore, I will draw upon the two main structural variables in social movement research: structure of political opportunities and mobilizing structures.[33]

In 1973 Peter Eisenger used the phrase "structure of political opportunities" to explain variation in protest behavior in forty-three American cities. He sought to identify the stable features of local political systems that affected "the degree to which groups are likely to be able to gain access to power and to manipulate the political system."[34] Eisenger's work inspired a new "political process" perspective in social movement research that seeks to explain why movements emerge when they do and how some succeed while others fail at accomplishing collective goals.[35]

Electoral rules are perhaps the most central formal dimension of local political systems. In cities, at-large electoral systems constrain political contention because they provide no incentives for elected officials to respond to claims of neighborhood challengers. Since the constituency of an at-large legislative body (for example, city council) is the city as a whole, members have no political obligation to advocate on behalf of a particular neighborhood constituency. At-large council members can afford politically to get behind legislation that may be unfavorable in one or more neighborhoods as long as they have the support of a majority of voters in the city. From the point of view of neighborhoods, at-large electoral rules create a more closed political system than district-based rules. Neighborhood leaders find natural allies in district representatives, who must be responsive to their concerns or risk electoral defeat. The implication is that neighborhood challengers in district-based systems should be more successful in getting government to respond to their claims than those in at-large systems, all things being equal.

Informal aspects of political opportunity structures are determined by analyzing a governing coalition's stability and its capacity to govern. I examine these measures for Pittsburgh in the two relevant periods of the study and find that in the early post–World War II period, the governing coalition was somewhat more stable than it was during the 1990s. Stable coalitions, or regimes, offer fewer opportunities for challengers to manipulate the political system than unstable coalitions, where weak or marginalized members might exploit external conflicts to strengthen their political positions. One key to stability in early postwar Pittsburgh was the concentration of substantial productive capacity in the steel industry and the control of much of the region's industrial wealth in the Mellon financial holdings. Governing arrangements in cities dominated by a single industry or firm tend to be more stable than those in cities with a decentralized economic structure. Dominant economic players such as Mellon hold the kind of systemic power that pushes them toward the center of governing coalitions, thereby maintaining the stability of governing arrangements over time. In a more diverse urban economy, as is illustrated in 1990s Pittsburgh, governance does not consistently revolve around the needs of a single firm or industry and the governing coalition is more prone to instability. The implication is that greater opportunities existed for marginalized stakeholders in the 1990s to gain access to government by challenging existing arrangements.

The governing capacity of Pittsburgh's growth coalition was a good deal more centralized in the earlier than in the later period. The ability to govern is expressed in preemptive power, "the power of authorities to implement adopted policies."[36] Urban coalitions with a strong and centralized capability to implement important policies can more easily ignore contentious claims of challengers than coalitions with a weak and/or decentralized capability. Building a strong and centralized ability to govern, as observed in midcentury Pittsburgh, leads to a greater political exclusion of those not formally incorporated in the governing coalition. It follows that coalitions with weaker, less centralized governing capacity must remain open to new participants in case they control resources commensurate to the governing agenda.

The phrase "mobilizing structures" refers to resources that challengers can access and convert into vehicles for mounting and sustaining collective actions. Examples of mobilizing structures include money, communications media, and meeting places, but also social structures such as family units, friendship networks, voluntary groups, work units, businesses, professional organizations, and government agencies that can facilitate resource mobilization.[37] The term "multiorganizational fields" encompasses the full range of social structures that have the potential to facilitate the mobilization (or demobilization) of a movement. The field of a movement may include local social structures or those with national or international scope.[38] In this study, the existence of national organizations as well as local groups connected to broader movements is a crucial structural variation. National and local federated organizations have been decisive in the outcomes of contention because of their independence from the growth coalition. Community organizations that depend heavily upon urban growth coalitions for operating resources are not likely to take the lead in challenging unwanted growth and redevelopment agendas because they might risk alienating their supporters and losing access to valuable resources. Autonomous organizations, those who depend less on the growth coalition, are better candidates for initiating a contentious collective action.

Regime theory and other familiar perspectives in urban politics have not paid enough attention to the role of autonomous national or local-federated mobilizing structures in urban political struggles. Too often urban political studies focus on the internal dynamics of coalition formation and their maintenance at the expense of a deeper understanding of the broader social context of community power. According to Gerry Stoker, the central challenge of urban political research today "is how to place the analysis within the context of wider processes of change . . . to connect local and non-local sources of policy change."[39] When cases of political contention are the unit of urban analysis, the investigator is forced to look beyond local boundaries to the broader multiorganizational field in which challengers are embedded. A comparison of the four case studies in chapter 3 with the fifth case in chapter 5 illustrates the decisive role that autonomous national and local federated organizations can have upon urban political processes and outcomes.

Integrating the structural ideas just discussed leads me to the following proposition: those who exert power by contentious means will be most successful when they face an open structure of political opportunities *and* benefit from access to autonomous mobilizing structures. Chapter 6 evaluates this hypothesis against the results of the five case studies. Are the outcomes in each case consistent with the expectations of the structural theory of social movements? For all but one, the answer will be yes. Challengers in case 1 had the benefit of neither an open structure of political opportunities nor autonomous mobilizing structures, but they did achieve concessions as a result of their collective actions. How can this anomaly be explained? More importantly, how did attributes of the structures of political opportunities combine with attributes of mobilizing structures to produce the predicted achievements in the other cases?

Dynamics of Contentious Urban Redevelopment

A mechanism-based approach to social explanation can provide answers to these questions. In the mechanism worldview, a complete explanation of an observed pattern between two variables, X and Y, consists of a description of how interactions among mechanisms $m_1, m_2 \ldots m_n$, emerging under condition X, generate outcome Y.[40] I follow Charles Tilly's definition of a mechanism as "a delimited class of events that change relations among specified sets of elements in identical or closely similar ways over a variety of situations." A well-known illustration of this is Robert K. Merton's "self-fulfilling prophecy," an event in which a false definition of a situation motivates behavior that makes the false definition come true.[41] A bank run is one of many situations produced by the self-fulfilling prophecy. Once a rumor of insolvency is started some depositors will withdraw their savings. This reinforces belief in the rumor, causing more depositors to withdraw, producing more withdrawals, and so on until bankruptcy becomes a reality. The same thing can occur in a wide variety of other circumstances, for instance in neighborhood segregation patterns or presidential primary elections.

Social processes in each case of contention are produced by interactions—"frequently recurring . . . chains, sequences, and combinations"—among specific types of mechanisms.[42] I selected mechanisms catalogued by Doug McAdam, Sidney Tarrow, and Charles Tilly, which I adapted for my purposes of analyzing the politics of place. Once a set of crucial mechanisms recurring across some or all cases was identified, it was then possible to construct a mode of representing their patterns of interaction that constituted or produced varying outcomes in each (see chapter 6). A mode of representation spells out how mechanisms, once activated, "produce the observable concatenations forming observable patterns."[43] Brief definitions follow for seven mechanisms depicted in all or some of the case studies: category formation, attribution of political opportunity, social appropriation of resources, brokerage, object shift, polarization, and certification.[44]

The mechanism of "category formation" creates new social identities. A social identity forms as members of a collectivity agree on a boundary distinguishing themselves from and relating themselves to some other actor or actors outside the boundary. In the politics of place social identities arise among neighbors who share the use of a locality from which they derive special values, as discussed earlier. When people perceive a threat to special-use values, they grow more reflexive about their underlying attachments to the threatened locality. Of course, a collective identity category does not take shape mechanically among neighbors once the physical structures in their neighborhood are threatened. Rather, identities are socially constructed. Challengers must invest resources to "align" the categories of potential recruits with those of the movement. Once stabilized, a category serves to both name an aggrieved group of people and to "underscore and embellish the seriousness and injustice of a social condition" experienced by the group that could motivate members into action.[45]

In the politics of place, the "unjust" use of eminent domain to acquire private property for redevelopment is a common source of collective identity formation. When multiple property owners are involved, they endure a common experience that facilitates the definition of a common grievance. But it takes skill and invention to define categories that withstand assaults from a hostile environment.[46] Robust categories evoke emotional reactions, such as anger at being excluded from a plan that demolishes one's place of business or a sense of injustice at having the state acquire one's property only to turn it over to a developer who can put it to more "productive" uses. Emotions are evoked through rituals, rhetoric, and popular symbolism, as the case studies in this book will demonstrate.

But urban growth coalitions attempt to prevent the spread of opposition to their plans by undermining the sense of injustice generated in the categories constructed by challengers. This can happen in two ways. The first is by articulating a "territorial ideology" that emphasizes the common interests of the residents of a city, regardless of the differences among them.[47] Promoters of redevelopment, for example, claim that their projects improve the economic standing of the city as a whole. All residents benefit when a city becomes "major league" or "world class," or when it achieves national visibility, even if residents or small businesses in redevelopment areas bear the disproportionate costs of these accomplishments. A second tactic of urban growth elites is to "try to make their projects *faits accomplis* by getting them as far along as possible without any kind of public input."[48] When public attention cannot be avoided, they can frame issues in narrow technical terms of relevance only to experts. This starves challengers of the information they need to make credible claims against the growth coalition. If the city is merely "conducting a feasibility study" for a new stadium but has "no immediate plans" to pursue such a project, there is little to create a burning sense of injustice among those who might be threatened by it.

"Attribution of political opportunity" occurs when challengers identify a change in the political environment as an occasion for making contentious claims. Contention increases when people perceive a lifting of existing constraints on their action or coming events and resources that might facilitate action. As an example, the Christian Right viewed changing electoral alliances in the Reagan era as an opportunity to organize a national movement through the Republican Party.[49] The attribution mechanism is different from the structure of political opportunities discussed earlier, for two reasons. First, it indicates that a shift is underway in a previously stable political structure, for example when growing internal conflicts weaken the governing capacity of an urban regime. Second, attribution operates through the perceptions of challengers, who mobilize when they both perceive structural changes and define those changes as occasions for mounting collective actions. Thus, attribution of political opportunity depends upon the previous formation of a collective identity category.

If mobilizing structures are the resources accessible to challengers, then "social appropriation" refers to the process of converting resources into vehicles for mounting and sustaining collective action. The existence of strong mobilizing structures, however, does not guarantee that a movement will take advantage of them in a timely or strategic way. With poor leadership, valuable resources available through social connections could be squandered or overlooked. Alternatively, people with few resources of their own could win respect and their movement gain support from sympathetic allies by demonstrating strong collective identity and strategic responsiveness to shifts in political opportunity. Thus, social appropriation often works in combination with identity formation and attribution of political opportunity.

"Brokerage" is another mechanism that can lead challengers to identify and gain access to resources not available to them prior to the emergence of contention. It occurs when two previously unconnected sites are linked by a third site that mediates relations between them. Sometimes in the course of a conflict previously unconnected people find themselves making contentious claims in the same time and place, which can lead them to share resources and struggle together on a common front.

"Object shift" transforms relations between challengers and the objects of their contentious claims. Herbert Gans illustrates object shift in his study of neighborhood resistance to federal urban renewal in Boston's West End.[50] Beginning in 1956 a Committee to Save the West End opposed the city's plans to demolish their neighborhood and relocate seven thousand low- and moderate-income residents. After failing repeatedly to prevent the Boston Redevelopment Authority from moving ahead with demolition, the committee shifted its object of claims to federal lawmakers, who ultimately had the authority to terminate Boston's West End urban renewal project. Students of U.S. social movements argue that the multilevel structure of American federalism provides multiple opportunities for object shift, which can reinvigorate waning social movements. For example, gay rights activism in the 1960s occurred at local, state, and federal levels simultaneously, and successes at one level frequently strengthened activism at other levels.[51]

According to McAdam, Tarrow, and Tilly, object shift is important for two reasons. First, it can activate new allies or opponents in contentious struggles, such as when national politicians are drawn into local policy debates. Second, object shift affects the "repertoires of contention" available to challengers.[52] For example, claim making in courts is governed by more restrictive rules than claim making in city council hearings. As illustrated in my first four cases, early postwar property rights battles against eminent domain tended to shift into the courts rather quickly, where judges determined their outcomes to the detriment of property owners. Property rights attorneys in the 1990s had learned from this experience and began advising clients to fight their struggles in the "courts of public opinion."

"Polarization" widens the differences between governing elites and challengers in contentious episodes. Conflict bystanders will often remain neutral, contributing nothing to either side and thereby sustaining an existing balance of power. Polarization infuses disputes with strong ideological and emotional content, activating new stakeholder categories and generating sympathy from observers who get drawn into conflict on one side or another. New contenders change the existing balance of power and ultimately determine the outcomes of social struggles.[53]

"Certification" of actors, their actions, or their claims by third parties is fundamental to the creation of allies who can sustain the momentum of a contentious challenge. Challengers generally welcome certification by legitimate authorities and experts, but also benefit from decertification of claims or actions of their opponents. Certification often acts in combination with the object shift mechanism. New actors such as courts can get drawn into a struggle through object shift and subsequently play a certifying role.

Each of these mechanisms is activated in at least two of the five cases studied in this book, as noted in table 1.1. Four are active in all the cases. But more important than the number of mechanisms is "the ways they combine, in what sequences they occur, and why different combinations and sequences, starting from different initial conditions, produce varying effects."[54] The cases produced three different outcomes for challengers—concessions,

TABLE 1.1
Mechanisms activated in five cases of contentious urban redevelopment

Mechanism	Cases
Category formation	1, 2, 3, 4, 5
Social appropriation of resources	1, 2, 3, 4, 5
Object shift	1, 2, 3, 4, 5
Certification	1, 2, 3, 4, 5
Attribution of political opportunity	1, 3, 5
Brokerage	3, 5
Polarization	1, 5

collapse, and strong participation. A complete explanation of each case involves identifying the processes that produced its outcome and locating the crucial causal mechanisms in those processes.

Conclusion

This study differs from other political research on urban redevelopment because it emphasizes how stakeholders struggle to gain a voice in policy making by challenging, disrupting, and rendering uncertain the structures of local governance. Such a research effort is valuable because it begins an exploration of how some instances of collective struggle create opportunities for meaningful citizen participation while others do not. Direct citizen participation in neighborhood land use and redevelopment projects gives palpable expression to our collective aspiration for a democratic way of life. It is therefore worthwhile to understand the conditions and processes that facilitate broader and deeper forms of neighborhood participation, especially in those cities where formal, citywide systems do not exist.

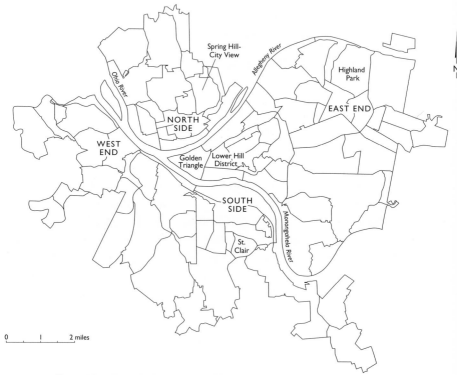

Spring Hill-
City View

Allegheny River

Highland
Park

Ohio River

NORTH
SIDE

EAST END

WEST
END

Golden
Triangle

Lower Hill
District

SOUTH
SIDE

Monongahela River

St.
Clair

N

0   1   2 miles

City of Pittsburgh. Map by Bill Nelson.

2

Urban Restructuring and the Formation of an Urban Growth Coalition, 1920–1947

■ Over the course of the nineteenth century, Pittsburgh became one of the largest and fastest growing places in the nation. Located at the confluence of three major inland waterways, the city served as southwestern Pennsylvania's connection to the world beyond. The advantages of river transportation were fully exploited during the Industrial Revolution, when the region's abundant supply of bituminous coal was tapped to meet escalating demand for iron and steel production.[1] By 1865 the region accounted for 40 percent of national iron production and by 1900 had captured 30 percent of national steel-making capacity. The rising output of Carnegie Steel, the region's largest metals manufacturer at the turn of the century, illustrates the velocity of this industrial growth. From 1888 to 1900 the steel behemoth increased production from 600,000 to 4,000,000 tons, about a million tons less than the total output of England at the time.[2]

Table 2.1 indicates how industrial expansion affected population growth in Pittsburgh's Allegheny County. By 1910 the county's population had grown to nearly six times its size at the start of the Civil War. This increase was reflected in the rising proportion of all U.S. production workers and the general population located in the Pittsburgh region between 1870 and 1920, as shown in table 2.2. Immigrants accounted for much of this growth. Thousands of newcomers, especially from southern and eastern Europe, were drawn to the unskilled and semiskilled jobs created by steel, glass, electrical equipment, aluminum, packaged food, and other industries that multiplied along the banks of the Ohio River and its tributaries. The abundance of immigrant labor kept wages down and was vital to Pittsburgh's success as a low-cost center of manufacturing. By 1890 a full 65.9 percent of Pittsburgh's residents were either immigrants themselves or children of foreign-born parents.[3]

The built environment of the city developed as rapidly as its economy and population. Between 1868 and 1900 Pittsburgh annexed numerous municipalities on its southern and eastern borders, increasing the city's land area from 1.77 to over 28 square miles. Streets were lit with natural gas, cable cars and electric trolleys replaced horse-drawn trolleys, and a central business district consolidated in the "Golden Triangle." "Skyscrapers" first appeared downtown in the 1890s, portending the gradual replace-

TABLE 2.1
Population growth in Allegheny County

Year	Population	Decennial Population Growth (%)
1860	178,831	–
1870	262,204	46
1880	355,869	35
1890	551,950	55
1900	775,058	40
1910	1,018,463	31
1920	1,185,808	16
1930	1,374,410	15
1940	1,411,539	03

Source: U.S. Census, *Population of States and Counties of the United States: 1790–1990, Pennsylvania, Population of Counties by Decennial Census: 1900–1990*, March 27, 1995; and U.S. Census, *Report on Population of the United States at the Eleventh Census, 1890*, table 4, Population of States and Territories by Counties, at each Census, 1790–1890.

TABLE 2.2

Pittsburgh region as a percentage of the United States in population and production workers

Year	Population	Production Workers
1870	1.02	1.9
1880	1.05	2.0
1890	1.25	2.5
1900	1.43	3.0
1910	1.60	3.0
1920	1.66	2.9
1930	1.65	2.6
1940	1.58	2.4
1950	1.45	2.4
1960	1.33	1.7
1970	1.17	1.4
1980	1.01	1.1

Source: Adapted from Houston, "Brief History," 46.

ment of factories and residences with corporate headquarters. Twenty-two major buildings, ranging from twelve to twenty-six floors, were erected between 1900 and the end of World War I, and another fourteen were constructed from 1923 to 1934. The boom in construction of downtown office towers, department stores, hotels, banks, and government buildings was paralleled by a wave of suburban residential development. More and more, Pittsburgh's professional and semiskilled office workers were becoming a population of commuters, delivered to and from the central business district each day by a vast network of electric trolleys.

Pittsburgh began to lose prominence as a hub of industrial production as quickly as it had gained it. Confronted with growing competition from emerging industrial regions and stabilizing world demand for manufactured goods, the Pittsburgh economy faltered after 1920, even as the economy of the United States continued to expand.[4] In terms of population, between 1900 and 1940 Allegheny County grew at an average of only 16 percent per decade, bottoming out at 3 percent in the 1930s. This represented a substantial reduction from the 44 percent average rate of growth in the decades between 1860 and 1900, which peaked at 55 percent in the 1880s (see table 2.1). In terms of employment, 1920 marked the end of six decades of job growth in manufacturing. In the 1910s the annual average number of wage earners in manufacturing peaked at 173,561 for Allegheny County. The number had dropped to 155,374 by 1930 and then to 124,216 by the start of World War II.[5]

Table 2.2 expresses these population and employment trends as a decline in the region's share of national industrial employment and population after 1920. Thus, in both absolute terms and relative to competing cities, Pittsburgh's industrial supremacy had peaked by the second decade of the twentieth century. By the 1930s the region's greatest challenge was to create a more diversified economic base. As the demand for steel began to fall rapidly during the Great Depression, Pittsburgh failed to nurture new industries to offset the loss of jobs in metals manufacturing. In contrast, Detroit, St. Louis, Cleveland, Milwaukee, and other Midwestern industrial regions were expanding into automobiles, household appliances, and other high-demand consumer goods.[6] Due to its overrepresentation of employment in coal and steel, Pittsburgh suffered more from the Depression than competing metropolitan areas.[7] In 1934 about one-third of Pittsburgh's labor force was out of work, and those fortunate enough to have jobs were forced to work at a fraction of pre-Depression wages.

For public officials the most alarming consequence of urban restructuring was the sharp decline in property values, which they depended upon for municipal revenues. The assessed valuation of downtown property values plummeted by some $18 million per year in the 1930s. The Depression forced many downtown businesses into bankruptcy, while those that survived often reduced their operations or sought cheaper office space in suburban locations. The net effect was a significant reduction in demand for downtown office space, where vacancy reached a peak of 40 percent in the years leading up to World War II.[8]

Residential properties also lost value. Rising unemployment

and the resulting downward pressure on real wages for employed workers helped fuel a wave of home mortgage defaults. In 1926, 400 homes were lost to foreclosure in Allegheny County, climbing steadily to 909 by 1929, and 3,406 by 1935. Not until after World War II did the foreclosure rate dip below its 1926 level.[9] Housing foreclosures reflected the more intricate problem of urban "blight" that spread across many parts of the city. One of the most distressed neighborhoods was the Lower Hill District, located at the northern edge of downtown. The Hill was a low-rent area that had provided thousands of immigrants with inexpensive housing in the peak years of industrial expansion. Among the city's most ethnically diverse neighborhoods, the Hill was a first stop for eastern and southern Europeans arriving in search of economic opportunity. The loss of manufacturing jobs after World War I, along with a gradual resettlement of the Hill's better-off residents into growing suburban areas, contributed to a steady erosion of neighborhood property values. Between 1914 and 1956, assessed valuation fell 45 percent in the Lower Hill, a much steeper decline than the citywide average of 16 percent. Creeping blight in the Lower Hill worsened the predicament of downtown, as more and more corporate executives questioned the desirability of the Golden Triangle as a place to do business.[10]

Severe environmental degradation was a further deterrent to real estate development in the central business district. The problems of flooding and coal smoke were deeply embedded in the collective memory of Pittsburghers. Downtown businesses had always lived under a constant threat of river flooding. The Saint Patrick's Day Flood of 1936, the worst in the city's history, reminded Pittsburghers of the vast destructive powers of their rivers. After a continuous day of rainfall and heavy ice melting, on March 18 the Ohio River crested at forty-two feet. This was twenty-one feet above flood stage, enough to put most of the Golden Triangle under several feet of water. Forty-six people were killed, 384 injured, and over 100,000 people went homeless. Thousands more went without transportation and clean water.

High-volatile bituminous coal was burned in southwestern

Pennsylvania as far back as the 1750s in the garrison at Fort Pitt. Environmental historian Angela Gugliotta finds that in 1804 local policy makers had already begun discussing coal smoke as a public problem.[11] Competition with Wheeling, West Virginia, and other nearby commercial centers, however, drove Pittsburgh to exploit its advantages in manufacturing, and by the Civil War bituminous coal had come into widespread use for domestic and commercial heating, materials processing, manufacturing, and railroad transportation. In 1889 the Ladies Health and Protective Association organized the first sustained antismoke movement in Pittsburgh. Emphasizing the health hazards of smoke, these middle-class women backed a series of ordinances to control the production of smoke in home heating devices.[12] Yet many local politicians and business elites resisted efforts to restrict smoke. Growth in the metals industry, virtually synonymous with smoke, was essential to local prosperity. "Expansion of industry," as Gugliotta puts it, "was regarded as a necessity, and complaints about smoke were characterized as threatening sustenance."[13]

In 1911 the prominent Mellon financial interests founded an institute for industrial research at the University of Pittsburgh, which began a major research effort to investigate the smoke control problem. The Mellon family had substantial regional investments in oil, aluminum, chemicals, glass, and real estate, in addition to steel. Since the family fortune was less dependent upon steel than the regional economy as a whole, it was not unthinkable for the Mellons to spearhead a new campaign against the smoke produced by coal-fired steel mills.

In the 1930s Richard King Mellon assumed control of the family enterprises and quickly emerged as a leading advocate for eliminating smoke, flooding, blight, and other pressing problems in the built and natural environments. He helped found the Golden Triangle Division of the Chamber of Commerce in 1939, and served as its first head. The purpose of the new division was to facilitate a broad effort to "stop depreciation of real estate values within the Golden Triangle" by improving mass transportation and automobile flow in and out of the central business district, dealing with the flood issue, enforcing the city's smoke ordinance, and other measures for making the Triangle "a better place in which to work and transact business."[14] The Chamber of Commerce viewed the physical transformation of the Golden Triangle as an important step toward attracting new corporate headquarters into the central business district and preventing existing businesses from leaving.[15]

Pittsburgh enjoyed a brief resurgence of growth from wartime industrial expansion during the 1940s. The federal War Production Board authorized approximately $511 million between July 1940 and June 1944 for new or expanded industrial plants in the region, most of which ran at full capacity throughout the war. While helping to bring unemployment down to manageable levels in the early 1940s, wartime investment also had the unwanted effect of reinforcing the region's dependence on the metals industry.[16] Over 90 percent of wartime expansion occurred in capital goods industries that were already dominant in the region. An article written in 1942 by Bervard Nichols of the University of Pittsburgh's Bureau of Research reflected the pessimistic attitude many urban professionals had adopted toward the region's postwar economy. Nichols wrote that in spite of wartime production, retail sales continued to decline and population gain was far less than in other regions. "The great involvement in war business," Nichols warned, "without important new industries to take up postwar slack, make the postwar outlook very discouraging."[17] There is no question that a war economy helped the city recover from the Depression, but in the long run it served only to defer and even worsen the onset of an impending economic crisis.

The Intergovernmental Context for Urban Regime Formation

As I will show later in this chapter, the civic involvement of R. K. Mellon exemplified a new generation of leaders in Pittsburgh who exhibited a conviction to urban regeneration unmatched by elites in earlier periods. It should be clear from the preceding discussion that if elite commitment to civic action was strengthened in the 1930s and 1940s it was commensurate to the escalating economic and environmental problems of the time. Nothing less than the total involvement of the wealthiest and most powerful individuals in the region would be sufficient to rectify the city's worst problems in the areas of flooding, smoke and water pollution, traffic and parking congestion, and urban blight.

The Golden Triangle Chamber of Commerce was one in a series of new organizational vehicles that would be used to define and carry out the renowned Pittsburgh renaissance. A "minor miracle" in terms of its repercussions for the built and natural environments, the renaissance symbolized the wealth of problem-solving capacity created when civic leaders and government authorities put aside their differences and establish a pattern of cooperation. With governing capacity highly centralized, however, regime insiders had little incentive to facilitate broad citizen participation. Moreover, the absence of autonomous structures for mobilizing neighborhood opposition meant that neighborhood leaders would meet with great difficulty in expressing their dissatisfaction with redevelopment planning (see chapter 3).

Before I discuss the nature of the urban growth regime that formed in the six years following the creation of the Golden Triangle Chamber of Commerce, I first want to outline important features of the intergovernmental context that set the parameters in which the regime took shape. How local leaders respond to opportunities and constraints of urban restructuring is shaped in important ways by their relationships with higher levels of government.[18] My main objective here is to locate in both national policy discourse and state and national legislation the origins of the public-private partnership form of governance on which Pittsburgh's regime was modeled.

Planning historian Mel Scott makes the case that the governmental context for postwar redevelopment in American cities was shaped significantly by a national movement organized during the war to prepare for eventual conversion to a peacetime economy.[19] As early as November 1939, once American combat overseas seemed inevitable, President Roosevelt instructed the National Resources Planning Board (NRPB) to concentrate on mobilizing the country in preparation for postwar planning. Under the authority of the National Industrial Recovery Act, Roosevelt had created the NRPB as a mechanism for coordinating state and local construction projects in order to stimulate economic recovery from the Depression. The NRPB, however, was no mere economic development agency. Board appointees such as Frederic A. Delano, uncle of the president, and Charles E. Merriam, founder of the Social Science Research Council, viewed their role as nothing less than a catalyst for changing national thinking about "the place of the urban community in the American economy."[20] As national urban problems intensified in the 1930s, these men believed that local officials would welcome federal support in the difficult battle against urban blight. The mobilization for postwar conversion was an opportunity to demonstrate the value of national planning in the effort to rebuild American cities.

In the early 1940s NRPB officials advanced their planning agenda along several fronts. They conducted research on urban problems; coordinated the actions of state and local planning bodies, private institutions, and other stakeholders in urban regeneration; and put together an innovative urban planning model for cities to follow as they prepared for the postwar conversion. In 1943 the planning model was outlined in a widely distributed booklet, "Action for Cities: A Guide for Community Planning." The model pointed out both immediate and far-reaching community benefits of rehabilitating or rebuilding deteriorated neighborhoods. Demand for construction workers would lead to immediate jobs for returning veterans, thereby keeping national unemployment low in the early postwar years. More fundamentally, redevelopment projects would make cities safer, cleaner, better places to live and conduct business over the long term. If done properly, redevelopment could protect America's massive investments in municipal infrastructure and regenerate existing urban communities.

The model's emphasis on physical rebuilding of communities, if far-reaching, was hardly controversial. In the Depression, the National Association of Real Estate Boards (NAREB) had sought government support for the assembly of dilapidated or abandoned properties for large-scale redevelopment.[21] But the lobby was downright hostile toward the bold approach to coordinating the rebuilding effort as outlined in "Action for Cities." All relevant community institutions, according to the booklet, needed to have a role in the redevelopment process, and each role would be defined according to a long-range community plan.[22] Moreover, "Action for Cities" assumed that federal officials would act as consultants in the broad areas of land acquisition and planning for new land use, which meant they could influence choices affecting whether projects would primarily be commercial or residential, serve lower or higher income groups, and so on. Some American communities had experimented with long-range planning, but few had succeeded in achieving the level of organization, and coordination with higher levels of government, suggested in "Action for Cities."

No sooner was "Action for Cities" released when congressional critics of comprehensive planning, prodded by NAREB and others opposed to comprehensive planning, voted to eliminate the National Resources Planning Board. Though it did not succeed in establishing the practice of comprehensive planning in American communities, the NRPB must still be credited with drawing national attention to the impending postwar conversion problem and arousing other, less controversial organizations into action.[23] One such group, the Committee for Economic Development (CED), assumed a prominent role in the planning movement after NRPB's demise. Founded as a national research organization in 1942, the CED advocated for limited government intervention in the economy as a means of curbing fluctuations that had dislocated people and undermined the security of economic assets during the Depression. Like the NRPB, the CED viewed changes in the built environment as a means of resolving long-standing urban problems. But the CED was an organization of businesspeople, and they differed from the national planning agency in advocating "the least possible government intrusion into the affairs of private enterprise."[24]

The CED urged private business firms to take the lead in forming "public-private" partnerships for planning the readjustment of urban areas to a peacetime economy. The idea behind the partnership model was that public expenditures and public authority (such as eminent domain for land assembly) could be used to prepare properties in distressed areas for private real estate investments that would regenerate U.S. cities. Insofar as partnerships were used to create investment opportunities in cities, NAREB and its research arm, the Urban Land Institute, supported the concept.[25] The real estate industry was deeply interested in the problem of urban blight, which had reached epidemic proportions in U.S. cities by the 1930s. From the real estate point of view, blight was the product of obsolete land uses (for example, unused rail yards adjacent to central business districts) and the exodus of affluent sectors of the population to outlying areas. Accordingly, NAREB supported government involvement in clearing obsolete structures and underwriting a part of the costs of preparing sites for private investment.

In the early 1940s many states established postwar planning commissions that embodied the principles of public-private partnership.[26] In Pennsylvania, Governor Edward Martin requested in 1943 that the state assembly form a Pennsylvania Post-War Planning Commission (PPWPC). The structure of the commission reflected the convictions of the planning movement that corporate executives rather than government officials should take the lead on community revitalization. First, PPWPC did not have resources of its own but relied upon support from businesses and nonprofit groups, giving them control over its direction. Second, the commission was chaired by a corporate executive and administered by people in government, business, and the nonprofit sector representing different regions of the state. It held no legal authority to coerce anyone to cooperate on a postwar development agenda, but focused on creating incentives for business, government, and nonprofits to allocate their resources around a shared vision of urban revitalization.

The PPWPC played an important role in establishing the legal and political framework for postwar planning in localities across Pennsylvania. Anticipating new federal legislation that would provide financial assistance to municipalities with "instrumentalities" to acquire land and clear redevelopment sites, the group lobbied successfully for the state Urban Redevelopment Law.[27] The legislation, which passed in 1945, enabled communities to establish quasi-independent development agencies with powers to issue tax-exempt revenue bonds, condemn and clear "blighted" properties using eminent domain, conduct studies of possible redevelopment areas, and buy, sell, lease, and manage properties. The anticipated legislation was the Federal Housing Act of 1949 (FHA), which distributed government assistance for local development projects and created incentives for cities to build affordable housing.

Title I of the act provided loans and grants enabling cities to cover losses incurred in the difference between the cost of acquiring and clearing "blighted" properties for development and the market values of prepared sites. Without the federal subsidy to cover the "write-down" cost, few cities could afford to engage in urban renewal. Title I was popular among national policy makers because it distributed benefits to a wide constituency. Businesses in central cities welcomed the new investment opportunities, mayors and city councils viewed it as a tool for increasing tax revenues, and social welfare leaders hoped it would clean up slums and improve the living conditions of the poor.[28] But the very popularity of the legislation led to a basic contradiction in how it was used. Liberal sponsors of the FHA intended it as a tool for improving housing conditions in inner cities, through rehabilitation or clearance and rebuilding of dilapidated buildings. But conservative business interests viewed the legislation as a tool for "upgrading" the character of the central city—including its buildings, public spaces, and the people benefiting from its use. A transformation in Pittsburgh was underway almost immediately after the war, after business interests began to establish a governing coalition.

Forming an Urban Growth Regime

In the early 1940s the Chamber of Commerce confronted several obstacles to its improvement plan for the Golden Triangle.

Perhaps the most intricate problem was the lack of any sustained interaction between civic elites—who viewed politicians with mistrust and tended to favor limited government—and politicians who acted more as "brokers" between interest groups than agents of the public good.[29] The Mellons and other prominent, wealthy families were personally distant from public affairs, preferring to support civic groups like the Chamber of Commerce and the Civic Club. These voluntary associations had played important roles in smoke control, housing, and other movements for civic betterment in the 1920s and 1930s, but progress often moved slowly, in decades rather than years. In order to forestall Pittsburgh's economic crisis and reverse its physical deterioration, a new form of partnership was needed that could organize top corporate and government leaders to act quickly on common objectives.

Another obstacle to postwar redevelopment was government weakness and fragmentation. No public agency had the financial, technical, or legal resources to acquire and redevelop deteriorating properties inside and adjacent to the central business district; no countywide legislation existed to control the production of smoke from railroads and outlying industrial boroughs; and there was no citywide agency capable of purchasing downtown properties, building badly needed parking facilities, and leasing or managing them as needed.

A declining tax base posed a third major challenge to rebuilding the city. Assessed valuations in the Golden Triangle recovered somewhat during the war years, but they continued to decline at the rate of about $10 million a year in the eight years following the Depression. In the city as a whole, assessed valuations fell from $1.2 billion in 1936 to $960 million in 1947. Thus, municipal revenues were shrinking when, in fact, a massive infusion of investment was needed for new projects. The decline of real estate in the Golden Triangle was "a matter of grave concern" to business and political leaders, who made it their top priority after the war to rebuild the "commercial heart" of their city and region.[30]

Democratic Party leader David Lawrence understood the political gains that a partnership with civic and business leaders could bring to his party, and he took the crucial step during his 1945 mayoral campaign of calling for a new era of cooperation in Pittsburgh. In the final days of Lawrence's campaign against his Republican opponent, the state Republican administration announced its support for construction of a new "Point Park" on the site of a dilapidated freight yard at the tip of the Golden Triangle, along with a limited-access highway in a nine-mile stretch connecting downtown Pittsburgh to its eastern suburbs. "The announcement was to embarrass me and make me lose the election," recalls Lawrence. But the candidate welcomed the news, a symbol of his desire to work alongside, rather than against, the Republican state administration. Lawrence praised Governor Martin's support for redevelopment in Pittsburgh: "It was such commitments from the state that I and the Democratic city administration had been hoping for, working for, begging for."[31]

In the first week of his administration, Lawrence gave an address to the Chamber of Commerce stressing the need for "teamwork" between his administration and the business community. "The future of Pittsburgh demands teamwork," Lawrence declared, "teamwork between government, business and labor. . . . That is the only way to protect our common future, which is our city's future."[32] Many Republicans in the business community were impressed with Lawrence's overtures and his apparent sincerity about solving the city's long-term problems. Business leaders who were aligned with the chamber's goal of central business district improvement understood that they needed cooperation from local government, regardless of which party was in control. This meant putting old rivalries aside and "giv[ing] the new Democratic mayor a chance and maybe some support."[33]

In 1946 Lawrence began a series of meetings with top business leaders in the Mellon corporate network to form a public-private partnership along the lines suggested by the Committee for Economic Development during the war.[34] The result of these efforts was an urban governing coalition hailed by the national press as a revolution in local public and private relations.[35] Several scholars have characterized Pittsburgh governance as "corporatist," a form of government that seeks to minimize unregulated political competition between business, workers, consumers, and other political groups. Members of a corporatist system tend to view excessive conflict as a misuse of resources that are better spent sustaining a capacity to carry out important policy agendas. The corporatist solution to conflict is to "incorporate" major interests into formal decision-making structures—to make them "partners" in government.[36]

As urban regime theory explains, the strength of participation in corporatist politics varies with the degree of a group's control over resources useful to a governing agenda; groups lacking valued resources get excluded from the corporatist agenda. Top business leaders became the main partners of government in early postwar Pittsburgh, with the universities as secondary participants. Neighborhoods, labor, and other community stakeholders had limited resources and lacked the organizational tools for allocating resources toward a public agenda. As a consequence, they played a very small role, if any, in planning the Comprehensive Program for improving Pittsburgh after World War II.

Beginning as early as the 1890s, a small number of downtown banks gradually came to dominate the financing of industrial expansion in Pittsburgh. Historian Edward Muller estimates that by 1941 Pittsburgh banks held more than 50 percent of the region's finance capital.[37] Mellon Bank, in particular, became the region's largest financial interest, with significant holdings in Gulf Oil, Koppers Company (chemicals), Alcoa (aluminum), U.S. Steel, Westinghouse Air Brake, Pennsylvania Railroad, Pittsburgh Plate Glass, Pittsburgh Consolidation Coal, and several other corporations in the region. Mellon's enormous financial interest in Pittsburgh made him an ideal figure to rally the corporate community around the goal of economic diversification and physical modernization that the PRPA, the Chamber of Commerce, and the City Planning Commission had been advocating since the 1930s.

The main instrument for consensus formation and coordination among executives was Mellon's extensive network of interlocking directors. The bank's twenty-eight directors held 239 seats on the boards of 185 different companies in the region. Mellon himself held twenty directorships, keeping him on familiar terms with corporate leadership across the region. The face-to-face relationships among directors of Mellon companies created a sense of mutual trust or "social capital" that Mellon could call upon when he needed leadership or political support for urban regeneration projects. From David Lawrence's point of view, Mellon was "a sort of bell cow in Pittsburgh; as he moved, others moved with him."[38]

In 1941 Mellon became president of the Pittsburgh Regional Planning Association (PRPA), a vehicle by which top business leaders sought to facilitate action on the improvement of downtown. To consolidate the effectiveness of the PRPA as an instrument for setting a postwar planning agenda, Mellon put considerable effort and money into creating the Allegheny Conference on Community Development.[39] The group was incorporated as a nonprofit organization in 1944 by six leaders in business and civic affairs. The main decision-making vehicle of the conference was an executive committee of twenty-four chief executives of Pittsburgh's top corporations. Executive committee members were required to participate personally in committee deliberations, a policy meant to ensure their familiarity with the objectives of the Pittsburgh improvement program and their ongoing commitment of resources to the effort.[40]

According to Wallace Richards, the first secretary of the executive committee, the conference was "a new kind of partnership . . . an intelligent, working group of potent citizens" created for the purpose of overcoming an "ingrown tradition of frustration and pessimism" in the area of civic engagement.[41] Park Martin, an engineer who spent much of his career as top planning officer in the Allegheny County Department of Public Works, served on the conference's first executive committee from 1944 to 1958 and as executive director from 1945 to 1958. He wrote a narrative of his experience in which he emphasized that the first fifteen years of conference activity centered on Pittsburgh and the central business district rather than other parts of the region. The thinking behind this emphasis began several years earlier in the Golden Triangle Chamber: diversification in the regional economy hinged on consolidating the Golden Triangle's strengths as a commercial center. "It was a matter of taking care of first things first," as Martin put it, and this meant "that the pressing problems in Pittsburgh must be solved if the region as a whole was to remain healthy."[42]

Martin took the crucial step of inviting selected public officials, including Mayor Lawrence, to serve as ex officio members of the conference sponsoring committee. In the early months after its founding, a broad cross-section of interests beyond the business community and government were involved in conference activities, including universities, professional planners, and even labor leaders. But by 1944, it had become evident that "the policymaking authority, the financing, and the day to day work of the conference fell primarily to its business and private-sector 'public' members who controlled the purse strings and were best able to cooperate among themselves to set priorities for the organization."[43] Over a period of five years, the United Smoke Council, previously an autonomous organization, was brought into the conference as an affiliated working group; the Chamber of Commerce was assigned various tasks under conference leadership; and the PRPA had become the planning arm of the executive committee. Under conference leadership, each voluntary group carried out a vital function in the program to improve Pittsburgh.

The Western Division of the Pennsylvania Economy League (PEL) was another important player in the postwar planning agenda. Originally founded in 1936 as part of the government reform movement that was sweeping through U.S. cities, by 1946 the PEL had become the primary research arm of the conference and was later placed under conference direction. The PEL, along with the PRPA, generated a wide body of research that was used to frame the postwar redevelopment agenda. In 1947 conference chairman Robert H. Doherty announced the "Pittsburgh Package," a far-reaching legislative agenda that ultimately paved the way for many of the achievements associated with the renaissance, including comprehensive, countywide smoke control, garbage and refuse disposal, transit and traffic improvements, and development of parks and recreation facilities. Doherty stressed that professional research conducted by the PRPA and PEL was essential to defining the package and to creating political support for it. The aim of the conference was "to have the most thorough and complete compilation of facts and information ever assembled on the Allegheny Region."[44] City agencies did not have the budget to conduct research of the same quality and consistency as the conference and its affiliates, and this severely restricted their role in the planning process. The conference "formulated the essential program" for postwar urban regeneration and then "submitted its plans to the city for approval and implementation."[45]

The conference and its affiliates defined the postwar redevelopment agenda, but they could not implement their plans without a corresponding degree of unity in the Democratic Party. The party owed much of its identity and strength to the leadership of David Lawrence himself. As chairman of the Allegheny County Democratic Committee since 1920, and the Pennsylvania Democratic Party since 1934, Lawrence rebuilt a moribund Democratic political machine and led it to victory over Republican rivals during Roosevelt's New Deal.[46] Lawrence was both mayor of Pittsburgh and chairman of the county Democratic Committee during the ascendance of Democratic politics in the 1930s. As county chair, Lawrence was responsible for selecting Democratic candidates for City Council and making informal recommendations for appointments to public agencies. He shared this role with a policy committee that consisted of elected officials in the city and county.[47]

The Democratic Committee had a policy of endorsing candidates it wanted to see in office and allocating party resources toward supporting them. The committee could also "purge" those in office for not performing according to expectations. The Democratic Party increased in popularity and strength under

Lawrence's leadership.[48] Candidates who were independent of the party were hard-pressed to prevail in an election against party-endorsed candidates, giving City Council members and other elected or appointed bodies strong incentives to "go along to get along" with the policy agenda of the conference and its affiliates. "Those who consistently opposed [Lawrence's] program," according to Lawrence biographer Michael P. Weber, "were almost without exception dropped in a subsequent election."[49]

Lawrence continued a practice established by council president Thomas Kilgallen of assembling council in private to air out differences, negotiate, and reach compromise on important issues. Private meetings were intended to ensure that council could resolve controversial issues before assembling for public sessions; hence, they were able to maintain an image of unity. Weber finds that as the public began to react favorably to the renaissance story, Lawrence's council meetings evolved into briefings on the policy agenda of the conference and its affiliates. Not even the city budget was passed without conference influence, as Lawrence would regularly give the budget to the Pennsylvania Economy League for review before presenting it to council.[50] Lawrence's control over council is illustrated in his success at getting council to approve his proposals. From the beginning of his first term in 1946 through his last day in office in 1959, council rejected under a half dozen proposals put forth by Lawrence.

The structure of local government was an important contribution to stability and unity in the public sector. In 1901 a business-backed charter created a "strong mayor" form of government, giving the mayor administrative authority over city departments such as the Department of Public Works. Another reform in 1911 replaced a dual council system, which elected members by district, with a single, nine-member council elected at-large. This second reform was good for the postwar redevelopment agenda because it freed the mayor's hand-picked legislators from pressures that might have caused them to voice strong independent views on renewal projects affecting residents and businesses in their districts.

Taking advantage of the 1945 state Urban Redevelopment Law, on July 1, 1946, the conference recommended to the mayor and City Council that they create a redevelopment authority in order to implement the rebuilding of the city.[51] On November 18, council and Mayor Lawrence established the Urban Redevelopment Authority of Pittsburgh (URA), and at the urging of the conference executive committee, Lawrence became its first chairman. The conference's sponsorship of the URA and Lawrence's appointment as chairman typifies the close working relationship between government and business that generated a capacity to make and implement important policy decisions. Following the successful model of the URA, council established a parking authority, public auditorium authority, sanitation authority, and tunnel authority, the key public institutions of corporatist governance during the renaissance years.

Louise Jezierski argues that the Urban Redevelopment Authority both extended the capacity of the mayor's office to guide regional development and shielded it from conflicts arising in electoral politics.[52] The same can be said for the other public authorities. Authority directors were appointees of the mayor, which made it hard for them to cultivate independent political followings. The "invisibility" of authority activities, moreover, tended to mitigate the extent to which they became subjects of political conflict.[53] Operating more like businesses than political organizations, the network of "quasi-independent" public agencies channeled resources away from the Democratic Party and thereby insulated the program of urban regeneration from patronage style politics.[54]

Urban Redevelopment and the Structure of Political Opportunities, 1943–1949

The corporatist regime in Pittsburgh created few opportunities for citizens not affiliated with the conference or the Democratic Party to participate in postwar planning. The closed structure of political opportunities was rooted in the systemic power of its corporate business members, resulting from the intersection of two conditions: a high concentration of manufacturing, especially steel, in the regional economy, and extensive Mellon financial holdings in the region's leading manufacturing industries. In the decade after 1953, when some of the biggest renaissance projects were underway, 44.1 percent of workers were employed in manufacturing, considerably higher than the national figure of 35.0 percent.[55] And even in the early 1950s, almost three-quarters of all regional manufacturing workers were employed in the metals industry.[56] With its enormous influence over the production of jobs and wealth in the region, the Mellon corporate network had a great advantage in dealing with local government. And Mayor Lawrence proved himself a capable and willing partner by pledging his full support for the conference's agenda for creating a more productive and dynamic regional economy.

But systemic power alone does not produce a closed political system. Only when systemic advantages are used to govern preemptively does a political system approach closure. Pittsburgh in the first half of the twentieth century was no exception, a point that is illustrated in the formation of a plan to manage growing problems of traffic, parking, blight, and obsolete land uses in the Golden Triangle. Traffic and parking problems in particular had grown steadily worse with increased automobile use after World War I. In 1918 fifteen influential businesspeople formed the Citizen's Committee on City Plan in order to "prepare and secure adoption of a comprehensive city plan."[57] Under the direction of executive secretary Frederick Bigger, the Citizen's Committee produced six reports between 1919 and 1923 that outlined plans for new playgrounds, major street changes, public transit, parks, railroads, and waterways. Bigger was a proponent of comprehensive planning and a vocal critic of the "short-sighted" attitudes toward planning in Pittsburgh and the "political accommodation" that obstructed serious action on the comprehensive plan during the 1920s and 1930s.[58] There was little sustained cooperation between civic leaders and public officials on long-term policy goals, and government decisions "were usually made on the basis of interest group pressures and coalitions, rather than commitment to a comprehensive plan that expressed the public interest."[59] The consequence was a city government that frequently agreed upon the ideals of comprehensive planning but did very little to put them into practice.

The challenge of long-term planning was made more difficult by the sheer number of organizations involved in land-use decisions. For example, five agencies were involved in highways and bridges: the city and county Departments of Public Works, a Civic Art Commission, the County Planning Commission, and a Joint Planning Conference, which included members from the County Planning Commission, City Planning Commission, and the Citizens Commission. No comprehensive plan could be carried out without cooperation from these and other organizations accustomed to making decisions based on the distribution of power. Until fragmentation of public authority and political competition could be overcome, there was little hope of overcoming the "piecemeal" approach to planning so loathed by Frederick Bigger.[60]

Fiscal strains caused by the Depression led the Citizen's Committee (renamed the Municipal Planning Association) to close its doors in 1933. But in 1936 the organization was revived by Richard King Mellon and other prominent industrialists concerned about growing urban distress and aligned with Mellon's vision of rebuilding the Golden Triangle—Howard Heinz of the H. J. Heinz Company, banker and publisher A. E. Braun, steel executive Ernest T. Weir, and chairman of Gulf Oil William Larimer Mellon. Wallace Richards, who later became secretary of the conference executive committee, was hired to run the new planning group, a role in which he "became one of the prime movers behind the civic spirit that created the new Pittsburgh." Frederick Bigger became the group's technical consultant until he resigned in 1940 after becoming chairman of the City Planning Commission.[61]

In 1938 the revived organization became the Pittsburgh Regional Planning Association (PRPA) and launched its first major effort, a $50,000 Arterial Plan for Pittsburgh by New York planner Robert Moses. Moses recommended a $38 million ten-year plan for correcting downtown traffic conditions. Additionally, he proposed an $8 million reconstruction of the Golden Triangle's "point" that would rid the area of a deteriorated railroad yard, facilitate traffic flow across two existing bridges, and create a landscaped Point Park. These suggestions advanced the Golden Triangle Chamber of Commerce's goal of making downtown a more desirable place to do business and reversing the spread of blight.[62] The Moses study succeeded in its intention to "coalesce all previous study and spur action" on the redevelopment of downtown. The PRPA immediately formed a committee, chaired by R. K. Mellon, to study and promote a parkway connecting the Point with the new Pennsylvania Turnpike to the east. Another committee, chaired by department store owner Edgar J. Kaufmann, studied and promoted capital improvements in the Golden Triangle. Mayor Cornelius Scully appointed a Point Park Commission in October 1940 to negotiate with the National Park Service over the possibility of reconstructing Fort Pitt as part of a national park.[63]

Creation of the PRPA marked a sharp increase in the commitment of private resources toward planning and implementing comprehensive improvements to the Golden Triangle. The stepped-up involvement of business and civic leaders in turn catalyzed greater commitment of public officials and more cooperation across the public and private divide. The foundations of a prevailing coalition for redevelopment were beginning to taking shape, though at some expense to city and county planning staff. They resented that the business community had gone "over the heads" of local planning officials in paying an "outsider" to conduct a study of Pittsburgh. Moses did not consult local planners before beginning his research, yet his own study "covered ground already studied and reported upon" by them. Although the overall recommendations of Moses's arterial plan differed little from earlier city and county studies, some of its priorities, especially regarding Point Park, did not reflect those of local planners. County planning officials viewed the park as a separate, less pressing, issue from the traffic plan. Frederick Bigger and his staff at City Planning favored the construction of a national park at the Point to commemorate Fort Pitt, a project that would have imposed such restrictions on the use of the land as to rule out the traffic improvements suggested in the arterial plan. In Moses's mind the two bridges already located at the Point, which would be extremely costly to move, "determined that traffic rather than history must be the decisive factor in the reconstruction of the apex of the Pittsburgh Triangle and in the establishment of Point Park."[64]

In July 1940 the PRPA hired Robert Moses's right-hand man, William Chapin, as their chief engineer, a move that suggested which planning priorities would ultimately gain the support of influential business leaders. Further action on the major improvements suggested by Moses would have to wait until after the war, at which point the construction of Point Park became a vehicle for consolidating the governing capacity of the postwar urban growth coalition.

Immediately after the war the Point Park Commission and City Planning Commission retained landscape architect Ralph E. Griswold as a consultant for a national historical park. "The City people were determined to have a national park at the point," Griswold later unhappily recalled.[65] He was frustrated with the national park idea, which in his mind restricted the site's potential to serve multiple needs, including the management of automobile traffic. Griswold's dissatisfaction with the historic interests led him to accept an offer by the PRPA in July 1945 to work on a broader concept for the Point that would tie it into a proposed state office building.[66] With the full support of the PRPA, Griswold and another landscape architect, Charles Stotz, set to work creating a plan for the Point that ultimately displaced the concept of a national park with that of a state park that allowed for new traffic interchanges connecting downtown with other parts of the region.

In October 1945 Park Martin and Wallace Richards presented Griswold and Stotz's "Point Park Development Study" to Governor Martin, who soon after announced the state's contribution of $57 million toward their proposed improvements to the Point.[67] With the priority and basic design of Point Park decided by the PRPA and the state administration, its implementation depended upon significant cooperation from public officials. This was all but assured when David Lawrence, in the midst of his first mayoral election, pledged full support for his Republican opponents' vision for Point Park.

The State of Pennsylvania acted as developer of the thirty-six-acre Point State Park, but support from the city was needed to vacate streets and from the county to remove the county-owned Point Bridge. To expedite these actions, the conference created a Point Park Committee, which included members of the conference and Chamber of Commerce, as well as Mayor Lawrence and County Commissioner John J. Kane. The composition of the committee illustrates the conference's basic strategy for building governing capacity in the postwar era, combining as it did top business and civic leaders with the highest-level public officials in the city and county. "The power and prestige represented in this committee," according to Park Martin, "was such as to guarantee success to the project."[68]

The City of Pittsburgh owned over half of the thirty-six-acre redevelopment area, including streets, wharves, and some buildings, which Mayor Lawrence readily agreed to donate to the state. But the largest private landowner was the Pennsylvania Railroad (PRR), where R. K. Mellon served as a director. Mellon was on the steering committee of the Point Park Committee, which took the lead in negotiating with PRR on a price for the properties. The nature of these negotiations illustrates how Mellon's extensive influence in the business community, in the context of the new public-private governing coalition, could serve to facilitate action on a controversial issue. R. K. Mellon's close advisor Arthur Van Buskirk represented the steering committee in negotiations with PRR, which began in March 1946. The railroad was unenthusiastic about the prospect of abandoning the crucial node in its interstate network located at the Point, and expressed hostility to the use of eminent domain to acquire the property. In his communications with PRR, Van Buskirk "included frequent reminders of the fact that he worked for Richard King Mellon . . . and could tap the resources of the Mellon enterprises." Several offers were made and one year passed before the two parties agreed on the selling price of $4.25 million.[69]

The chain of events—beginning in 1936 with the founding of the PRPA and ending in 1947 when the conference secured the largest parcel of land for the building of Point Park—illustrates how the accumulation of governing capacity among business and civic elites came at the expense of other legitimate stakeholders in the redevelopment process. The privately financed PRPA, rather than constituted planning authorities, effectively determined that Point Park would become a top priority in postwar planning. Along with the conference, the PRPA also determined the shape of the park and its uses. These organizations underwrote a set of architectural plans for the park, arranged for Governor Martin to view them, and organized the leadership necessary to overcome commercial resistance to their full implementation.

Conclusion

The essential political vehicle for rebuilding Pittsburgh at the end of World War II was a store of preemptive power created by business and civic leaders in the form of the Chamber of Commerce, PRPA, the Allegheny Conference, and the public and private governing coalition. The corporatist-style system of decision making that resulted from the new institutions offered limited opportunities for participation by those not aligned with the goals of the conference or the Democratic Party. Corporatist planning aimed at minimizing conflict through efficient policy decision and implementation.

The systemic power of business also played a role in closing the structure of opportunity for those wishing to express dissatisfaction with the planning process. With the region overwhelmingly dependent on industrial wealth and jobs, especially in the metals industry, the Democratic Party of David Lawrence had every interest in meeting the preferences of R. K. Mellon and his network of industrial leaders, and he worked closely with them to revitalize the city. With substantial control over much of the region's wealth in the hands of R. K. Mellon, the corporate business community could act with uncommon unity in support of urban growth projects, which Lawrence and his council would approve with matching unanimity. There was no well-organized audience for opposition, in government circles or in the broader community.

Despite the closed structure of political opportunities, collective struggle did occur after 1949 as the renaissance moved into Pittsburgh's neighborhoods. In the Point Park project the city owned a large share of the needed properties, with the remainder held by railroads, warehousing companies, and other businesses represented on the conference. Residential and mixed-use neighborhood renewal involved a new set of stakeholders, those seeking to preserve the special-use values attached to places in which they lived and worked.

3

Contentious Politics of Neighborhood Redevelopment, 1949–1960

■ From 1949 to 1960 redevelopment in Pittsburgh grew contentious as it moved into the city's neighborhoods. Strategies for neighborhood revitalization during this period included both the rehabilitation of existing structures and the demolition and rebuilding of structures considered "blighted" according to the broad criteria established in the state urban redevelopment law. In those areas designated for demolition and rebuilding, the procedure in the 1950s was for the Urban Redevelopment Authority to condemn and acquire properties by eminent domain, to remove some or all residents and businesses, demolish some or all existing structures, and then to rebuild according to plans financed, researched, and formalized by the Allegheny Conference on Community Development and its affiliates with minimal input from neighborhood residents.

In this chapter I will discuss how four communities reacted to the city's attempt to condemn and acquire neighborhood properties during this period. In each case community leaders responded by mounting collective and public challenges to the condemnation process. Similar mechanisms and processes propelled contention in each instance, producing similar results for neighborhood challengers. With one exception, challengers failed to prevent the city from authorizing the redevelopment of their neighborhood. The one exception, I will argue, resulted from temporary shifts in political opportunity brought about by the collective struggle itself. Generally, however, neighborhood activists suffered from a lack of autonomous mobilizing structures and faced a corporatist-style regime in which public officials had little incentive to include their voice in the decision making.

Case 1: Condemnation and Resistance in Highland Park, July 1949

Neighborhood challengers of growth politics win concessions when officials change or withdraw a contested land-use proposal but stop short of including their challengers into an expanded governing coalition. Residents in the East End neighborhood of Highland Park won concessions in 1949, after a long summer of protest against the conference's land-use plan for their community. The Highland Park case illustrates how neighborhood resources commensurate with a governing agenda can be discovered in the course of the collective struggle and then be used by neighborhood leaders to bargain for concessions from public officials. Highland Park was the first widely controversial neighborhood redevelopment proposal of the Lawrence administration, and the only one in the decade after 1949 that ended favorably for the challengers.

Beginning in 1946, the Pittsburgh Civic Light Opera (CLO) established a national reputation in musical theater through performances at the University of Pittsburgh stadium. Active conference member Edgar Kaufmann was a loyal patron of the arts who understood that an athletic facility was hardly suitable for the Broadway-quality musicals produced by the CLO. When he offered the opera a $500,000 gift for construction of an amphitheater, Mayor Lawrence responded immediately with a matching contribution from funds secured in municipal bonds. Kaufmann contacted conference chairman Edward Weitlein to get corporate support behind the proposal. The executive committee referred

Kaufmann's request to the PRPA, which responded with a site selection study paid for by the conference.[1]

The PRPA proposed that any new public facility be owned and
maintained by the city and receive private financial support.
Highland Park was the top choice of the site selection committee.
Due to its thinly settled population, the neighborhood had an advantage over the alternatives considered by the committee, such
as the Lower Hill and North Side, because it did not involve expensive land acquisitions requiring relocation of thousands of existing residents. In late spring 1949 a team of civil engineers
entered Highland Park unannounced and began surveying several neighborhood properties. Alarmed by rumors that the city was
starting a major redevelopment project, residents formed a committee to appropriate resources for a protest campaign.[2] They so-
licited ten dollars per household to hire lawyers to defend their
interests against the city. On June 17 they contacted City Council,
whose members claimed to know nothing about a survey or construction project in Highland Park.

Then, on July 5, 1949, City Councilman A. I. Wolk introduced
an ordinance "authorizing the taking, using, appropriating and
condemning by the City of Pittsburgh" of six acres of property on
North Negley Avenue in Highland Park.[3] The proposed location
contained most of the estate of Robert B. King, uncle of R. K. Mellon, and sections of several smaller residential properties. Immediately after the ordinance was announced, the Highland Park
committee circulated a petition door-to-door, which collected
over one thousand signatures, and encouraged residents to have
their voice heard at one of the scheduled open meetings or public hearings on the condemnation issue. In meeting other residents face-to-face, the committee sought to form a category, a
common grievance defining residents in opposition to the city
that could motivate subsequent collective action. According to
the committee, the city was perpetrating an injustice against the
residents by destroying their special-use values, the "tranquil and
pleasant" residential character of Highland Park that would be
overcome by arena-generated noise and traffic. Members of the
committee also believed that the city would be acting unfairly and

perhaps illegally in taking private property for purposes of building a cultural facility, especially because affected residents were not included in the decision making about the civic arena. Attorney for the protesters Vincent J. Burke claimed that the proposed condemnation would have a "disastrous effect" on neighborhood property values, privacy, availability of parking for residents, and the enjoyment of their front porches. Burke identified the main injustice suffered by his clients as "the terrible power of eminent domain" that the city would invoke to acquire properties once condemnation was approved. Residents were seeking to protect the quality of life provided by the local community setting—its quiet, residential character, availability of parking, and high property values. But in order to protect the community, they believed, they had to protect their property from the city's land-use agenda.[4]

Overwhelmed by the swift reaction to Wolk's ordinance, City Council agreed to a request by Burke to hold a public hearing the same week for the benefit of the residents. In making the request, Burke framed the question for council: "Why take property from private citizens for this project when there is plenty of space available in other parks?" Over three hundred residents of the neighborhood crammed into council chambers to protest the condemnation at the public hearing. Residents were boisterous and unruly during the session. Council introduced an array of experts supplied by the conference and its affiliates to explain the reasons for the selection of the Highland Park site. Each was booed and mocked continuously, to the point that presiding councilman William Stewart announced he had given up hope of maintaining order.[5]

The neighborhood challengers benefited from certification of their claims against the city by Burke's team of attorneys. A central issue facing council and the URA was the legality of the use of eminent domain for purposes of creating an entertainment center for the city. Burke argued on behalf of the residents that the city "could not lawfully condemn and take private property for amusement purposes," and that "if they can do this, they could build a ball park like Forbes Field in your back yard."[6] Burke had raised a legitimate concern, since the use of eminent domain for such purposes had not yet been tested in the courts. He explained further to council that Philadelphia and St. Louis recently had built new theaters without the taking of private property. In addition to Burke's comments, sixteen residents spoke about issues ranging from traffic and parking problems resulting from the proposed arena, its effect on property values, and the destruction of the overall quality of life in the neighborhood.[7]

The three hundred Highland Park protesters attributed political opportunity to temporary divisions among elites within the urban growth regime. During the spring primary election cycle City Council members Edward Leonard and Joseph McArdle had been falling out of Mayor Lawrence's favor due to the mayor's inability to control them on important policy issues. From the beginning of his tenure in council, Leonard had consistently attacked Lawrence for his alliance with the wealthy interests of the city and his ignorance of the problems of the "Little Joe." McArdle's grievance with Lawrence had developed after the mayor dropped him from the Democratic slate in the primary election.[8]

During the public hearing, Leonard blasted Lawrence and the conference several times to loud cheering from the crowd. "Everyone knows," Leonard proclaimed, "that the Allegheny Conference controls both political parties." He also attacked council itself for "shoving people off their homes." McArdle likened Mayor Lawrence to dictator Joseph Stalin: "You can't be here as a member of council if you don't listen to the dictates of David L. Lawrence, the Stalin of Pittsburgh." Leonard shifted the object of attack to the Urban Redevelopment Authority (URA). He denounced John Robin, executive director of the URA, for lobbying on behalf of a bill to "seize private property" for the Highland Park site. Robin, Leonard claimed, was "hiding behind the sham of urban redevelopment" in his attempts to explain the use of eminent domain. Leonard's object shift exposed the inner workings of the otherwise "invisible" URA and thereby challenged the legitimacy of the urban growth regime.[9]

In addition to their rhetorical attacks against the governing regime, Leonard and McArdle became direct allies of the Highland Park protestors. The two council members sponsored a resolution to accept an offer by Robert King to give all his property to the city on the condition that it not be condemned and that the city turn it into a park and bird sanctuary after his death.[10] In King's estate the protesters had discovered a resource for bargaining with the urban growth regime. The contribution of park land was clearly commensurate with the environmental agenda of the renaissance. A park and sanctuary would serve to enhance the quality of life in the East End and thereby bolster property assessments in the neighborhood.

Despite direct protests from Leonard, McArdle, and Highland Park residents, the petition of one thousand, and King's offer to the city, Lawrence and key members of his council did not relent. The mayor called a secret council session, not attended by Leonard or McArdle, where they agreed to approve condemnation of several thousand feet of residential property in Highland Park.[11] The result was greater polarization between the two sides of the conflict. When the ordinance was up for a final vote on July 18, the two rebellious councilmen made every effort to prevent it from passing. Leonard demanded that no vote be taken until the legal department could evaluate the legality of eminent domain property-taking for cultural usage. McArdle added that the "bill has not received a lot of study—it was presented in this Council on July 5th; reported out of the Committee on Finance one week later and is now before us for final passage."[12]

Council president Thomas Kilgallen retorted that the issue "has been under discussion for many months. . . . Had Mr. Leonard's request been made more timely I would have been agreeable to favor it, but here on the threshold of the vote Mr. Leonard desires to call the City Solicitor before City Council to interrogate her as to the legality of the matter."[13] Kilgallen overlooked the fact that as recently as June 17 he and his council had claimed to know nothing about the Highland Park proposal, meaning it was perhaps discussed in secret sessions but not at council meetings or in public hearings. The land-use proposal had been on the public agenda for only two weeks and City Council passed the ordinance, effectively condemning the properties in Highland Park and declining Robert King's offer.

After the council vote Vincent Burke announced his intention to bring equity action in common pleas court to restrain the city from condemning the properties. McArdle accused City Council of trying to "confiscate private property and homes for the purpose of putting in an objectionable outdoor theater." Backed by lively applause from attendants, he continued, "This is the boldest and cruelest thing ever to happen in Pittsburgh."[14]

Newspapers were attracted to the Highland Park story. It was a narrative about the first visible conflict over a renaissance project, and the petition and ensuing drama in City Council involving Leonard and McArdle were newsworthy material. Nearly all the major stories about the Highland Park controversy were run on the front pages of the city's largest newspapers. In July 1949, when the most contentious activity occurred, the *Pittsburgh Press* ran a front-page story on the issue every day of the first half of the month, and about every other day in the second half.[15] Moreover, considerable feedback in the form of opinion pieces reveals that the *Press* readership, including those who lived outside Highland Park, generally sympathized with the protestors.

In a July 14 letter, a Dormont resident begins, "If they need a site for the Civic Opera, why take somebody else's property out at the end of the Highland Ave. car line? The City already owns a good site." In a July 15 letter, a resident of Chislett Street writes: "I sympathize with the people in the Highland Park area, especially Robert King. The City wants to take away his property and build an amphitheater in his backyard. . . . We want to commercialize everything. Some years ago we passed a zoning law to protect such residential districts from commercialization. But now the City wants to break its own law for the law of eminent domain." In a July 20 letter a Bellevue resident draws an analogy between Pittsburgh politics and communist oppression in a manner similar to McArdle's earlier attack on Lawrence in council chambers: "We in America today are very vitally concerned with the advances made by Communism throughout the world, and still the people of

Pittsburgh sit by and do little to stop their representatives from performing this land grab in a manner very similar to the methods used behind the iron curtain." A resident of Bridgeville ends his letter of July 24 with an attack on the Lawrence administration's motives in choosing the Highland Park site, a primarily Republican district: "Maybe the officials are not really interested in providing the most people with the best recreation at the lowest cost. Their choice of Highland Park indicates that they might be thinking of pleasing the few regardless of the cost."[16]

There were other opinion letters, all of which reflected the language and tone of those stated above. Not a single opinion published in the *Press* favored the city. This is especially striking since the *Press* generally published very favorable views on the renaissance. Judging from the letters and front-page coverage of the Highland Park story, it seems obvious that opposition to the urban growth agenda, if not a direct challenge, existed well beyond the directly aggrieved residents of Highland Park.

Mayor Lawrence took action to end the controversy in Highland Park shortly after Vincent Burke took the case into the courts. In August Lawrence reversed his position and wrote a letter to the City Planning Commission requesting a recommendation for an alternative to the Highland Park site.[17] According to historian Michael P. Weber, Lawrence's reversal was strongly influenced by his wish not to get the city entangled in a protracted legal battle that could delay the project indefinitely. The courts also might have rejected the city's liberal interpretation of eminent domain law. "The city had in effect decided that any project deemed to be in the public good was permissible," says Weber, "and the planning office followed that philosophy in exercising its power to designate an area as blighted. A more restrictive ruling by the courts would place the entire renewal program in jeopardy."[18]

To be sure, legal aspects of eminent domain created much uncertainty around urban renewal in the early years. Yet Lawrence was prepared to invoke it again and again in subsequent development projects. Eminent domain law had to be tested eventually, and it would be in the next year as Point Park development expanded into the Lower Triangle. An alternative account of Lawrence's reversal points to the polarization of conflict revolving around temporary divisions within City Council. Rebellious councilmen allied with the residents and endorsed a proposal by one of them to save the neighborhood from redevelopment. Robert King had something to bring to the table of urban redevelopment, an environmental asset commensurate with the regime's regional capital and industrial development agenda. If the agenda had been different, Robert King's land gift may not have possessed the same value it had in Lawrence's environmental renaissance. At its core, the corporatist agenda of renewal was to make the city a more desirable place to live and invest capital. This meant more parks and more housing in parklike settings. If Mayor Lawrence had declined the opportunity to expand the environmental assets of the city, it could only erode the legitimacy of the postwar renaissance, already tainted by the struggle in Highland Park.

Case 2: A Movement to Challenge Neighborhood Land-Use Intervention Downtown, December 1949–May 1950

Just months after City Council withdrew the ordinance condemning properties in Highland Park, the lower Golden Triangle was threatened with eminent domain. The problem facing landowners and tenants in the Lower Triangle began in 1946 when the conference created the Point Redevelopment Committee. The Wabash Terminal, located adjacent to the proposed Point Park in the Lower Triangle, was destroyed by fire in the spring of that year, creating an opportunity for another section of downtown to be rebuilt. The Point Redevelopment Committee researched the area and decided to build new office towers in a parklike setting adjacent to Point Park. The idea was to utilize the massive Point Park project as a catalyst for new development in surrounding areas.[19] From a legal perspective the Lower Triangle was a much riskier project than what had been attempted in Highland Park. It involved acquiring private properties, through negotiation or eminent domain, and turning the properties over to private owners for commercial use. The URA was the first redevelopment authority in the country to use eminent domain in this way.

Members of the conference executive committee believed there was a demand for new downtown office space because no new office buildings had been constructed downtown since the 1920s and office occupancy had reached 99 percent by spring 1946. A group of leaders in the conference searched for a suitable private investor for the project, which they found in the New York–based Equitable Life Assurance Society. Negotiations with Equitable began in March 1947 and continued until February 1950, when the company signed an agreement to undertake the redevelopment, conditional upon firm commitments for twenty-year leases on half the space in the proposed buildings. Conference executive committee member Arthur Van Buskirk persuaded several Pittsburgh corporations to relocate into the proposed buildings under the terms demanded by Equitable. Among the original lessees were Jones & Laughlin Steel Corporation, Westinghouse Electric Corporation, Westinghouse Airbrake Company, Pittsburgh Plate Glass Company, the Joseph Horne Company, and Mellon Bank.[20]

In early 1948 Equitable bought a tract of land in the redevelopment area and shortly thereafter the URA sold a $150,000 bond issue in order to begin acquiring properties in the Lower Triangle that would be subsequently turned over to Equitable. This was the first long-term debt issue to an urban redevelopment authority in the United States.[21] The composition of the redevelopment area was very different in character from the adjacent parcels slated for Point Park. By 1945 the thirty-six acres intended for Point Park were covered mainly by warehouses and old rail yards. As noted in the last chapter, the city's main challenge there was to negotiate with the Pennsylvania Railroad, a single, albeit large and powerful, corporation. In contrast, the twenty-three-acre commercial neighborhood selected for the new Gateway Center office tower complex contained over ninety buildings held by over one hundred property owners. Records kept by Reed

Smith Shaw & McClay, who represented Equitable in the land acquisition process, describe a wide variety of owners and tenants that had to be removed to make way for Gateway Center. In addition to dozens of small businesses and professional offices, there were several voluntary organizations in the neighborhood, including the Congress of Clubs and Club Women of Western Pennsylvania, the Elks Club of Pittsburgh, the Pittsburgh Association for the Improvement of the Poor, the Junior League, and the Girls Service Club. There were also a number of residential apartments, social clubs, restaurants, a hotel, and Duff's Iron City College. While some of the structures were dilapidated, most were well-kept homes of thriving organizations and businesses.[22]

In order to initiate eminent domain proceedings, the URA and the City Planning Commission had to first certify the area as "blighted" and then demonstrate that the desired redevelopment would serve a public use. With so many thriving businesses in the area and many of the buildings—some fewer than twenty years old—in sound condition, it was by no means obvious that the neighborhood would benefit from wholesale demolition. In order to make a plausible argument for the blight designation, the conference and URA took advantage of the broad language in the Urban Redevelopment Law allowing the use of eminent domain in cases of "inadequate planning" of a neighborhood, or when the uses to which land had been put in the past were viewed as "economically or socially undesirable" to an extent that it hindered future development of the city.[23]

Utilizing the conference's impressive technical capacities, the Point Redevelopment Committee quickly established two subcommittees—planning and zoning, and area redevelopment—to determine how the conditions in the area could qualify under the Redevelopment Law's broad language for the use of eminent domain. Research by the committees culminated in an official report, delivered to the public by the City Planning Commission in March 1947. The report concluded that the Lower Triangle neighborhood adjacent to the Point was blighted due to its inadequate planning in relation to the proposed adjacent park. To demonstrate the public benefit of the redevelopment proposal, the URA claimed that "eradication and renewal of a privately-owned blighted area was a public need, because it was important to the health, safety, and welfare of the community as a whole." The blight designation occurred quietly with little reaction by residents in the area.[24]

Before demolition for Gateway Center could begin, the Urban Redevelopment Law required City Council and the Planning Commission to approve the redevelopment plan. On November 28, 1949, URA chairman David Lawrence sent a letter to City Council requesting that they consider the renewal plan and schedule the required public hearing. The Planning Commission had already reviewed and approved the plan and Lawrence expected swift action from City Council. Landowners and businesses in the Lower Triangle read about the plans in the newspapers. Their reaction was sharp. On December 8, thirty owners of buildings slated for demolition by the URA met in the William Penn Hotel to begin appropriating resources to challenge the Gateway Center project. Spokespersons for the group told reporters they "did not feel they are located in a blighted area since they have spent large sums of money in putting their buildings into shape." Protesters in the Lower Triangle were organized into an informal ad hoc group. Their objectives were straightforward and immediate: to prevent the acquisition and demolition of the buildings in which they worked. The resources to be appropriated toward the effort were limited mainly to locating places for the group to meet, allocating time to show up for meetings and public hearings, making protest posters and signing petitions if necessary, and hiring attorneys to represent them against the city.[25]

The group defined their common identity and grievances in much the same way as the Highland Park residents. They believed they were threatened with an injustice—the taking of private properties by eminent domain—that would destroy the values attached to places in the neighborhood they had themselves created from years of sacrifice and hard work. The group of thirty formed a committee to meet with Mayor Lawrence before council held its public hearing on the project on January 3, 1950. The URA, the conference, and Equitable had meanwhile joined with

Albert Schenck, a property owner in the redevelopment area, in filing a "friendly" lawsuit in the Pennsylvania Supreme Court to determine the legality of the URA's plan to use eminent domain to secure properties in the area.[26] Officials wanted to be sure that their proposal, pursuant to the Urban Redevelopment Law, would hold up in court before any demolition began.

On January 2, 1950, the group of landowners, tenants, and their attorneys prepared for an attack on the conference, URA, and Equitable. Spokespersons for the group told reporters they would not give up their properties "without a fight." The group of thirty stormed council during the hearing, which was attended by more than a hundred people.[27] Objections came in many forms but were framed mainly in terms of the injustice of using eminent domain to transfer property between private owners and the destructive effects such actions would have upon the valuable community institutions that had evolved to serve residents, workers, businesses, and owners in the Lower Triangle. The testimony of Ira Marshall, president of the Congress of Clubs at 408 Penn Avenue, was exemplary: "We've heard a lot about greenery, but not a word about women. We've been at 408 Penn Avenue for 26 years, yet your plans make no place for a most essential factor, women and their welfare work."[28] Marshall went on to point out that over two hundred clubs regularly met at that address and not all would be able to meet the cost of replacing the space lost through displacement. Several other owners, tenants, and their families and friends spoke of the hardship of displacement and the unlikelihood that they could ever find adequate replacement space with relocation funds provided by the city.

Protesters found no allies to their cause in Lawrence's council, which had restored its unity after purging Joseph McArdle.[29] This left them with limited opportunities to leverage their numbers in council's public sessions. Like their counterparts in Highland Park, the downtown protesters hired professional attorneys experienced in property rights litigation who certified their claims against the city. City Council maintained that the courts, not legislators, should determine the legality of using eminent domain to clear downtown. The attorneys were therefore not able to persuade council that approval of condemnation would amount to an illegal action. Four property owners decided to file suits against the URA in the Pennsylvania Supreme Court, challenging the legality of transferring private property for commercial use. On January 11 the court dismissed the suits. Two separate suits were also filed, one in common pleas court, and the other in federal court, each challenging the method by which properties in

Demolition for Gateway Center, 1950. Source: Library and Archives Division, Historical Society of Western Pennsylvania.

Aerial view of Golden Triangle showing the cleared site for Point Park with Gateway Center on the lower right, 1954. Source: Library and Archives Division, Historical Society of Western Pennsylvania.

the district were designated as blighted and the violation of due process of law of the property owners. Both suits were also dismissed.[30] The full authority of the URA could now be invested in commercial development adjacent to Point Park. With the site studies and plans completed, private sector investors lined up; with no remaining legal questions about the URA's authority to transfer private property for commercial use, council approved the Gateway Center proposal and the URA began to acquire property.[31]

The lawsuits against the URA enacted an object shift in pushing the issue from the legislative system into the judiciary system. The movement would certainly have gained a boost from favorable decisions by the courts. After the defeats, however, many protesters gave up hope of preventing further action by the city.[32] But a small group of them shifted objects again by appealing the decision to the U.S. Supreme Court. Andrew Gamble, owner of 416-418 Penn Avenue, organized a group of tenants and owners to continue their fight. They formed the Property Owners and Tenants Protective Committee (POTPC), which focused its efforts on winning the battle in the Supreme Court.[33]

The POTPC also managed to mount a public protest using the newspapers and posters printed by member Francis Roney, owner of the Colonial Press.[34] On May 8, they published a half-page announcement in the *Post-Gazette* entitled, "Here's a Pittsburgh Example of How You Can Throw a Going Business into the Street."[35] The announcement was framed in terms of the now familiar conflict between special-use values and commercial values of property. Big business and big government, allied against small business and community values, were viewed as the adversary of ordinary neighborhood residents:

> When the plans for Point Park were laid, the Equitable Life Assurance Society of the United States, a big private business corporation from New York, came to town and offered to build three large buildings . . . if it could have unobstructed park view of the point and a lot of fat 20 year leases. . . . You could do the same if you were big enough. . . . Now naturally a lot of the companies in the area didn't want to be kicked out, but those who dared object were little people. In the eyes of the Urban Redevelopment Authority they weren't as good as grass, so the area was declared "Blighted" through the use of a statute on the books of the State of Pennsylvania designed primarily *to remove slums.* (Emphasis in original)

In the last few lines of the announcement, the committee said they intended to "carry their fight all the way to the Supreme Court of the United States." Attorney for the committee G. E. Morecroft announced the lawsuit at a weekly luncheon of the Pittsburgh Real Estate Board.[36] But this struggle was in vain, like the other cases filed by landowners since December 1949.[37] To make matters worse, protesters in the Lower Triangle did not enjoy the kind of favorable press coverage or groundswell of support that occurred in Highland Park. No opinion pieces were printed in any of the major newspapers about the situation, even after the POTPC article.

The conference, Point Redevelopment Committee, Equitable, and the URA had been planning extensively for Gateway Center since 1946. They held prodigious preemptive power to produce and finance a plan before landowners and tenants even knew what was going on. The protestors demonstrated their solidarity and had their claims against the city certified by legal experts. But the formation of a category and the appropriation of resources occurred long after plans for Gateway Center had been drawn, redrawn, and financed. They put forward no resources to bargain for influence over the Gateway Center plan, unlike their predecessors in Highland Park. The movement collapsed shortly after the May 8 article, and demolition began at the Point on May 18.[38]

Case 3: Federal Structuring, Low-Income Housing Development, and Neighborhood Revolt, August–September 1950

Redevelopment in Pittsburgh received a great boost by the passage of the Federal Housing Act (FHA) in July 1949. The legislation created the Housing and Home Finance Agency (HHFA) to construct public housing and distribute subsidies to cities involved in slum clearance and rebuilding. Local redevelopment authorities responded to FHA incentives by intensifying the effort to rebuild blighted neighborhoods. Since the clearance of slums would displace thousands of low-income residents from their homes, construction of public housing became imperative. Urban professionals had identified relocation as a potentially significant obstacle to urban renewal. The FHA required client cities to demonstrate the existence of adequate replacement housing in their reapplications for federal renewal funds. The executive director of the URA, attorney Theodore Hazlett, was constantly reminding the conference executive committee that rehousing problems threatened the flow of federal renewal funds.[39] In public statements executive director of the URA John P. Robin warned that $5 million of slum clearance planned for Pittsburgh would not go forward "until there is enough low-cost housing for families uprooted in the slums."[40] Officials were also aware that physical displacement imposed significant technical and financial burdens. As discussed earlier, the city initially chose Highland Park over the Lower Hill for the proposed amphitheater because the Hill was "occupied by thickly built areas presenting a re-housing problem."[41]

The FHA provided the legal and financial basis for implementing a two-pronged strategy of urban restructuring in Pittsburgh. It enabled officials to begin acquiring properties throughout the city for clearance and rebuilding while at the same time constructing public housing projects into which qualified residents displaced from renewal could be relocated. The first project requiring substantial relocation of moderate-income residents was Jones & Laughlin (J&L) Steel Company's massive extension of its facilities on the South Side. In 1949 the URA and J&L reached a redevelopment agreement similar to the one initiated in the Lower Triangle. The URA would acquire and clear a residential neighborhood and the city would extend the utilities necessary for the plant to install new furnaces.[42] The expansion of J&L involved the displacement of over 235 families and the destruction of their homes. The city was fortunate that most of the displaced residents were steelworkers who perceived they were gaining from expansion of the plant. Organized labor was involved in the expansion early on and helped Lawrence to "interpret the project not as a case of a large corporation acting at the expense of workers but rather as a chance to create industrial jobs and secure the economic future of the City."[43] The URA and a committee of affected residents reached a friendly agreement, the city agreed to help relocate the families into suitable dwell-ings, and City Council approved the plan with minimum controversy.[44]

Other clearance and renewal projects, some on a much grander scale, were already in various stages of planning as the J&L expansion got underway.[45] In the spirit of the renaissance, the Pittsburgh Housing Authority took maximum advantage of the benefits of FHA and began applying to the HHFA for funds to construct public housing for residents displaced by redevelopment plans in the Lower Hill, North Side, and East End areas.[46]

Three months after the Property Owners and Tenants Protective Committee shifted the object of their claims to the U.S. Supreme Court, the Pittsburgh Housing Authority contacted residents of the St. Clair neighborhood in the city's South Side. St. Clair had been an independent borough and suburb of Pittsburgh until 1872, when the city absorbed it in a wave of annexation that increased the city's size by 4.2 square miles and its population by 36,000. In August 1950, the authority requested conferences with forty-four property owners to arrange selling prices of their land, which stood in the vicinity of a proposed seven-hundred-unit public housing site.[47] St. Clair was a tight-knit German community whose many families traced their ancestry back over one hundred years. The community was composed largely of steel workers, truck drivers, other skilled workers, and artisans, many of whom built new houses after the war to accommodate their growing families.

St. Clair residents reacted immediately to the letters from the housing authority by forming a group to prevent the agency from acquiring their properties. On August 28, Ida Imhoff, chair of a committee of six hundred St. Clair homeowners, sent a formal communication to City Council protesting the building of public housing in St. Clair.[48] As in the earlier neighborhood protests, the St. Clair group was informal, temporary, and defined by the single goal of protecting special-use values attached to the places they lived. One young landowner defined the collective sentiments attached to the St. Clair neighborhood: "There's more to this fight than just houses and land. My forefathers helped clear frontier forest from this hill. My grandpap . . . helped build St. Joseph's Church and even they stayed here in St. Clair Borough. There's a sentiment to this land that money can't buy."[49]

St. Clair residents mobilized the same personal, rather than organizational or institutional, resources as their counterparts in Highland Park and downtown, though they did hold a much stronger sense of ethnic solidarity than the others, as reflected in their militant defense of the special-use values manifest in neighborhood buildings, sidewalks, and open spaces. Resources were first appropriated for what reporters called a "gigantic protest rally" at St. Joseph's Hall. Over five hundred residents participated.[50] At the rally, residents launched several campaigns to define their grievances against the housing authority, URA, and the mayor's office. They also sought the attention of a broader public believed to be sympathetic to their claims. "Only political pressure can halt [the project]," attorney for the residents Al Sloan stated. Because attorneys did not believe the housing authority was engaging in illegal action, they realized that they had to win the sympathies of the broader public if officials were to reverse their plans.[51]

The group launched an editorial campaign in the *Pittsburgh Press* on September 2, with six letters of protest against the housing authority. Reflecting a theme in the Highland Park controversy, one resident repudiated the housing project as a "Communistic type of government-controlled home." A second letter makes the same reference: "[The housing authority] is demanding to buy most of the homes adjoining the land, at their price, and giving us to understand if we don't sell, the homes will be condemned. Is this the good old U.S.A. or is this Russia?" Another letter offers an alternative way for the city to develop the Henger farm: "Why not put the [Henger] farm up for sale and let private enterprise develop it?" The references to patriotic loyalty contrast the community values of the landowners with an oppressive and insensitive local state. Similar references to community loyalty and patriotic sentiment were made in the Highland Park and downtown protests; for example, council members McArdle and Leonard had also drawn analogies between Pittsburgh government and communism in their fight for Highland Park.

After the editorial campaign, the group sent letters to Mayor Lawrence and the housing authority requesting an opportunity to "build on the land with their own money." One letter stated that the residents of St. Clair would "like to see a group of small homes built on Henger's farm and we don't want to be pushed out of our homes for the project."[52] The group formed a committee with the goal of presenting their grievances to city officials in a formal meeting and getting their response to each grievance.[53] Officials from the mayor's office and housing authority agreed to a meeting, at which residents claimed they were reluctant to give up the neighborhood because their "ancestors had settled in old St. Clair Borough and had instilled a pride of community that has come to present times."[54]

Despite the persuasive story about community and property in St. Clair, officials dominated the meeting by presenting a series of technical experts who explained why the housing authority selected the St. Clair neighborhood. Officials even used the opportunity to promote other renaissance projects—a Lower Hill District cultural complex, a crosstown boulevard, and a new sports arena —all of which would "bog down completely if public housing is not provided for low-income families." Officials left the meeting resolved to move ahead on the housing development, an action protesters responded to with their greatest campaign to date, a four-hundred-strong march on city hall.[55]

Within a week of the planned march on city hall, Spring Hill–City View residents in the North Side neighborhood launched another wave of protest against a different public housing project. When the housing authority requested to annex two tracts of land in the abutting Reserve Township, news of its plans for a 1,600-unit public housing project were leaked into the surrounding neighborhoods of Spring Hill–City View. Tentative plans called for construction on two hundred acres of hillside land presently divided by the City of Pittsburgh–Reserve Township boundary line. North Siders mobilized with a thousand handbills circulated throughout City View, Spring Garden, Spring Hill, and Summer Hill advertising a mass protest meeting against the project. The new wave of protesters borrowed the familiar language of community use values and property rights. Protest chair Madeline Lyon declared that "residents of this area have lived here a long time, and have built new homes and fought to make the community a better place to live. Now the authority intends to take our land and homes."[56]

Journalists covering the protests acted as brokers of connections between the North Side and South Side neighborhood protesters. North Siders immediately identified with the struggles of

The neighborhood of Spring Hill, 1951. Photo by Clyde Hare. Source: Carnegie Museum of Art, Pittsburgh; gift of the artist.

the St. Clair group, which they learned about through the newspapers, and resolved to join with them in a "common front against housing projects."[57] Eight hundred people, including St. Clair residents, turned out for the North Side protests against the housing authority. The state congressional representative of the North Side was in attendance and announced his support for the residents, which they treated as a political opportunity. They viewed the politician's support as a signal that grassroots protest was working and resolved to form an organization, the North Side Protest Committee (NSPC) to fight the battle. The NSPC circulated a petition, door-to-door, and urged the North Siders to join in the St. Clair march on city hall. Handbills and a sound truck were used in the neighborhoods to promote the demonstration; leaders even requested that people take off work in order to join in. On September 27 four busloads of protesters arrived at city hall and presented a petition of five hundred names of persons opposed to government housing developments in Pittsburgh neighborhoods. Protesters, who were mainly working-class Democrats, also staged a mass threat of withdrawal from the Democratic Party if the city did not back off its plans.[58]

Despite the large numbers of neighborhood residents activated in the North and South Sides, their innovative repertoires of protest, and promise to the administration that "Democratic voters will turn against you," the housing authority went ahead with property acquisitions. The authority was an autonomous body that did not require consent from City Council to buy land or even to change an existing zone classification. City Council agreed to listen to the protests, but they could not prevent the authority's actions.

The NSPC followed earlier protesters in pursuing a legal strategy, this time against the Pittsburgh Housing Authority. Lawyers certified the claim that the housing authority had acted arbitrarily in choosing the North Side sites, that it had not conformed to state and federal laws governing the actions of local authorities, and that plaintiffs were deprived of their property without due process of law. This shift in the object of claims from the authority to the courts kept the movement activists hopeful and held up the project until the Pennsylvania Supreme Court finally ruled in favor of the Pittsburgh Housing Authority in 1954. The public housing facilities were completed by 1962.[59]

Case 4: Urban Renewal in the Lower Hill District: The Rise and Fall of a Preservation Movement, March 1958–September 1960

The problem of relocating displaced residents in redevelopment areas grew vastly when the urban growth agenda moved into the Lower Hill District. The Lower Hill was by far the largest neighborhood rebuilding project attempted in Pittsburgh up to this point in time. It may not have occurred but for changes to federal housing legislation in 1954 that lifted restrictions on the use of urban renewal funds for commercial construction and allocated $400 million more in federal funds for local projects. The original legislation of 1949 required that loans and grants be distributed only to projects of a "predominantly residential" character, reflecting the goal of addressing a national shortage in low-income housing for residents of the inner city. John Mollenkopf describes the program of urban renewal after 1954 as shifting "from a nationally directed program focusing on housing to a locally directed program which allowed downtown businesses, developers, and their political allies, who had little interest in housing, to use federal power to advance their own ends."[60] As a result of these changes in the federal context for local redevelopment, by the mid-1950s many U.S. cities had initiated major federally subsidized clearance and renewal programs that were predominantly commercial in character.[61]

Street scene in the Lower Hill before demolition, 1956. Source: Library and Archives Division, Historical Society of Western Pennsylvania.

Lower Hill District before demolition, with East End in the background (date unknown). Source: Library and Archives Division, Historical Society of Western Pennsylvania.

While portions of the densely populated Lower Hill suffered severe poverty and physical decay, the neighborhood as a whole remained a source of affordable housing as well as a vibrant center of African American businesses, community institutions, and culture.[62] The poverty and physical decay in the Lower Hill, however (rather than its affordable housing and thriving social networks), became the topic of widespread concern in Pittsburgh. In the 1940s the conference and its affiliates began calling for extensive demolition of the Lower Hill. They believed the momentum of the renaissance that had been established downtown would be curtailed, and property values in the Golden Triangle suppressed, by the proximity of a "slum" capable of supporting more prestigious and profitable uses. Clearing and rebuilding the Lower Hill, they claimed, would "remove the blighted barrier to the east of the metropolitan business district and may pave the way for ultimate future rehabilitation of the entire Hill District."[63]

Early in 1947 the Chamber of Commerce announced plans

for a new "metropolitan cultural center" in the Lower Hill. The focal point of the proposed center was a public arena for conventions, entertainment events, and other large gatherings, which would be accessible from all directions through a new crosstown expressway. The conference's main concerns in moving forward on the project were the enormous financial cost of purchasing hundreds of properties and the problem of relocating thousands of residents from the thickly settled Lower Hill. Construction of new public housing in the early 1950s alleviated the relocation problem, while the availability of federal urban renewal funds enabled the URA to manage the financial risks by securing properties and reselling them to developers without fear of financial loss.[64]

In 1953 the conference and the URA released a study that redefined the Civic Light Opera amphitheater as a civic arena and proposed locating it in the Lower Hill to anchor the proposed cultural center. A central goal of the official plan for the Lower Hill was "redevelopment of a portion of the site to provide a higher classification of housing in proximity to [the] downtown core."[65] Eventually, the report envisioned, the entire Hill District could be transformed in much the same way as the Lower Hill. A revitalized Hill District would connect downtown to Oakland, Pittsburgh's center of educational and research institutions located along the eastern border of the Upper Hill District.

By 1955 the URA had submitted all the paperwork required by the Housing and Home Finance Agency to receive federal subsidies. The federal agency granted a package of $17.4 million in loans and a capital grant of $8 million for the Lower Hill.[66] In 1956 the URA began purchasing and demolishing the first of 989 properties that would eventually be incorporated into the area redevelopment. Clearance continued until 1959, ultimately destroying 1,324 buildings and displacing 1,551 mostly African American families and an additional 413 businesses.[67] The magnitude of displacement was nearly eight times that of the South Side J&L project, the second largest removal up to that point in time.[68]

Relative to the massive scope of displacement in the Lower Hill, however, the organized response of neighborhood residents

Concept drawing of the Lower Hill redevelopment by architects Mitchell & Ritchey, 1956. Source: Library and Archives Division, Historical Society of Western Pennsylvania.

was minimal, especially in the early period of renewal. At first, many of the Hill's black residents believed in the promise of urban renewal. Historian Laurence Glasco surveyed *Pittsburgh Courier* articles written on the Lower Hill redevelopment and found they were generally supportive of the project. This consent for renewal is understandable given the extent of decay in the neighborhood. Unlike Highland Park and downtown, many buildings in the Lower Hill were dilapidated, and "many residents—with insufficient appreciation of what they would lose—looked forward to the better housing they had been promised."[69]

Other observers see not consent but a collective sense among Hill residents that they simply could not reverse the power and momentum behind the cultural center. Morton Coleman, a native of Pittsburgh and senior social planner for the Planning Department's Community Renewal Program (launched in 1961), observes that many residents of the Lower Hill were deeply skeptical about the postwar redevelopment, but had not defined any specific or compelling grievances around which to mobilize opposition. "[People] were really suspicious. It was before the civil

Lower Hill clearance near completion, August 1957. Source: Library and Archives Division, Historical Society of Western Pennsylvania. Photo by John R. Shrader.

rights movement, so there wasn't the same kind of mobilization that you'd see. There was just an anger that was not an articulated anger. . . . There was no big rousing meeting like we had in the sixties. It was just sort of an angry acceptance."[70] Sala Udin, lifelong resident of the Hill and current City Council representative for the neighborhood, expresses a similar observation, but he emphasizes the limitations upon collective action imposed by the lack of mobilizing structures and the closed structure of political opportunity facing residents of urban renewal neighborhoods: "People were not empowered. They didn't have representatives in government. There was not a large hue and cry . . . but there was some hue and cry. They just didn't have the muscle."[71]

Pittsburgh's corporatist regime provided few opportunities for participation by African Americans, due in part to their lack of representation on Lawrence's tightly controlled City Council. State representative Homer Brown, a Hill District native, was the most prominent black politician in Pittsburgh at the time. Brown ran Lawrence's black "sub-machine," delivering the black vote in return for patronage that would sustain black loyalty to the Democratic Party. He was deeply involved in Lawrence's renaissance agenda. For example, he played a key role in gaining support for the conference's Pittsburgh Package in 1947.[72] The accommodation of black political leaders to Democratic machine politics provided them with incentives to support the goals of urban renewal and become associated with its success.

Despite quiescence in the African American community, beginning in 1958 a contentious preservation movement formed among white parishioners of the Lower Hill's St. Peter's Church. The historic preservation movement in Pittsburgh had developed partly out of a defensive reaction to the famous Pittsburgh Survey of 1907–1908. The Survey painted a very dismal picture of the city's environment, institutions, and architecture, to which many middle-class reformers responded with efforts at restoring and preserving the city's greatest assets, including its historic architecture. Historian Roy Lubove writes that Pittsburgh's preservation tradition is based largely on "piety," emphasizing "house museums commemorating social or political notables, patriotic sentiment expressed in military parks and memorials, [and] historical restorations."[73]

The pietistic tradition turned contentious in the late 1940s when a group of architects "got incensed" in reaction to a movement to demolish the jail and courthouse structures designed by architect H. H. Richardson.[74] The transition toward preservation activism was sharpened by events in the Lower Hill that began in 1958. In March rumors had begun to spread among parishioners of St. Peter's Church that their place of worship was designated for demolition in June of that year. Most of the buildings surrounding the church had already been destroyed in the first of three phases of clearance. Hill residents had begun to grow skeptical about the whole renewal process, as the demolition of residential units displaced people more quickly than replacement housing was being built. Resistance to new public housing projects in neighborhoods like St. Clair and Spring Hill–City View was further aggravating the housing crisis. Many in the Lower Hill had begun to believe strongly that demolition should be stopped outright, the renewal process slowed, and time set aside for a community-level decision about the future of the entire Hill and its residents.[75]

Under such conditions parishioners decided to battle the city to preserve St. Peter's Church. In early March a group was formed around a collective grievance against the URA for planning to demolish a neighborhood building that embodied special-use values in both its religious symbolism and its physical proximity to the homes of people who worshiped in it. Utilizing their own resources, the aggrieved parishioners printed 30,000 cards containing a message to the mayor that read, "Stop the unnecessary and wanton destruction of this magnificent landmark together with the inspirational Lourdes Shrine which has a place in Pittsburgh's renaissance."[76] The group distributed cards to office workers, city employees, and train and bus commuters who attended the noon services held daily at St. Peter's. They also managed to collect 10,000 signatures on a petition that they presented to City Council. According to the protesters, council had the right to reject any proposals of the URA and could, therefore, save the church.

Lawrence's council, pressured by the conference and URA to

proceed with the clearance, claimed they had "nothing to do with St. Peter's or any other church in the Catholic Diocese."[77] The parishioners followed the path of other protesters by hiring attorneys and filing suit in state court against the URA and the City of Pittsburgh, thereby shifting the object of claims to the court system. Attorneys certified their clients' claims in court by arguing on legal grounds that defendants had violated the parishioners' Fourteenth Amendment rights by seizing property without due process of law. The court ruled against the group on the argument that Bishop Dearden, who sold the property voluntarily to the URA, was the rightful owner in trust for the parish as a whole.[78] Thus, the parishioners had no legal rights to prevent sale of the property, despite the emotional and monetary investments they had made in the church and its parish for generations.

The St. Peter's group felt deeply betrayed by the city as well as their own bishop, who had accepted a $1,240,000 compromise damage settlement for the church from the URA. In their final efforts to save St. Peter's, the parishioners shifted the object of their claims a second time. They made direct appeals to the pope, beginning with a letter signed by all parishioners, to intervene in the local controversy. The group then launched a campaign to get all Catholics in the city to write letters to the Vatican in support of their claims. Over the course of the two-year battle, the Vatican reported receipt of some 50,000 letters from Pittsburgh.[79] Yet Vatican officials decided to stay out of the conflict, even after a lead attorney for the group met with the pope personally in Rome.

Adding further drama to the St. Peter's controversy, the newspapers ran a series of front-page stories covering the efforts of an elderly Hazelwood woman who, since 1955, had set out each day on a pilgrimage throughout the city with a sign that read, "In Jesus' Name Save St. Peter's Church." She took her daily tours by streetcar, which lasted from noon to 10 PM. The woman became somewhat of a folk hero as well as a public symbol of faith and religious conviction that served to constantly remind people of the great losses suffered by Pittsburgh communities as a result of the urban renewal bulldozer.[80] St. Peter's was finally surrendered to the Urban Redevelopment Authority in September 1960 and razed the following month.[81]

Conclusion

In 1949 Pittsburgh's renaissance moved into a new phase, the demolition and rebuilding of residential and mixed-use neighborhoods. The result was a continuous stream of contentious politics in the affected neighborhoods that tested the social control power of the corporatist regime. A core set of mechanisms recurred across all four cases: category formation among an aggrieved group of people, appropriation of social resources for mobilizing contention, certification of protesters' claims by legal experts, and multiple shifts in the object of claims. Other mechanisms were activated in cases 1 and 3. But only in case 1 were challengers able to gain concessions from the city. Mayor David Lawrence backed off his proposal to locate the new civic arena in Highland Park after two of his opponents in council—in the midst of intense polarization—presented Robert King's conditional offer of land to the city. In chapter 6 I account for how case 1 ended differently from the subsequent three through a comparison of the timing, sequence, and combination of mechanisms that generated contention in each.

RI - 1945-1970
RII -D 1977 1990   Pittsburgh most livable,
                     revitalizing early
key players: Joseph
              Barr,
          Pete Flaherty,
              David Lawrence

Public Housing Authority
i) Neighborhood Composition Rule
L) integrate
- work @ % area then segregate

4

Another Wave of Urban Restructuring and Governing Realignments, 1970–1997

Riots of 1968
put Trenze to end
- AC ran about

Dem
Public Housing
no temporary

- Due Diversity
New Dire Totmer
Flaherty
appoints
first black
to housing authority
- Churchhill Khelman, 1972
-> outsider
- Reform

He
Employment Agency
- credit union
Health service
HACP spenans
1hm 69,1 7.1972
Black emp 1951
- Security Force

HKH
urban
redevelop
authries

■ My fifth case study is set in a very different context, some thirty-seven years after the early postwar wave of neighborhood contention discussed in the previous chapter. Initial conditions for case 5 differed in important ways from those of the first four. Specifically, protesters in case 5 benefited from more developed mobilizing structures and a more open structure of political opportunities than their counterparts at midcentury. Recent community leaders who mounted contentious claims thus had a greater chance of gaining a strong voice in redevelopment projects. In order to explain changes that occurred in the local context of redevelopment over the thirty-seven-year period, I turn again to the urban restructuring tradition. Pittsburgh's renaissance occurred at a time when the United States was the unchallenged leader in world industrial production. In the years immediately following 1945 it exported capital goods and manufactured items at unprecedented high levels, while state leaders in Europe, North Africa, and much of Asia focused on rebuilding their war-torn economic infrastructures. By 1963 the United States produced 40 percent of world industrial output, over four times the amount held by West Germany, its closest rival.[1] The economic preeminence of the United States continued until the end of the century, but only after significant shedding of its older industrial capacity.

A major stimulus for restructuring in American industry came from the economic ascendance of Japan and a group of low-cost manufacturing states in east and southeast Asia. In 1963, Japan, South Korea, Taiwan, Hong Kong, Singapore, Thailand, Indonesia, the Philippines, and China held a combined share of 5.9 percent of world manufacturing output. By 1994 these same countries held 29.2 percent of manufacturing output, while the United States' share fell to 26.9 percent.[2] As manufacturing employment in developing countries increased steadily after 1960 it dropped precipitously in the older industrial economies of North America and Western Europe. In the United States manufacturing jobs declined from 28.3 percent of total employment in 1960 to 17.5 percent in 1991. A sharp rise in employment in producer services (finance, insurance, real estate, engineering, law, accounting) and social services (medical, education, welfare, nonprofit, government) occurred alongside the shift away from manufacturing in the United States. Employment in these services increased from a combined 22.9 percent to 39.5 percent of total employment during the 1960–1991 period.[3]

Employment shifts in the American steel industry mirrored those in the economy generally, as steel manufacturers introduced labor-saving technologies at home, shifted significant production to offshore locations, and divested from steel production altogether. In the 1970s Pittsburgh-based U.S. Steel accumulated investments in over a dozen subsidiaries in developing countries that were exporting steel to the United States. The company announced in 1979 that it would permanently close twelve steel plants, half of which were in Pittsburgh, resulting in the loss of 14,000 jobs in southwestern Pennsylvania. In the same period Mellon Bank acquired controlling interests in the LTV Corporation, which bought out J&L Steel, closed its Pittsburgh plants, and entered a partnership with Sumitomo Steel Company of Japan.[4]

All told, deindustrialization in Pittsburgh resulted in the loss of over 100,000 manufacturing jobs between 1979 and 1987.[5]

Table 4.1 illustrates the sweeping effect of deindustrialization on manufacturing employment in the region. In 1995, employment in manufacturing was less than a quarter its level at midcentury, having dropped from 44.1 percent to 11.3 percent of the total workforce. A sharp growth in service employment compensated for losses in manufacturing, with over 170,000 service jobs created in the region between 1970 and 1990. For those who lost jobs in manufacturing, however, the service sector offered inferior employment opportunities. In 1990, the average annual wage in manufacturing was $36,989 in the region, compared to only $24,442 for service workers with equivalent educational backgrounds.[6] For thousands of workers the postindustrial transition in Pittsburgh was a period marred by economic hardship rather than opportunity.

As employment prospects diminished, out-migration from the region increased. Net out-migration peaked at 50,000 annually in the early 1980s and continued into the 1990s at an annual average of 5,000. The economic factors that boosted out-migration after 1980 primarily affected young adults. More than half the population decline in the 1980s is attributable to the loss of twenty- to thirty-nine-year-olds. Retaining this age group is fundamental to the long-term economic growth of a region. Since most people find partners and settle down in their twenties and thirties, they

TABLE 4.1
The decline of manufacturing in Pittsburgh

Year	Manufacturing as percentage of total employment
1953	44.1
1960	38.1
1969	33.6
1979	26.7
1985	17.9
1995	11.3

Source: Bureau of Labor Statistics, State and Area, Employment, Hours, and Earnings

are much less likely to relocate after the age of thirty-nine. Regions that lose young people thus have significantly more trouble sustaining a vibrant and productive labor force over the long run, an idea illustrated by Pittsburgh's poor performance in job creation. In the 1980s and 1990s it ranked near the bottom of U.S. metropolitan areas in growth of employment and household income.[7]

The serious economic challenges associated with population aging were compounded by another demographic pattern, the continued spreading out and hollowing out of the population.[8] Table 4.2 shows that Pittsburgh city lost 45 percent of its population between 1950 and 1990, while the region as a whole lost only 7 percent in the same period. Older jurisdictions near the urban core suffered much greater declines than newer municipalities on the periphery. In fact, outlying Butler County actually grew in jobs and population at the same time that human capital, businesses, and tax revenues were emptying out of the urban core. This trend indicates a highly inefficient pattern of land use in the region. Total urbanized land area grew by 42.6 percent in the six counties while population shrank by 8 percent between 1982 and 1997. The costs of such extreme inefficiency in land use include increasing traffic congestion, consumption of valuable environmental as-

TABLE 4.2.
Population trends for Pittsburgh and metropolitan area, 1950–1990

Year	Pittsburgh city	Pittsburgh MSA[a]	Ratio of city to MSA population
1950	676,068	2,213,136	.30
1960	604,332	2,405,435	.25
1970	520,089	2,401,362	.21
1980	423,938	2,218,870	.19
1990	369,879	2,056,705	.18

Source: U.S. Census Population Division
[a] Pittsburgh Metropolitan Statistical Area (MSA) includes the counties of Allegheny, Beaver, Washington, and Westmoreland. The 1990 figure reflects a revised six-county area, including Butler and Fayette counties.

sets and farmland, a growing spatial mismatch between the location of new entry-level jobs and the people who need them, and declining property values in the urban core.[9]

Patterns of urban restructuring in Pittsburgh after 1970 indicate that the accomplishments of the renaissance, while significant, were not sufficient to reverse economic decline and population loss. Civic leaders and public officials continued to search for the appropriate strategic response to the demographic and economic challenges facing the region. The intergovernmental context in which strategic decisions were made also shifted significantly after 1970. The era of strong federal intervention in urban redevelopment gradually came to an end, and more than ever public officials were forced to partner with business leaders, state governments, foundations, and other nonfederal actors to solve local problems.

Federal Restructuring and the Decline of National Urban Policy

The election of Richard Nixon in 1968 marked the beginning of a long period of federal retrenchment from urban policy that continued with the Carter, Reagan, Bush, and Clinton administrations. Nixon's New Federalism emphasized greater discretion in how localities used federal funds and relied more on the discipline of the market to guide urban growth. Against a background of national recession, unrestrained inflation, and global economic restructuring, urban constituencies came to support Nixon's efforts to reduce federal intervention in urban economies.[10] The heart of his urban policy was the 1972 State and Local Fiscal Assistance Act. The legislation, which came to be known as "general revenue sharing," returned a portion of all federal tax revenues to state and local governments with minimal requirements on how the funds were to be spent.

In 1974 Nixon also signed into law the Housing and Community Development Act, which consolidated a multitude of existing categorical grant programs into large community development block grants (CDBGs). Grantees were required to give priority to activities that benefited low- and moderate-income persons but otherwise enjoyed flexibility in how they spent federal funds. Whereas earlier federal programs were targeted to large cities in the Northeast and Midwest, the CDBG formula redirected funding to smaller cities, those in the South and Southwest, and suburban municipalities. The new formula rewarded Nixon's Republican constituencies in the fast-growing Sun Belt region to the detriment of Democratic strongholds in the older industrial Rust Belt.[11]

Economic recession grew worse during the Nixon administration, and when Jimmy Carter took office in 1977 the fiscal distress of big cities had become a priority issue on the national agenda. Carter advanced a $16 billion economic stimulus for distressed cities and enacted a change in the CDBG formula that increased intergovernmental aid to big cities by 25 percent. Beyond this, however, the Carter administration's policies did little to reverse the federal government's retrenchment from national urban policy. As Richard Nathan finds, nonwelfare grants from the federal government to states and localities actually declined in real terms by 3.3 percent in 1979 and 6.8 percent in 1980.[12]

Carter advocated for "new partnerships" between private investors and local governments in big cities that had suffered the greatest distress. The partnership initiative reflected recommendations of a 1977 policy statement of the Committee for Economic Development entitled *An Approach to Federal Urban Policy*.[13] The CED urged national policy makers to recognize the diversity of local conditions and needs, and to design federal policies that enhanced the capacity of local leaders to deal with problems facing their cities. National policies were to be highly selective, targeted toward priority needs, and molded to fit specific local conditions. The CED also emphasized that government could not solve urban problems on its own and required the capital, skills, and commitment of local business and civic leaders. Carter's Urban Development Action Grant program (UDAG) embodied the main principles of the partnership model. It provided $4 billion for redevelopment projects in 2,200 cities under the provision that grantees raise local matching funds. Revenue sharing, block grants, and the UDAG matching-grant formula encouraged local politicians to seek support from business leaders and foundations that would allow them to engage in more risky revitalization projects.

Federal urban programs suffered further cuts under the Reagan and Bush administrations. Reagan radicalized the CED public-private partnership model by arguing that "national funds for local development encourage inefficient locational decisions and, consequently, a suboptimal national economy."[14] His Omnibus Budget Reconciliation Act of 1981 (OBRA), which cut domestic spending some $35 billion, was passed at a time when U.S. industrial corporations were closing their domestic plants, eliminating thousands of union jobs, and shifting production overseas. Advocates for OBRA touted it as a mechanism for reducing the growth rate of federal spending and improving the competitiveness of the national economy.

Urban programs were hit hard by Reagan and Bush spending cuts. Funds allocated through CDBG funds were cut by 54 percent, UDAG and general revenue sharing were eliminated altogether, and the remaining economic development assistance was cut by 78 percent. By 1992 federal aid provided an average of only 7.5 percent of city government revenues, down from a peak of 17.3 percent in 1978.[15] The Reagan and Bush administrations expected cities and states to fill the void with greater commitment of local resources. But as Demetrios Caraley argues, the capacity to replace federal aid varied widely among municipal governments. Generally, those jurisdictions with high taxable assets and low concentrations of needy populations were able to adjust to the loss of federal resources. Most of the places in this category were located in emerging technology districts and high-income suburbs. Jurisdictions with low taxable resources and high concentrations of needy populations, on the other hand, "had little or no capacity to substitute locally- and state-generated revenues for lost federal aid."[16]

Older industrial cities in the Northeast and Midwest suffered the most from Reagan and Bush era budget cuts. Pittsburgh provides a good illustration of some of the consequences of lost federal funds. Increases in local taxes only provided incentives for high-income families and thriving businesses to move out. The steady decline in Pittsburgh's population during the 1980s further eroded the city's fiscal capacity, causing greater increases in tax rates to make up for a smaller tax base and pressures to cut city services, especially those targeted at unemployed workers and other needy groups.

Federal policy was not significantly affected by the election of Democrat Bill Clinton to the presidency in 1992. Like Reagan and Bush, Clinton relied heavily on market forces and private organizations to revitalize regional and local economies.[17] The hallmark of his policy was the urban empowerment zone, which expanded upon an effort by President Bush to create a more competitive environment for local development. Empowerment zone funding earmarked grants to distressed communities on a competitive basis and provided tax breaks and other incentives for businesses that located within them. The program was designed to encourage a "bottom-up" strategy of national support for local initiatives. Communities were chosen to participate through a multiagency designation process that encouraged government, private, nonprofit, and community agencies to cooperate on shared developmental goals. As Susan Clarke and Gary Gaile have said of the Clinton empowerment zones, "There is a deliberate and conscious effort to emphasize initiatives that reconnect citizens and jobs, citizens and information, citizens and community organizations. In contrast to the hands-off mentality of the 1980s, the Clinton administration spoke of covenants and compacts of 'reciprocal responsibilities.'"[18]

Economic and demographic decline in Pittsburgh continued until the end of the century against a background of shrinking federal support and greater emphasis on local, multisector partnerships as a means of solving urban problems. And governing arrangements and urban redevelopment agendas in Pittsburgh changed alongside these broader structural shifts.

Urban Governing Alignments and Realignments since 1970

In 1957 the Allegheny Conference on Community Development founded the Allegheny Council to Improve Our Neighborhoods (ACTION-Housing, Inc.), a nonprofit agency for the construction of low- to moderate-cost housing in the region. The conference established the housing agency in part as a response to growing neighborhood demands for participation in redevelopment after 1949; it was the first effort at expanding the system of corporatist governance to include the neighborhood voice.[19] Reflecting the achievements of a national movement, Pittsburgh neighborhoods acquired greater representation in the corporatist system in the three decades after the founding of ACTION-Housing. Populist mayor Pete Flaherty (1970–1977) must be credited with initiating the first major reforms in city government that led to a more open structure of political opportunities for neighborhood challengers of urban growth politics.

The Mellon and Lawrence partnership was a one-time phenomenon in Pittsburgh, and it ended in 1958 with Lawrence's election as governor of Pennsylvania and Democrat Joseph Barr's successful bid for the mayoralty. After the death of Lawrence in 1966 and Mellon in 1970, local leaders sought in vain for successors with equal influence and legitimacy. Flaherty lamented that he did not have a partner in the business community with the stature of Mellon. "I wish there had been a General Mellon to whom I could relate," Flaherty said in a retrospective interview. "I wanted someone in the business community like that I could turn to. But there wasn't any."[20]

But Flaherty's actions as mayor seemed to belie his wish for a union between government and business. He was a product of the machine-style politics characteristic of the Lawrence era. Serving on City Council from 1965 to 1969, he then broke with the machine to run for mayor on the platform of being "Nobody's Boy." Flaherty's independence appealed to many Nixon Republicans who had grown skeptical of Community Action, Model Cities, and other expensive federal programs targeted toward cities in Mayor Barr's era. Flaherty's break with the party paid off. He beat the Democrats' endorsed candidate, Harry Kramer, in the primary and went on to rout his Republican opponent by a margin of almost two to one. As mayor, Flaherty did not sustain the local Democratic Party organization. He did not get involved in council races, as his predecessors had, and he raised campaign funds independent of the Democratic Party. This radical departure from patronage politics gave City Council members a great deal more autonomy from the mayor's office than had been the case in the Lawrence and Barr administrations.[21] Flaherty was no more friendly to corporate leaders than he was to party officials. He distanced his administration from the Allegheny Conference and ended the policy of subsidizing redevelopment in the Golden Triangle begun under Lawrence. By eliminating staff linkages between the URA, City Planning, and the conference, Flaherty effectively cut ties between local government and the corporate business community, and redirected resources from downtown to the neighborhoods. The implication was to empower the community development movement while eroding trust and cohesion between local government and corporate business leaders. "[Flaherty] has a bitter distrust for everything that happened in the past," said one senior Conference official. Remarks by Flaherty's executive secretary reflected the mutuality of cold feelings: "The Conference is a special interest group which tries to influence and run the city government. . . . They are not able to accept the change."[22]

Historic preservationists were a major impetus behind the community development movement in Pittsburgh. In 1964 the executive director of the Department of City Planning, several local foundations, and over seventy civic leaders came together to incorporate the Pittsburgh History and Landmarks Foundation (PHLF). Preservationists mobilized around a common concern for the "widespread decay and demolition of the significant architecture of Pittsburgh."[23] The group began with an ambitious undertaking to revitalize the racially and economically mixed Manchester neighborhood without removing its historic buildings or inhabitants. Located in the North Side, Manchester was filled with older Victorian homes slated for clearance under federal urban renewal. As reflected in the comments of PHLF's first president, preservationists believed that "urban renewal has been in some cases a very destructive, sociologically destructive force."[24] The Manchester project combined two innovative funding mechanisms: grants and loans from federal urban renewal, and a revolving loan established with $100,000 from the Sarah Mellon Scaife Foundation. Manchester was the first preservation program in the country to use urban renewal funds for the restoration of houses for low- and moderate-income residents.[25] After the 1968 riots in the wake of Martin Luther King Jr.'s assassination, the largely black population of Manchester dropped to a low of 1,200, down from a postwar high of 18,000. Landmarks helped create the nonprofit Manchester Citizens Corporation (MCC), which contracted with the URA in 1979 to manage a program for rehabilitating older residential buildings in the neighborhood. The URA hired the PHLF to recommend ways of preserving existing buildings with funds that would have gone toward construction of new public housing. While the PHLF was glad to have support from the URA in its Manchester restoration project, it advocated a voluntaristic, private-sector-driven philosophy of redevelopment. As discussed in the previous chapter, the modern preservation movement was born in reaction to the destruction of older neighborhoods by public-private growth coalitions. It shared Mayor Flaherty's populist skepticism toward large-scale redevelopment projects promoted by corporate and government officials. In the words of PHLF executive director Arthur Ziegler, the "more voluntary and resident involvement and less from government," the better chances a revitalization project had of succeeding.[26]

According to preservation philosophy the purpose of citizen participation is to increase neighborhood commitment to project outcomes by giving residents an opportunity to have a stake in the restoration of their community.[27] Through its involvement in other restoration projects on the North Side and South Side, the PHLF also learned to engage in contention with local officials who did not always appreciate the principles of adaptive reuse and historic preservation. As Ziegler has put it, "We learned very quickly that we would have to engage in pitched battles with authorities to prove that preservation is a practical goal."[28]

Mayor Flaherty accommodated the rising demand for community participation by creating a citywide system of neighborhood participation known as the Community Planning Program (CPP). The program divided the city into seven sections and assigned planners to work with community organizations in eighty-eight neighborhoods. Planners provided technical assistance to communities in land-use planning and conducted research on conditions and progress in the neighborhoods. They advocated for the needs of neighborhoods and helped give them a voice in private redevelopment projects. The CPP also sponsored community meetings that facilitated communication between officials and neighborhood leaders around capital budget formation and other fundamental policy decisions. As planners Robert Lurcott and Jane Downing wrote of the community planning mechanism, it "ensure[d] participation of *all* neighborhoods at an early stage of planning on all important issues."[29]

Flaherty's reforms were facilitated by Nixon's CDBG program. Since block grants were "noncategorical," the Flaherty administration faced no restrictions on channeling them through the Department of City Planning into neighborhood redevelopment programs. One significant accomplishment of CDBG neighborhood allocations was a citywide home improvement loan program for rehabilitation of older residential buildings. In contrast to the Lawrence and Barr era, when the mayor's office channeled the majority of federal funds to large-scale redevelopment projects in and around downtown, by 1975 one-half of all federal money was going directly into incremental neighborhood redevelopment programs such as the home improvement loan.

Richard Caliguiri (1978–1988) faced a major crisis in economic restructuring during his two terms as mayor of Pittsburgh. The region suffered sharp losses in the well-paying industrial sector while major cutbacks in federal aid to cities continued.[30] Reductions in the CDBG program reduced Pittsburgh's annual entitlement from a high of $26 million in 1980 to $17 million in 1986, which made it more difficult to allocate funds to neighborhood programs. Caliguiri reacted to the predicament with a broad effort to diversify the region's economy and strengthen the city's role as regional capital. "The steel industry is down," Caliguiri lamented in 1987, "it might come back, and I hope it will, but in the meantime we must attempt to revitalize our economy. . . . The future, as I see it, is in High Technology, it is in our educational and health institutions, in our research and development."[31]

To carry out his regional capital strategy Mayor Caliguiri used his charismatic personality and cooperative style of management to reorganize the urban growth coalition and initiate another round of large-scale redevelopment. As illustrated in chapters 2 and 3, the Allegheny Conference set the agenda for the Pittsburgh renaissance, while the city promoted the required changes in law and government. Under Caliguiri the division of labor between the public and private sectors was reversed. The necessity for government leadership in redevelopment planning was created by the erosion of preemptive power in the corporate business community. In the 1980s business executives were preoccupied with managing the global restructuring of their enterprises, and few were able to make community issues a priority. In a 1987 survey, Roger Ahlbrandt and Morton Coleman found that corporate executives believed they had far less time and fewer overall resources to devote to public affairs than their predecessors of the 1940s and 1950s.[32] The emphasis on high technology development positioned the city's major research institutions, the University of Pittsburgh, Carnegie Mellon, and Duquesne University, to compensate for loss of corporate leadership in the new urban growth coalition. When Caliguiri embarked on a second wave of bricks-and-mortar redevelopment targeted at economic diversification and the regional capital strategy, the universities became key partners.[33]

Redevelopment planning under Caliguiri was centralized in the Mayor's Development Council (MDC). John P. Robin, URA chairman in the Caliguiri era, conceived the idea of the new agency, which was chaired by the mayor's secretary and made up of directors of City Planning, Economic Development, Housing and Public Works, the URA, the parking authority, and the heads of two external organizations, Pittsburgh Area Transit, and the Regional Industrial Development Corporation. Among the major projects facilitated by the MDC were five mid- and high-rise buildings containing new office, retail, and residential space; a new hotel next to the David L. Lawrence Convention Center; the East Busway (an exclusive bus road connecting downtown to the universities and eastern neighborhoods), and a rapid transit system connecting the South Hills suburbs with downtown.[34]

Caliguiri also included the neighborhoods in his reconstructed urban growth coalition, but the mechanism of participation was community development corporations (CDCs) rather than the Community Planning Program. The CDCs partnered with the city to carry out small-scale commercial and residential real estate projects in the neighborhoods. One notable collaboration began in 1980 with the formation of the Oakland Planning and Development Corporation (OPDC). The Department of City Planning provided technical assistance and research support to the group to give it a role in planning several high-technology projects initiated by the city and universities.[35]

If neighborhoods gained a strong voice in the redevelopment process under Flaherty, they evolved into redevelopers in their own right during the Caliguiri era. The administration took an active role in the transition. Along with several nonprofit groups it created the Community Technical Assistance Center, which served as a vehicle for extending information and technical support to community leaders interested in creating CDCs in their neighborhoods. In 1983 the Ford Foundation, the Howard Heinz Endowment, the Mellon Bank Foundation, the Department of City Planning, and the URA joined with several community leaders to create a more permanent CDC funding mechanism. In its first years of operation the Pittsburgh Partnership for Neighborhood Development distributed funds from private foundations and banks to underwrite the operating costs of five core CDCs in Pittsburgh. The city also created a neighborhood fund with community development block grants to encourage CDC formation beyond the core organizations.[36] The Allegheny Conference sponsored the Local Initiatives Support Corporation in 1982 to provide further financial assistance for CDC real estate projects.[37] As a result of these extensive organizational efforts, twenty-two CDCs had formed in neighborhoods across the city by the end of the decade.

The Pittsburgh History and Landmarks Foundation launched its first large-scale commercial rehabilitation project in 1976 and completed the initial phase of construction in the Caliguiri years. The group received national acclaim for the project, which consisted of redeveloping an old rail yard along the Monongahela River into Station Square, a mixed-use "festival" marketplace.[38] In

an interview with fellow preservationists Richard Moe and Carter
Wilkie, Ziegler said that his organization was unable to garner
support from local authorities to redevelop the site. The "city
planning agency even tried to stop us," he claimed. Of government institutions that promote redevelopment, Ziegler opined,
"Bureaucrats are not known for having a lot of imagination. . . .
We're free to go out and do what comes to mind."[39]

Basic financing for Station Square was provided by a $5 mil-
lion grant from the Allegheny Foundation, one of the prominent
Scaife family trusts. The foundation was interested in a project
that could demonstrate how an incremental but focused redevelopment process, driven by private investment, could revitalize historic buildings in an economically viable way. With a commitment
to making older buildings serve new uses, the PHLF focused first
on serving the local population, then shifted toward building at-
tractions for tourists. Station Square stimulated the creation of
over 140 businesses and 3,000 jobs. In 1994 PHLF sold its substantial interest in the development—which had grown to become the most visited attraction in Pittsburgh—for $25.5 million.
The proceeds were used to endow more preservation work.[40]

In 1987, at the end of Caliguiri's administration, Pittsburgh
voters passed a referendum to establish district elections for City
Council. In 1989 the city elected its first district-based council
since 1911. The new electoral system represented another degree
of separation between the mayor's office and City Council, as
council members would now be elected to serve constituents of
their districts rather than the city as a whole.

Pluralism and Conflict in the Corporatist System:
Mayor Tom Murphy, 1994–2005

While the community development movement went a long
way toward empowering residents to participate in the revitalization of their neighborhoods, it was powerless in stemming the loss
of manufacturing jobs and population from the region. Pittsburgh and Allegheny County continued to suffer net population
losses, especially of college-educated young adults, through the

1990s. Continued contraction of the population reflected a longer trend of economic decline in southwestern Pennsylvania. In 1992 Pittsburgh had the slowest employment growth in the country and in 1999 suffered the slowest growth in wages among the twenty-five largest U.S. cities.[41]

A white paper report commissioned by the Allegheny Conference in 1992 framed the problem as stemming from a "lack of consensus about vision and strategies. . . . Key stakeholders from business, labor, government, education, civic organizations and foundations in Southwestern Pennsylvania do not have a widely shared vision of what the region's economy can be."[42] In underscoring the consensus problem, the report's authors were reacting in part to the sheer proliferation of public, private, and nonprofit organizations involved in community revitalization since the era of Lawrence and Mellon. By 1993 over two hundred such organizations were active in the region, in many cases with little coordination among them. The white paper claimed that these organizations were beset by "factionalism, fragmentation, and overlapping agendas which divert attention from solving real problems." By contrast, fewer than twenty-five agencies were active in the Mellon-Lawrence era.[43]

Many community development groups in the 1980s and 1990s were created with significant financial and technical support from the urban governing coalition. In addition to the CDCs, two other important groups in this category are the Pittsburgh Downtown Partnership (PDP) and the Pittsburgh Urban Magnet Project (PUMP). With the backing of philanthropic foundations and the mayor's office, the Allegheny Conference created the PDP in 1994 to foster "a clean, safe, accessible, and vibrant downtown." The group works with other agencies to help market downtown as the business and cultural center of the region. In 1997 the PDP established a business improvement district to pay for cleaning, marketing, and other services for businesses in the Golden Triangle.

PUMP was formed in 1995 with a network of support similar to that of the PDP. A University of Pittsburgh graduate student founded the membership organization in order to advocate issues affecting "young and young-thinking people" in Pittsburgh. The foundations, the city, and the conference embraced the group's mission of making the region more attractive to young professionals by engaging them in politics and civic affairs. The twenty- to thirty-nine-year-olds in Pittsburgh knew they were a highly valuable population for the city's economic future and their declining numbers created a justification for involving them in important decisions. As proponents of growth in Pittsburgh, PUMP's greatest benefit may be its effect on the image of the city. By getting more young people to sit on organizational boards, by engaging them in policy controversies (for example, transportation, education, redevelopment), and by profiling their civic and professional accomplishments in ceremonies such as the highly popular "40 under 40" annual event, PUMP has helped to foster a younger image for the region.

Some groups involved in community development in Pittsburgh are a good deal more autonomous than the CDCs, the PDP, and PUMP. For example, independent environmental groups such as the local Group Against Smog and Pollution (GASP), the statewide Citizens for Pennsylvania's Future and 10,000 Friends of Pennsylvania, and the national Sierra Club are deeply involved in community development issues in Pittsburgh. Their relative independence from the city and the downtown corporate business sector gives them greater freedom to openly challenge redevelopment agendas that they oppose. Three autonomous nonprofit groups were instrumental in organizing participation in my fifth case study and therefore warrant a more detailed description: the Pittsburgh History and Landmarks Foundation, the Allegheny Institute, and the Institute for Justice.

As I mentioned above, the PHLF has an endowment, as well as membership fees, that help support its activities. The group also uses foundation grants, especially from the Scaife family trusts, to underwrite new, risky projects. The Scaifes have long invested in initiatives to challenge the dominance of Pittsburgh's corporatist governing coalition,[44] as illustrated above in their involvement with Station Square.

The Pittsburgh History and Landmarks Foundation has organizational capacities and an operating strategy that inevitably involve them in activities beyond financing and planning historic restoration projects. Education and advocacy are essential aspects of their mission, which they have carried out with support from the national preservation movement.[45] The National Trust for Historic Preservation is a membership organization that raises awareness about the benefits of preservation, provides technical support for historic rehabilitation projects, and conducts public advocacy for preservation issues. The PHLF's local advocacy efforts benefit from the national movement's success at building public support for preservation issues.

The local Allegheny Institute for Public Policy was founded in 1995 as an educational nonprofit organization with a mission to "champion the interests of the taxpayers through its commitment to free markets, small government, individual liberty, and the protection of property rights."[46] Like PHLF, the institute was started with seed money from the Scaife foundations. It earned a reputation as a powerful critic of corporatist politics in 1996–1997 by leading a successful community movement against a referendum that would have raised the sales tax in eleven counties to finance construction of professional sports stadiums in downtown Pittsburgh. As a result of this and subsequent successes, the institute attracted significant support from membership subscriptions and foundations other than Scaife.

In 1991 the Institute for Justice was founded in Washington DC as a "civil liberties law firm" to defend people against "arbitrary and oppressive" government in areas such as free speech, small business entrepreneurship, school choice, and private property rights. The firm intervenes in cases of eminent domain "abuse" in local redevelopment, which it views as use of government authority to acquire and transfer property from one private owner to another. This institute is another beneficiary of Scaife seed money, but by 2003 it had 9,000 donors, with no single one contributing more than 7 percent of its annual budget. With an annual budget rising from just over $1 million in 1993 to $3.5 million by 2000, the firm has maintained a policy of giving free legal services to property owners threatened by eminent domain abuse. It took its first property rights case in December 1996 when it applied to the New Jersey Supreme Court to join a lawsuit challenging the use of eminent domain by New Jersey's Casino Reinvestment Development Authority for the purpose of acquiring residential properties that would then be transferred to the Trump Company for construction of a casino parking lot. Although the Institute for Justice was incorporated as a nonprofit law firm, staff attorneys have invested considerable effort in assisting and training grassroots activists to fight against eminent domain. They hold workshops and conferences that train activists in how to get important information about a redevelopment project they want to oppose, how to work effectively with the media, how to build community support for their struggles, and how to network with activists in other places.[47]

The emergence of independent organizations, autonomous from local growth coalitions but with stakes in local redevelopment issues, began to create a more pluralistic system of redevelopment politics by 1993 when State Senator Tom Murphy was elected mayor of Pittsburgh. Mayor Murphy, a former activist in the Manchester neighborhood, responded to the region's continued economic decline with an aggressive urban growth agenda that emphasized investing in the preservation and strengthening of downtown and reusing older industrial sites for business retention, expansion, and relocation opportunities.[48] One goal of the investment strategy was to increase opportunities for entertainment, shopping, tourism, and housing in the downtown area, which had clearly suffered from the growth of accessible shopping and entertainment options in other parts of the region.[49] The Murphy administration believed that making Pittsburgh a "twenty-four-hour city" would, among other things, facilitate capital investment by attracting the twenty-one-to-thirty-nine-year-old college graduates demanded by advanced technology companies.

In Murphy's first year as mayor, the Urban Redevelopment Authority acquired five hundred acres of property for the city, the largest land purchase in its history. "We bought this property," Murphy said in an interview, "because it was not particularly attractive to anybody, it wasn't producing taxes, and we believed that we could, with aggressive management, get it back to adding value to the city."[50] In order to finance his ambitious redevelopment agenda, Murphy started the Pittsburgh Development Fund (PDF) and the Strategic Investment Fund (SIF). The Development Fund was created with a budgetary commitment from the city of $7 million a year. Banks and foundations agreed to match the contribution, resulting in $120 million for low-interest, flexible financing of redevelopment projects. The Strategic Investment Fund was capitalized with $40 million of private contributions from thirty regional corporations, foundations, and individuals. It provided financial incentives—for example, flexible loan terms and deferred interest—for private developers to partner with the city on large-scale redevelopment projects.

Architecture and the built environment were Mayor Murphy's proudest accomplishments, and his most influential changes upon the cityscape were financed by the PDF and SIF. The largest is the 1.5 million square foot David L. Lawrence Convention Center, an environmental award-winning symbol of the new Pittsburgh. Another important product of the funds is Penn Avenue Place, a $56 million historic renovation of a turn-of-the-century dry-goods department store into a 560,000-square-foot office and retail complex. The PHLF designated the building as a historic landmark and it was carefully adapted into a high-energy efficient office and retail space. A third major project, a downtown Lazarus department store, embodied the same quality of design and engineering as the other major projects. But it is unique in the extent of its commercial failure. The store closed its doors in 2004 after absorbing $48 million in public subsidies and operating for only five years.

I will expand on the Lazarus story in the next chapter, but here I want to emphasize that the Lazarus project was similar to several other large redevelopment deals—including retail projects, sports stadiums, and industrial expansion projects—in the extent to which it suffered under public scrutiny. In the pluralistic political environment of the 1990s, major redevelopment packages involving substantial public financing and use of government authority (that is, eminent domain) to assemble properties were vulnerable to criticism from taxpayers and property rights advocates, preservationists, and neighborhood groups. The pro-

fessional staff, organizational resources, and technical expertise
of autonomous nonprofit groups like the PHLF and the Allegheny Institute for Public Policy were instrumental in mobilizing
credible challenges to corporatist-style redevelopment projects.
Mayor Murphy also advanced a massive housing redevelopment agenda through the creation of the Pittsburgh Housing
Development Corporation (PHDC), a government-sponsored
citwide CDC. The PHDC worked closely with the URA to construct both upscale housing meant to attract and retain young
professionals and affordable housing for the region's low- and
moderate-income population. The PHDC allowed the mayor,
instead of just the URA or neighborhood CDCs, to exert control
over neighborhood housing projects. Perhaps the greatest
achievement of the PHDC is the nationally acclaimed Crawford
Square, an eighteen-acre racially and economically mixed residential neighborhood in the Lower Hill. Crawford Square was the
first residential construction project in the Lower Hill since the
neighborhood was razed thirty-five years ago.

Political Opportunity and Mobilizing Structures, 1994–2000

The focus of the Murphy administration's urban growth agenda on construction of large-scale regional assets and mixed-use
neighborhood projects represented one solution to the problem
of economic restructuring and long-term economic and population decline in Pittsburgh. In the context of continued economic
decline, federal withdrawal from urban redevelopment, and the
apparent failure of CDCs to reverse urban problems, the Murphy
administration attempted to gain greater control of the redevelopment agenda, which created some tensions between the neighborhoods and Murphy's growth coalition.[51]

Despite the continuing struggles of neighborhood groups,
those seeking to influence the policy process through contentious
politics benefited from a more open structure of political opportunities when compared to their counterparts at midcentury.
Mayor Pete Flaherty began a tradition of mayoral nonintervention in council politics that destabilized elite alignments and cre-

ated incentives for council members to form alliances with neighborhood groups in opposition to growth agendas. The transition to a district electoral system in council in 1987 created even greater potential for division among the branches of government. The corporate business sector maintained systemic power over other actors in the community due to the continued importance of private capital for the creation of wealth and jobs in the local economy. But with the disinvestment of steel in the 1980s and the corresponding diversification of the regional economy, high technology and other industries grew in relative importance. No longer could a single individual such as an R. K. Mellon speak for the entire corporate business community. This pluralism in the private sector compromised the capacity of corporate leaders to preemptively control the urban redevelopment process. The decline in resources, especially time, that corporate executives could devote to community issues further eroded the preemptive power of the business community.

Contentious challengers of urban growth politics in the 1990s also benefited from autonomous mobilizing structures that did not exist in the early postwar era, as exemplified by the Allegheny Institute for Public Policy, the Pittsburgh History and Landmarks Foundation, the Institute for Justice, and the National Trust for Historic Preservation. In the next chapter I will show how these organizations shaped the dynamics of a neighborhood challenge against one of Mayor Murphy's most ambitious redevelopment projects—the transformation of the city's downtown retail district.

5

Contentious Politics
of Downtown Revitalization,
1997–2000

■ My fifth case study begins in September 1997, when a
Chicago developer, Urban Retail Properties, signed a development option and consulting deal with the City of Pittsburgh.
According to the agreement, Urban Retail was to explore the pos-
sibility of initiating a large-scale redevelopment project in the
city's downtown retail district.[1] Existing businesses in the district
were predominantly small, locally owned stores that served workers and residents in or near the Golden Triangle. For over thirty
years merchants in the district had been losing business to regional malls, a problem that public officials, civic leaders, and businesses agreed had to be addressed. The mayor's office, however,
did not ask these stakeholders to participate in the initial stages of
planning with Urban Retail, which led journalists to characterize
the relationship between Urban Retail and the city as one of "secrecy" and exclusion.[2]

The city made its first public announcement on the status of
consultations with Urban Retail in March 1998, when AMC Entertainment of Kansas City signed a letter of intent to build a four-
thousand-seat theater in the retail district.[3] At that point
newspaper coverage began to rise steadily and it became clear
that Urban Retail was planning to add 400,000 to 600,000 square

feet of new retail space along Fifth and Forbes Avenues downtown. Yet neither the developer nor the Murphy administration indicated where this new space would be located or what existing buildings and properties might be displaced by their plan. When Murphy's staff discussed the issue publicly, they framed it as a component of the Pittsburgh Downtown Plan, a comprehensive ten-year development strategy completed in 1998 after a yearlong process of citizen participation. By defining the contract with Urban Retail as a step in the implementation of the downtown plan, rather than a planning process in its own right, the Murphy administration hoped to benefit from the plan's legitimacy in the community.[4]

Pittsburgh History and Landmarks Foundation and Conventional Politics

On September 30, 1997, Arthur Ziegler of the Pittsburgh History and Landmarks Foundation wrote a letter to Murphy's director of development requesting a meeting with Urban Retail to "review with them what we feel are the significant buildings in the area."[5] Ziegler had learned about the arrangement between the city and Urban Retail through a *Pittsburgh Business Times* article. According to Cathy McCollom, PHLF director of marketing and public relations, it is common practice among preservationists to take action well in advance of official announcements of redevelopment projects that potentially threaten older buildings or historic districts. Since much of the Fifth and Forbes project area was located inside the Market Square historic district, preservationists had cause for concern. After several phone calls to the city following the letter of September 30, the mayor agreed to meet and discuss which buildings should be protected against demolition. At the meeting, officials revealed the basic outline of Urban Retail's plan, from which Ziegler concluded that it was a "demolition and rebuilding project." He recommended against significant demolition and made specific suggestions regarding the treatment of forty-three historically significant buildings and facades in the area.[6]

The city continued to work with Urban Retail into the spring of 1998 without giving any firm indication to PHLF that their recommendations for saving specific buildings and facades would be taken seriously. In June, Ziegler offered his foundation's services to the city for organizing an "open forum" on preservation issues in retail redevelopment. The purpose was to provide input to the city from professional designers and preservationists and also to allow interested members of the community to have their views heard. On several occasions Ziegler contacted both City Planning and the mayor's office to secure approval for such a forum.[7] While officials said they were friendly toward such an idea, they avoided settling upon a date to hold the meeting. The deputy mayor was concerned that the "open forum" idea would significantly slow down the planning process and lead to requests for changes that Urban Retail might not wish to make, such as allowing various existing retailers to have a place in the final plan. The PHLF responded to these concerns by changing the open forum concept to a "working committee on saving facades"[8] that included architects from PHLF and Preservation Pittsburgh, another local historic preservation group.[9] After convening once in July, however, the city and Urban Retail neglected to maintain the discussions with PHLF that were begun in their initial session.[10]

On July 22, City Council passed a nonbinding resolution approving the URA's exploration of a $17 million tax increment financing plan (TIF) for several redevelopment projects. Tax increment financing is an innovative but controversial public financing mechanism that many states have implemented in response to the decline in federal funding for urban redevelopment. It enables cities to appropriate additional property taxes generated by new development in order to pay for expenses incurred in supporting the development. To take advantage of the mechanism, officials must first create a TIF district, which requires approval by all taxing bodies in the proposed area (the county, the city, and the school district), as they are required to forgo revenues from the increment of value added to taxable real estate during the period of the TIF.

Market Square. Photo by Beth Conant. Used by permission of the photographer.

The Warner Centre and Lazarus Department Store, Fifth Avenue, downtown Pittsburgh. Photo by Beth Conant. Used by permission of the photographer.

Seven million dollars of the TIF approved by council was to be used to help prepare Fifth and Forbes Avenues for retail redevelopment.[11] This was an important victory in the mayor's effort to advance his agenda for retail revitalization, but it alarmed an increasingly frustrated Arthur Ziegler, who saw the Urban Retail plan beginning to come together while he still had no assurance that the values of preservation would be respected. On July 29 the mayor scored another important victory when Pennsylvania Governor Tom Ridge released $10 million in state aid toward the city's effort to "purchase land, demolish buildings and relocate existing businesses" in the retail redevelopment district.[12] The next day Urban Retail officials went public with the most detailed description to date of their plan for downtown redevelopment. The International Council of Shopping Centers held an "idea exchange" at the Pittsburgh Hilton and Towers, where the president of Urban Retail announced that his company had reached "an agreement with the City of Pittsburgh" to create a 600,000 square foot retail and entertainment corridor downtown. Dubbed Market Place at Fifth and Forbes, the redevelopment was estimated to cost $170 million.[13] The agreement was not a formal contract, but represented the intention of both parties to work toward a contract once the developer lined up a "critical mass" of companies intent upon participating in the project.

The retail component of Urban Retail's plan featured more than forty "high-end" specialty chain stores such as Tiffany & Co., FAO Schwarz, and Victoria's Secret, while the entertainment element included franchise restaurants like Planet Hollywood and All-Star Café, along with the twenty-four-screen movie theater proposed by AMC. Urban Retail would own most of the land, lease the space, manage the buildings, set the hours of operation, and market the project to visitors and shoppers. The company would provide the URA with $23 million up front for demolition and relocation expenses, while the URA would acquire buildings, move businesses, clear the land, and sell the properties to Urban Retail for fair market value.[14]

Category Formation and the Rise of Opposition to Market Place at Fifth and Forbes

From the point of view of Murphy's development team the only steps remaining in the Market Place plan were for Urban Retail to sell the idea to national retailers, secure letters of intent from them, and then begin the process of land acquisition and demolition. But not everyone in the community was satisfied. The city had yet to provide details on which buildings were slated for demolition, which merchants would be removed, and which properties possibly taken by eminent domain. Further, the city still had not invited people who worked, lived, shopped, or owned property in the neighborhood to participate in shaping the project. Had these stakeholders been allowed to view details of the plan, they would have seen that many national chain stores were sketched in locations of existing Pittsburgh businesses.

In autumn 1998, Bernie Lynch was executive director of the Market Square Association, an organization that marketed and promoted retail, dining, and entertainment in the lower third of the Fifth and Forbes retail corridor. After reading about the plan in the newspapers, Lynch began "going into people's businesses [in the district] and saying, 'Did you hear about the plan and what they are going to do?'" According to her it took a lot of convincing to get people concerned about the possible fate of their properties, businesses, and historic buildings. Most were unconcerned mainly because they did not take the efforts of the city seriously. Rumors about major changes downtown had circulated periodically since the Caliguiri era, but nothing had come of them. Besides, most believed that if the city were really planning large land acquisitions, the community would be involved at an early stage.

Lynch held an unusual belief that the city had an obligation to allow public input into the creation of the Urban Retail plan as it appeared to involve such a massive dislocation of downtown businesses and property owners. Like the PHLF, Lynch believed the Murphy administration was creating a plan in private with Urban Retail that would then be presented to the community at some future point when it would be too late to change or oppose it. Lynch brought together a group of aggrieved stakeholders in downtown redevelopment, which included merchants, property owners, workers, and others who depended on special-use values attached to the built environment of downtown. Her message to them was that they were threatened by the city's preparations to demolish the buildings and displace existing businesses.[15]

In October a local journalist suggested to Lynch that she contact the Institute for Justice for advice on how to oppose the city's plans. The institute eventually performed a crucial role in appropriating resources to mobilize opposition to Market Place at Fifth and Forbes, as I will discuss later. At this stage, the public interest law firm began advising her on how to win any future battle with the city. Their central piece of advice was to "let everyone know about the injustice of the plan. . . . Shout long, hard, and loud, and don't stop shouting until justice is served."[16] Institute attorneys were not hopeful that opponents could stop public authorities from approving a plan to transfer property from one private party to another, but they believed opponents could "win in the court of public opinion."

October was also the month in which urban critic Roberta Gratz gave an important talk, as part of the PHLF Making Cities Work lecture series, on "three years studying what is working in revitalizing downtowns and what isn't."[17] She addressed a capacity audience that included invited public officials, business leaders, preservationists, planners, and civic leaders. In her lecture Gratz distinguished the "reborn" from the "rebuilt" city. A reborn city utilizes existing buildings and businesses; a rebuilt city starts from scratch. The problem facing Pittsburgh, according to Gratz, was how to cultivate a rebirth through the collective efforts of the community and support of local government. The city, in her view, could assist local businesses by helping them market their products and services by improving roads and sidewalks, and by creating incentives for owners to improve building facades. Gratz attacked the mayor's plan as a rebuilding project that would destroy existing buildings, remove tenants, and transfer control over the tenant mix to a single management company.[18]

Accompanied by journalists, Gratz toured the redevelopment area after her talk. En route, she defined a gap in the public's understanding of what was at stake in the redevelopment of downtown: "This is a replacement, not a rebirth project. I don't think people know how many local businesses will be displaced."[19] Gratz went on to argue that downtowns under single management are never as successful as those in which buildings are owned individually. Her comments were not only critical but well informed from research documented in her popular book, *Cities Back from the Edge*.

The persuasiveness of Gratz's ideas helped to legitimize other kinds of criticism. For instance, Sala Udin, City Council representative for downtown, attended the lecture and expressed concern that the whole approach for revitalizing downtown was occurring in a top-down fashion that excluded important stakeholders in the community. "There is an absence of public planning process and lack of public dialogue," he told the audience. "I don't see the forum for the public who lives in and uses the downtown area to come together and develop a policy for the city. That's what is missing."[20] Udin defined a somewhat broader category of stakeholders than Bernie Lynch—all those who lived in and *used* downtown.

Despite growing discontent among preservationists and neighborhood activists, the city and Urban Retail continued to assemble the Fifth and Forbes project without public input. The day after Gratz's visit the mayor announced the completion of another major component in the realization of his downtown vision. At a news conference held in front of the former Mellon Bank building downtown, Murphy announced that department store Lord & Taylor had agreed to move into the building upon the city's offer of $11.75 million in subsidies to the company.[21] Lord & Taylor would be the fifth major department store within an area of a few blocks in the retail district. The city was also negotiating with Nordstrom of Seattle to become the sixth and final department store to participate in the project. Officials viewed department stores as crucial participants in the retail redevelopment. As "anchors" they would draw large crowds to the district and generate foot traffic on the sidewalks along the forty or so expected boutiques in Market Place. The Lord & Taylor deal would make the project more attractive to prospective tenants.

Yet the city's agreement with Lord & Taylor served only to widen the growing rift between public officials and preservationists, who were particularly concerned about the department store's intention to renovate the interior of the Mellon Bank building to fit the needs of a retail establishment. Built in 1924 in the neoclassical style, the interior of the building consisted of twenty-four marble Ionic columns supporting a dramatic sixty-two-foot-high ceiling. According to PHLF, the Mellon building housed one of the city's "most magnificent interiors." The preservation group wanted to be part of any negotiations between the city, the bank, and the department store to be sure that no tax subsidies would be used to destroy the bank's interior. When the three parties neglected to include the PHLF in their negotiations, preservationists took this to mean destruction of the interior was imminent.[22]

Preservationists Appropriate Social Resources for Contention

Landmarks geared up for a longer battle with the city. On November 9, the group placed the first in a series of preservation "alerts" on its Web site and into its quarterly newsletter, the *PHLF News*. The alerts were designed to draw the attention of members and other preservation-minded people to any preventable threat to historic buildings and to provide an immediate and practical means of minimizing such a threat. The November alert began by framing Market Place as a subsidized "new downtown retail complex which could involve the total demolition of almost ten blocks of buildings." It listed ten recommendations for revising the plan, including the saving of some historic buildings and facades, inclusion of housing in the plan, and retention or recruitment of unique Pittsburgh retail businesses not represented in Market Place at Fifth and Forbes. The alert ended with the statement, "To support our recommendations and oppose total demolition, write or call the mayor's office or the office of your council person."

The Web page contained a link to the mayor's office. The alert framed an issue of potential injustice (the possible "total demolition" of ten blocks of buildings), around which another category of stakeholder was created—all those people who view historic buildings as a community asset. In addition, through its links to elected representatives, the alert was a resource for interested parties to take direct action to prevent the injustice from occurring.

On November 10, PHLF created a memorandum of agreement with Preservation Pittsburgh to convene a Fifth and Forbes Preservation Working Group in order to "advocate the preservation of buildings and facades . . . advocate a balanced involvement of local businesses and landowners in the [Fifth and Forbes] project . . . [and] advocate a complete and timely public review of the project concept through an appointed task force and a public 'town meeting' process." The working group outlined a strategy by which they would appropriate resources to raise public awareness about preservation issues related to the mayor's downtown agenda and mobilize people to get involved in redefining that agenda. Key elements of social appropriation included setting up a Web site and e-mail alert system, developing a public relations kit (a slide show with scripts for outreach presentations to CDCs, planners and architects, and other organized community groups), printing flyers and white papers analyzing the hazards of Market Place, sending a mass mailing to all major organizations in the community, meeting with organizations to coordinate a "community planning process," applying for grants and financial support for the cause, and preparing worst-case tactics in advance, which would define "when we go ballistic."[23]

Beginning in January 1999, the Fifth and Forbes project was on the monthly agenda of the Historic Review Commission of Pittsburgh, which had to give its approval to building alterations in the Market Square historic district. No date had been set for the commission to make a decision on the approval of Market Place at Fifth and Forbes. Their purpose at this point was to review the plan and provide the developer with recommendations on which buildings were worth preserving. The commission's meetings were, by statute, open to the public. Preservationists saw the open meetings as an opportunity to communicate their concerns about Fifth and Forbes to an authority designated to approve the plan. They showed up at monthly meetings with maps indicating which buildings they wanted to protect from demolition and ideas for an alternative to Market Place. In attributing political opportunity to commission meetings, preservationists also shifted the object of their claims from the mayor and his invisible bureaucrats to an independent authority invested with the responsibility of preserving the city's historic assets.[24]

The commission meetings also served to broker a connection between preservationists and another group of stakeholders, Bernie Lynch and a group of business owners she had been trying to organize since October. They, too, used the meetings as an opportunity to communicate concerns about the Fifth and Forbes agenda that the city had yet to hear.[25] The two groups discussed their grievances at the meetings, discovered common concerns, and eventually formed a Fifth/Forbes Planning Group for purposes of creating an alternative to the plan of Urban Retail Properties. Four statutory authorities—the City Planning Commission, the Historic Review Commission, the URA, and City Council— had to approve Market Place before work could begin.[26] All except the URA were required to hold public hearings before voting on a proposal, though the City Planning Commission, the Historic Review Commission, and the URA were staffed by mayoral appointees who would feel pressure to approve Murphy's plan as quickly as possible. The alternative plan was to serve two purposes. First, it would be "open to everybody and anybody" in the city interested in participating and would thus create public sentiment favorable to their cause. Second, having a plan of their own could provide critics of the Urban Retail plan with bargaining power in City Council, the one approving agency not appointed by the mayor.

The first phase of the alternative planning process consisted of provoking a broad cross-section of the community to begin questioning and criticizing Market Place at Fifth and Forbes. To this end, in the spring Preservation Pittsburgh and its state-level affiliate, Preservation Pennsylvania, placed the downtown area on their annual listing of Pennsylvania's "most endangered historic properties."[27] In the summer, PHLF followed up with Web site alerts and hundreds of letters clipped to copies of a special issue of *PHLF News* addressed to downtown tenants, landowners, and leaders of organizations across the region.[28] Several articles in the newsletter criticized the city's willingness to destroy historical properties, to replace local tenants with national chains, to give control over the future of downtown to a single out-of-town developer, and to create the entire agenda without public input. One essay presented suggestions for an alternative to Market Place and invited readers to show their support for the suggestions by contacting City Council, the mayor's office, or the newspapers. All the major newspapers received PHLF's mailing and each wrote a lead story on the opposition to Market Place. The *Post-Gazette* referred to the newsletter as "a call to arms" because it urged readers who shared PHLF's views to communicate their concerns to elected officials and to participate in the planning of their downtown.[29]

As the planning group entered phase two—enlisting the growing audience of critics to participate in an alternative planning process—PHLF again assumed the lead role. Ziegler commissioned New York architects Ehrenkrantz, Eckstut, and Kuhn, who were experienced in incremental downtown revitalization, to study the area, collect input from participants, and create an alternative plan. The planning group agreed to hold a series of six open meetings for public participation beginning on September 22. Ziegler explained the purpose of the public process: "We need the benefit of grassroots opinions, merchants' opinions, building owners' opinions, [and] customers' opinions.[30]

The whole process would take eight weeks, beginning at the first meeting with architect Stan Eckstut "standing in the front of the room asking people what they wanted," and then returning with a preliminary plan that would be subject to further public commentary and refinement until a plan that satisfied all participants was established.[31] In addition to posting announcements on its Preservation Alert Web site, the PHLF publicized the planning process through direct invitations to six hundred organization leaders and through newspaper, radio, and cable television advertisements.[32]

Polarization and the Unveiling of Market Place at Fifth and Forbes

Downtown landowners and businesses had still not received official word from the mayor's office by the end of summer 1999. In June, business owner Patty Maloney first heard about the mayor's plans from a construction worker on the street in front of her store. The worker, who was replacing sidewalks for the opening of the Lazarus department store, told Maloney her block would not be getting new sidewalks because it was "slated for demolition." In the same month, newspapers reported that Urban Retail had begun marketing its Pittsburgh project at national shopping center conventions. The papers published marketing materials specifying where the project, now estimated to cost $400 million, would be situated downtown. The renderings showed that some buildings would be left alone while others would get absorbed into the development, displacing existing tenants.[33]

Before the marketing materials were published, many members of the Market Square Association were "kind of waiting for the day to come" when the mayor would contact them to discuss his plans.[34] To be sure, people were frustrated that the city was not sharing more information with them, but they learned as much as possible from the newspapers and took every opportunity, such as the Historic Review Commission meetings, to communicate concerns about the security of their businesses and property. When people in the neighborhood heard that Urban Retail had begun marketing a completed plan prior to any formal word from the city, their frustration was transformed into anger. The "wait and see" approach was no longer their operating principle.

Bernie Lynch told reporters, "It's ludicrous. They're lining up new tenants without letting current ones know what is happening." An owner of a small bookstore, whose shop would be replaced by a Borders Books and Music, reacted to the news: "If big chain stores were all we had to worry about, that would be fine. It's the city that causes us the most problems. . . . I'll pick up a newspaper story and there'll be a map of our street and a Banana Republic store in the space where we are. . . . You pay your business privilege tax only to have it used against you to force you out." The owner of a Market Square restaurant responded to the news in a similar way: "The city is just sucking the blood out of the smaller businesses in town and putting all of its money into projects where the developers and businesses are from out of town. . . . It just doesn't make sense." "If it wasn't for people like us," reacted the owner of another Market Square restaurant, "Market Square wouldn't be on the map. . . . Now we're going to see the [Murphy administration] turn its back on us."[35]

The growing polarization between the neighborhood and the city caused Patty Maloney and other business owners to join with Lynch in challenging Market Place at Fifth and Forbes. These new challengers found a creative outlet for their anger in the alternative planning process and were joined by hundreds of others enlisted by the Fifth/Forbes Planning Group. The mayor had to move quickly on his plan or risk having the redevelopment process co-opted by a growing coalition of his opponents. While his opponents enjoyed far greater legitimacy, Murphy had much of the money required to make his plan work. On September 9 the URA approved two additional sources of funding, a $17 million loan from the Pittsburgh Development Fund and a $10 million loan from the Strategic Investment Fund. Adding these funds to the $10 million given by the state in July 1998, the $14 million in TIF money approved by City Council in November 1998, and a recent $10 million grant application to the state's Redevelopment Assistance Capital Program, Murphy had over half of the public funds called for in his financing plan, and Urban Retail had promised $169 million upon public approval of the project.[36]

The mayor announced his plan at a special news conference on October 4. In all, 125 businesses, occupying 62 properties, would be relocated to accommodate the new development. Murphy moved swiftly to gain the required approvals. In a special board meeting that same afternoon the URA approved the plan, and within days the URA's director of real estate mailed letters containing information about property acquisition and relocation to affected property owners and occupants.[37] By November, well before other authorities had approved the plan, demolition experts were surveying the properties slated for removal. Patty

Maloney recounts how the demolition person first showed up at her business on the day before Thanksgiving: "A guy comes into the store and . . . he looks at me and says 'I'm from the City and I need to get into your basement.' And I said 'For what?' And I'm thinking, is it for the sidewalks or what is it? And he said 'I'm the demolition person and I need to look at the structure to see where the dynamite is supposed to go.'" Sixty-one other property owners had experiences similar to Maloney's. She characterizes the general reaction of people who met after Thanksgiving to discuss the issue: "[We became] so unbelievably hostile. . . . I mean it really hit the point where the principle of the thing, of using eminent domain to replace retail with retail, of subsidizing retail, I mean the whole thing was just so egregious that, at a really visceral level people were just saying no."[38]

For two years officials had effectively kept the community out of the planning process by not inviting participation and by keeping a tight grip on information that opponents would have needed to adequately respond to the plan. "There will be plenty of time for debate once a contract is signed with URP," was the refrain from the mayor's office.[39] During this time, the plan was linked with the financing required to make it withstand criticism that was sure to come after its placement on the public agenda. With the plan now on the agenda, the city moved as quickly as possible to implement it with minimum debate, responding to public criticism by reminding people that Market Place at Fifth and Forbes was a proposal with a developer and financing already in place.[40] For example, when in December PUMP offered to sponsor a "side by side" comparison of the plans of Ehrenkrantz, Eckstut, and Kuhn and Urban Retail, the URA director of development responded, "When approached about a 'side by side comparison of the two plans,' we are happy to provide information to clarify and detail our plan. However, I believe that the format of this comparison is like comparing apples to oranges. For instance, our Market Place at Fifth and Forbes plan is an economically viable plan, with a developer and financing in place. The EEK [Ehrenkrantz, Eckstut, and Kuhn] column is based upon an architectural exercise."[41]

From the opponents' point of view it appeared that city officials were not serious about their promise for a public debate
"once a deal is struck." Instead, officials urged a streamlined approval process in order to get their project underway. The resulting polarization between the Murphy administration and the
critics of Market Place at Fifth and Forbes was revealed in a protracted public planning process, which would stretch out four
times longer than the administration had hoped.

Brokerage and Attribution of Political Opportunity in the Alternative Planning Process

Between October and December 1999 public participation
unfolded in two arenas, one sponsored by the Fifth/Forbes Planning Group and the other, required by law, in the public agencies
reviewing Market Place at Fifth and Forbes. A group of about 250
"usual suspects" attended both sets of meetings, most of them
learning of the controversy from the planning group's media
campaign earlier in the summer.[42] The meetings mobilized a
broad range of community interests. As one participant put it,
"You ha[d] your preservationists. . . . Then you had . . . people
who were all about dollars and taxes. . . . You had a lot of libertarians showing up. . . . There was this very strange amalgam of people."[43] Property rights advocates protested the city's threat of
eminent domain, urban planners attacked the city's failure to include housing in its plan, and taxpayer groups insisted that the estimated $100 million in public financing[44] for Market Place was
an irresponsible use of government resources.

An important consequence of the planning group's meetings
was to bring previously unconnected stakeholders together in the
same place, brokering new relations. Pat Clark, who worked
downtown for a successful national retailer, showed up regularly
for the meetings. He characterized the brokering function this
way: "I sat down [at the meetings]—you know I'm a bleeding
heart liberal Democrat who . . . has voted for [Mayor] Tom Murphy in the past—sitting next to a guy who was as far right as I'd
ever want to be associated with. [We were] all fighting the same

battle."[45] It was through the relationships formed at the public meetings that previously unconnected people began to combine their efforts to redefine or stop the Fifth and Forbes project. Participants joined one another's mailing and e-mail lists and declared their support for subsequent collective actions.

Opponents welcomed any opportunity to delay action in proceedings by the Historic Review Commission, the City Planning Commission, or City Council, because it would give them more time to prepare and advocate for alternatives to Market Place at Fifth and Forbes. Arthur Ziegler played an essential role in this endeavor. He began by persuading the Planning Commission to delay action on the mayor's proposal from its original November 9 scheduled date to November 24 in order to provide time to review the Ehrenkrantz, Eckstut, and Kuhn plan.[46] The delay bought time and created further opportunities for challengers to have their voices heard, but it failed to prevent the Planning Commission from approving Market Place at Fifth and Forbes. On November 23 the Planning Commission certified the redevelopment area as blighted—a first step in taking properties by eminent domain—and approved the redevelopment proposal.[47]

After three public hearings, the Historic Review Commission also decided to put off its scheduled December 10 vote because of "opposition . . . and a lack of specifics" about how the plan would affect significant buildings in the district.[48] In preparation for the rescheduled vote of January 8, Ziegler invited a representative of the National Trust for Historic Preservation to join him in testimony against Murphy's plan. After three hours of testimony, however, the Historic Review Commission voted unanimously to approve Market Place at Fifth and Forbes. The representative for the National Trust reacted: "I'm totally shocked. If you read the city ordinance, if you read the guidelines, the design and preservation guidelines that the city has adopted for the district and the commission has established for review, there is no way they can legally support this project."[49]

Opponents enjoyed greater success in the district-elected City Council than in the other decision-making agencies. New relations formed in the dozens of meetings from October through

December, when the mayor expected council to make a decision, resulted in a new sequence of contention revolving around a second alternative to Market Place at Fifth and Forbes. Bernie Lynch's neighborhood activists established the Golden Triangle Community Development Corporation to create a downtown "Main Street" plan based on principles of incremental change through partnerships between government and existing local businesses. Representatives of the Pittsburgh History and Landmarks Foundation sat on the board of the new CDC and put the group in touch with the Main Street Center of the National Trust for Historic Preservation and the Pittsburgh-based firm Edge Architecture, which provided professional support in formulating the plan. Though the PHLF had already invested $40,000 in its own alternative planning process, the group was open to approaches of any type. "We offered an alternative to show that there were alternatives," PHLF's Cathy McCollom said, "but not to monopolize the planning process."[50]

Volunteers from the Golden Triangle CDC set up meetings with ten of the largest, most active CDCs in Pittsburgh to sell them on the Main Street approach and to persuade them to actively oppose the mayor's plan. City Council was aware of this process in the neighborhoods because council member Jim Ferlo, a longtime community activist, was working closely with the Golden Triangle people. In January he held a community meeting in council chambers, attended by over three hundred people, to protest Market Place and drum up support for the Main Street approach.

With so much controversy surrounding his plan, the mayor finally put on the brakes. Instead of submitting the plan for council's approval, he directed Urban Retail to respond to the critics with a reformed Fifth and Forbes concept. The delay led council member Sala Udin, along with the Pittsburgh Downtown Partnership, the Allegheny Conference, and the H. J. Heinz Foundation, to initiate a Downtown Planning Collaborative in order to provide the community with "accurate and comprehensive information" on the proposed Market Place, to gather their input, and to provide an official avenue for communicating that input to government.[51] The collaborative, which first met in February 2000, engaged a diverse group of over six hundred participants, including property rights and taxpayer advocates, preservationists, Main Street adherents, and proponents of Market Place. It was organized around a "stakeholder group process," by which people interested in different issue areas—merchandising, financing, eminent domain, disruption mitigation, relocation, or urban design—could compare the three existing plans.

By March, seven of nine council members had said they would vote against Market Place unless substantial changes were made, such as including local retailers in the mix and taking eminent domain off the table. Three members, Bob O'Connor, Alan Hertzberg, and Jim Ferlo, introduced a resolution establishing a Pittsburgh Main Street Task Force and urged Mayor Murphy to endorse the Main Street concept.[52] The momentum of the planning process had shifted toward the Main Street approach, and this signaled a political opportunity to an entirely new group of challengers. In the winter, a group of about two hundred people identifying themselves as "young professionals" had begun meeting regularly to "discuss, vent, rant, praise, invent, solve, and create ideas relating to Pittsburgh as a 'Center for the New Economy.'" Many of them were frustrated by the lack of a voice for young people who wanted to change Pittsburgh's culture and politics.[53]

The young professionals created the Ground Zero Action Network, an informal group held together by regular meetings and e-mail announcements, which functioned as a resource for members to garner support in advancing their own civic projects, such as improving public transportation, renovating older buildings, and fighting the mayor's Fifth and Forbes plan. Pat Clark quickly became involved in Ground Zero when the group contacted him to help locate a downtown meeting venue. According to Clark, the Fifth and Forbes controversy was "the core around which [Ground Zero] formed. It was the issue that drove them to mobilization."[54] The group issued a statement endorsing the Main Street approach and the architects and designers among them participated in developing a plan for downtown.[55] They opposed Market Place because it lacked a substantial housing component, because it did not include mixed-use spaces for artists and start-up companies, and because it was created by an "undemocratic" process that was totally inconsistent with the cooperative values they espoused. The founders of Ground Zero created a wholly new form of collective action, the action network, without officers or formal organizational roles. Being a member of the network involved nothing more, or less, than advancing a civic project through personal leadership. In this sense it represented what McAdam, Tarrow, and Tilly call "transgressive" contention. Contention becomes transgressive when at least one party to the conflict identifies itself as a new political actor and "adopts means that are either unprecedented or forbidden within the regime in question."[56] Innovation contributed to Ground Zero's appeal to younger people who were looking for points of entry into the local political system. The open, nonhierarchical structure of the network served as both an organizing strategy and a metaphor for the strong vision of democracy held by members.

Certification, Object Shift, and Social Appropriation: The Role of Autonomous Mobilizing Structures

In the last chapter I stated that challengers of urban growth elites in the 1990s had the benefit of mobilizing structures—autonomous national and local nonprofits—unavailable to their counterparts in the 1940s and 1950s. This point has been illustrated by the prominent role in Fifth and Forbes played by the Pittsburgh History and Landmarks Foundation and other preservation groups. In spring 1998 the PHLF was the first to draw public attention to the city's "secretive" planning process. The group invested over $40,000 to commission Ehrenkrantz, Eckstut, and Kuhn and spent thousands more in the alternative planning process. They provided technical assistance to the Golden Triangle CDC and its Main Street plan. The PHLF also attracted the most consistent media attention. For example, the *Tribune-Review* cited them more often than any other group challenging Urban Retail's plan.

Two other autonomous nonprofit groups—the regional

Allegheny Institute and the national Institute for Justice—played crucial roles in challenging the city's plan. In addition to the claims about historic preservation and community participation that I have emphasized up to this point, critics made two other types of claim against the mayor's plan. The first was that the plan did not make good economic sense and consequently represented an injustice to the region's taxpayers. Critics argued that the estimated $100 million investment of public money would have been better spent on basic infrastructure and other needed improvements to city neighborhoods. Moreover, it was unclear how the plan could produce the promised results in terms of economic development. The second type of claim was that the plan called for what many considered to be an unconstitutional and unjust use of eminent domain power to acquire properties from existing owners and resell them to Urban Retail Properties. The expert economic and legal analyses by Allegheny Institute and the Institute for Justice played an important role in certifying these economic and legal claims. The two organizations also invested their own resources to make those claims visible to a broad audiance and to direct claims making to higher-level decision-making authorities.

Department stores were the cornerstones of Murphy's retail redevelopment strategy. Marketing research shows that they draw large numbers of shoppers into retail districts, creating heavy foot traffic beneficial to smaller, specialty stores and to the overall ambience of the district. Moreover, most of the specialty stores Urban Retail was trying to recruit followed a general strategy of locating in districts bounded by department stores and other anchors. Kaufmann's department store and Saks Fifth Avenue already had a presence in the Fifth and Forbes area in 1997 when Urban Retail began its consultation. At that time officials were seeking to relocate an existing Lazarus department store in the cultural district to a new 251,000-square-foot facility on Fifth Avenue in the redevelopment area. They were also trying to lure two other department stores—the New York–based Lord & Taylor, and the Seattle-based Nordstrom—to create the critical mass necessary to make the Urban Retail plan work.

City and state tax dollars provided more than half the financing to support the $60 million relocation of Lazarus, including an $11.8 million tax increment financing plan (TIF). When the new store opened in November 1998, Mayor Murphy called it the cornerstone of future development in the Golden Triangle. *Tribune-Review* journalist Jeff Stacklin contacted the managing director of Allegheny Institute, Jake Haulk, for his expert view on the probable impact of the new Lazarus on the Fifth and Forbes redevelopment. Stacklin cited Haulk in his subsequent story on Lazarus: "Lazarus won't be the keystone store Murphy and others tout it to be. . . . We had a Gimbels and a Horne's, and they all failed." Haulk went on to say he was "not sure that the retail strategy [downtown] is something that the government should be subsidizing."[57]

On May 27, 1999, Allegheny Institute sent its weekly *Behind the Headlines Newsfax,* which presented data to support the claim that the TIF used by the URA for the new Lazarus department store was "a prime example of misuse of tax incentive development programs."[58] The claim of misuse of a tax incentive program was based upon calculations showing that the Lazarus store would not generate enough tax revenue to pay off the TIF-backed bonds that the city had invested in moving it to the new location. According to the news fax, the URA overestimated the post-project assessment of the Lazarus property by $1 million when it put the TIF plan before the approving agencies. Because of this, taxpayers in the city, county, and school district would have to cover these uncounted costs of moving the department store.

Over the course of the following year, Allegheny Institute released four more news faxes, as well as a thirty-page report, analyzing problems with the recent use of tax increment financing in Pittsburgh.[59] The *Tribune-Review* and *Post-Gazette* followed up each release with stories that quoted Haulk and made reference to Allegheny Institute. The releases emphasized two issues: First, under Pennsylvania law, TIFs were allowed only for projects that eliminated or prevented the spread of "blight," a designation that had always been ambiguous in Pennsylvania law. Designations of blight for Lazarus and Market Place relied upon this ambiguity, since downtown was still an economically viable area, according to the institute. Therefore, the resulting TIFs were not used appropriately. Second, according to the institute, retail redevelopment was generally not an appropriate use for TIF, which was designed for economic growth projects. Unlike in manufacturing and professional services, new retail does not create jobs in a region but shifts them from one place to another. Tax increment financing plans for retail construction, therefore, served only to subsidize competition between retail companies located within the same region, and this was unfair to retailers outside the TIF district.

Allegheny Institute's economic and legal arguments about TIF provided credibility to the barrage of claims that the plans for Market Place were economically irrational and an injustice to local taxpayers. This circulation of professional research reports and faxes was essential in certifying the contentious claims of other, nonexpert, challengers of the city's plans. The institute provided the only consistent stream of criticism of the mayor's redevelopment strategy by public policy professionals. Bernie Lynch's neighborhood activists, the PHLF, Preservation Pittsburgh, Ground Zero, and other critics of the Fifth and Forbes process depended heavily upon research by Allegheny Institute to establish the logic and data for their economic criticisms.

The institute also appropriated resources for a campaign aimed at repealing county approval of the Fifth and Forbes tax increment financing plan, which represented another shift in the object of claims since it brought county-level authorities to bear on the planning process. The institute obtained the five hundred signatures from voters in the county that were required to bring a petition before County Council.[60] On why they were drawing the county into the controversy, Allegheny Institute attorney Doug Reed explained, "[The] Fifth-Forbes corridor is at the very heart of the city and the city is at the very heart of the county. This project is very important to everybody in Allegheny County."[61]

Following the same basic strategy of the TIF campaign, the institute also certified contentious claims over the threat of eminent domain in the Fifth and Forbes area. In this effort the group was joined by the Institute for Justice, which pledged free legal representation for the Fifth and Forbes businesses and property owners who did not want the URA to acquire their properties. The Allegheny Institute and the Institute for Justice believed that the U.S. and Pennsylvania constitutions did not permit the state to transfer property from one private owner to another and that Pennsylvania eminent domain law was created for the limited purpose of either clearing "blighted" neighborhoods or providing public goods such as roads, bridges, or utilities. The state's ambiguous criteria for establishing blight, however, made it quite difficult to limit the uses of eminent domain.

After Mayor Murphy went public with Market Place at Fifth and Forbes in October 1999, Allegheny Institute sponsored a talk by Clint Bolick of the Institute for Justice on the issue of eminent domain and property rights. Bolick argued that the intended use of eminent domain in Market Place was a form of "social engineering [that has] totally failed to fulfill the promise of social equality." "We're not talking about building hospitals or roads, we're talking about Starbucks Coffee shops," which are "totally inappropriate" uses of the eminent domain power. [62] Also in October, Bolick, with support from Allegheny Institute, moved ahead with Bernie Lynch's group on a public campaign to fight eminent domain "abuse" by the city.

The battle was pitched simultaneously at the city, county, and state governments. Allegheny Institute released a twenty-two-page report proposing an eminent domain code for the Allegheny County Council to study and consider adopting in its administrative code. [63] The new code would establish a board of eleven members, an executive director, and a solicitor, who would review all eminent domain issues in the county. The code would also tighten blight designations and prohibit eminent domain transfers from one private entity to another. At the state level, Allegheny Institute and the Institute for Justice contacted lawmakers to pursue a similar bill in the state legislature. The local eminent domain fight in the city took the form of another drive to create a ballot referendum, this time amending the city charter to prohibit the city from taking private property for the use of other private businesses. [64]

The Allegheny Institute and Institute for Justice also organized a wave of protests. Allegheny Institute held a boisterous rally in Market Square on November 6, which drew an estimated 150 people. According to Jake Haulk, participants were recruited from the institute's mailing lists consisting of "conservative grassroots groups . . . gun rights people, school vouchers people, libertarians," and others ideologically motivated to defend property rights. The "usual suspects" also attended. While most did not identify themselves as property rights defenders, they wanted to support any action that opposed the Fifth and Forbes redevelopment plan. Allegheny Institute and the Institute for Justice advertised the rally heavily on the radio, through phone trees and e-mails, on their Web sites, and through fliers circulated in the Golden Triangle. The rally was followed by another one in March 2000, with an estimated 250 people attending.[65]

On the economic and eminent domain issues, both institutes played an important certifying role in their delivery of expert testimony at hearings held by the Historic Review Commission, the City Planning Commission, and City Council. They made the same arguments in the hearings that they printed in their news faxes and reports.[66] Such expert testimony was important because many of the people who stood up in hearings to oppose the Fifth and Forbes redevelopment expressed strong critical views about the economic, legal, and constitutional aspects of the project, much like their counterparts had in the 1940s and 1950s. Yet Fifth and Forbes opponents were certified by attorneys and policy experts making very similar claims and supporting them with theory and carefully analyzed data. While expert testimony was ineffective in persuading the mayoral appointees of the Historic Review Commission and City Planning Commission, members of City Council regularly cited research by Allegheny Institute and the Institute for Justice when declaring their reservations about the mayor's redevelopment strategy.

On June 1, 2000, the Urban Affairs Committee of the Pennsylvania Assembly had scheduled a date for action on the proposed legislation to change the use of eminent domain under the state's redevelopment law. The committee scheduled a public hearing in Pittsburgh and a tour of the Fifth and Forbes area for interested lawmakers. The protesters were well prepared and stormed the meeting in large numbers.[67] The Institute for Justice, Allegheny Institute, and the PHLF all delivered testimony opposing the use of eminent domain in Market Place and arguing for stricter laws governing its use in Pennsylvania. The Institute for Justice decided to capture the statewide publicity generated by this event to launch a media campaign attacking Mayor Murphy's threat of eminent domain in downtown Pittsburgh. They created ten billboard advertisements criticizing the use of eminent domain in Pittsburgh, with messages such as "Mayor Murphy: Pittsburgh was built on steel, not stealing. Fight eminent domain at Fifth and Forbes," and "Murphy's Law: Take from Pittsburgh families. Give to a Chicago Developer."

Conclusion: The Death of Market Place at Fifth and Forbes and the Birth of "Plan C—for Compromise"

The Downtown Planning Collaborative continued its work amid the turmoil over eminent domain. By the end of summer 2000 the coordinating committee had completed ten of twelve meetings and was compiling its results and recommendations.[68] On October 21, the collaborative held its closing conference, where Patty Maloney and Bernie Lynch gave an extensive presentation of the Main Street Plan.[69] Before closing they brought senior Institute for Justice attorney Scott Bullock to the podium. He endorsed the Main Street approach, mainly because it did not rely upon eminent domain, and he reminded the audience that his law firm would represent property owners in court if the city pursued eminent domain in the Fifth and Forbes corridor.

No sooner did the collaborative hand its final report to the mayor when Nordstrom Inc. decided against a new store in Pittsburgh. On November 22 the company released a statement that it was no longer interested in pursuing a store in downtown Pittsburgh.[70] Nordstrom had begun to reexamine its business initiatives in light of the national economic downturn that began in early 2000. Since the department store was the principal component in Urban Retail's plan, the change of strategy signaled to the mayor's office that the "big bang" approach to retail redevelopment that relied on participation from national chains and large department stores could no longer be supported, financially or politically. Mayor Murphy responded to the statement from Nordstrom with a press conference in which he announced his decision to "rethink how we move forward with the revitalization of the central business district."[71] In the press conference the mayor announced the beginnings of "Plan C—for compromise." "I want a revitalization effort that will look for the consensus forged in the Pittsburgh Downtown Collaborative," Murphy said, and, "to that end, I have notified Urban Retail Properties that the Market Place at Fifth and Forbes Development is no longer on the table, and that we will be moving in a new direction."[72]

Before his press conference, the mayor personally contacted many of the stakeholders in the Fifth and Forbes process, including Golden Triangle CDC members Patty Maloney, Bonnie Klein, and Bernie Lynch. His intention was to form a "Plan C Task Force," to which he appointed Maloney and Lynch as co-chairs. The Landmarks Foundation's Arthur Ziegler and Albert Hatley of the Hill District CDC were among other Murphy opponents selected for the committee. Bally Design Co., which had employees involved in Ground Zero, was selected to facilitate the task force meetings. The challengers of Murphy's redevelopment agenda for downtown Pittsburgh were now leading the city's effort to determine the future of the Golden Triangle.

6

Contentious
Urban Redevelopment
and Strong Democracy

■ How is it that some urban social movements succeed while others fail to create opportunities for strong democratic participation? Up to this point, I have approached this question by describing the historical context and dynamics of three movements that have "failed" to produce strong democratic participation (cases 2–4), one that "succeeded" (case 5), and one (case 1) that fits somewhere in between success and failure. In this chapter I will evaluate the strength of participation generated by each movement. In what sense was citizen participation in Fifth and Forbes stronger than in the other cases? Answering this question begins with a description of the criteria of strong democracy.

Participation and Democracy

Few statements were more influential in the development of twentieth-century democratic theory than Joseph Schumpeter's formulation of democracy as "an institutional arrangement for arriving at political decisions in which individuals acquire the power to decide by means of a competitive struggle for the people's vote."[1] Robert Dahl accepts Schumpeter's basic premise and seeks to specify how voting in competitive elections serves to maximize the accountability of democratic leaders.[2] According to Dahl, competition is the characteristic of elections that makes them specifically democratic because it forces potential leaders to shape their ideas and proposals so as to fall within the limits set by the expectations and preferences of the electorate. Political leaders are central to the democratic theories of Schumpeter and Dahl. Citizens play the role of discussing alternatives and voting for leaders, but only leaders have direct responsibility for the content of public decisions. In the words of critic Benjamin Barber, "citizens use the franchise only to select an executive or judicial or legislative elite that in turn exercises every other duty of civic importance."[3]

Barber is a proponent of strong democracy, which is defined by norms of deliberation that hold leaders accountable to a process of exploring the common interests of citizens and the benefits of alternative choices to the political community as a whole. Common interests are most easily identified through "the give and take of discussion in a face-to-face setting." Face-to-face meetings help members to identify with one another and with the group as a whole, thereby facilitating decision making by consensus rather than political competition. Thus, the objective is not to control leaders so as to keep their actions in line with the preferences of those who put them in office. Rather, in a strong democratic system elected leaders govern by promoting dialogue about the content of the common good that lies beneath the diverse interests expressed in political competition.[4]

But what are the common interests binding the various stakeholders in local redevelopment? How does a political community judge a land-use or investment decision to be in the common good? If Paul Peterson is correct that land-use policies are by definition those government decisions designed to improve the status of the community as a location for investment, then the search for common ground ends with the discovery of the optimal growth policy. Redevelopment is cast largely as an administrative matter in which decisions are "closed to the broader public, until technical and political feasibility is fairly well determined."[5] According to this view, developers, redevelopment experts, and public administrators deserve a "privileged hearing" in the dialogue about what is in the public good. They use technical knowledge to define what public decisions must be made in order to facilitate growth and prosperity for the community as a whole. Peterson's approach to discovering the common good is difficult to reconcile with the case studies in this book, which suggest that under some circumstances citizens want to participate directly in shaping the city and often have ideas about the common good that are at least as enlightened as those of developers and experts assembled within the urban growth coalition. Stephen Elkin has proposed an alternative criterion for shaping decisions about the common good that is both consistent with the strong democratic emphasis on deliberation and attentive to the economic requirements of the city in the American federal system. There is no question, Elkin argues, that citizens must have a vigorous concern for the commercial interests of the city. Yet he sees the idea that developers and redevelopment experts deserve a privileged hearing in the dialogue about community prosperity as fundamentally flawed, since it denigrates the value of contributions by small businesses, neighborhood residents, and other stakeholders, and "precludes and otherwise displaces other definitions of what is at stake."[6]

The alternative to a policy debate guided strictly by the commercial interest of the city, according to Elkin, is one in which the "commercial public interest" is kept foremost in mind. A genuine concern for the commercial public interest will recognize not only the views of developers, experts, and local officials, but also others invested in the special-use values of places under consideration for redevelopment. In a genuinely deliberative form of government, advocates of redevelopment proposals are required to give reasons for their ideas and to listen to and take seriously the views of others, including those outside the governing coalition.

Adopting the commercial public interest as a criterion for regulating decisions about redevelopment demands much stronger forms of citizen engagement than is typically found in cities without participatory institutions. This raises the question of what counts as an appropriately strong participation opportunity for those citizens wishing to articulate their views and have them taken seriously by policy makers. In the introduction I referred to the "breadth" and "depth" criteria that Jeffrey Berry and colleagues use to evaluate participation efforts in formal citywide systems. I have adopted these criteria here since they are equally applicable in measuring participation that grows out of contentious collective action.

The concept of breadth expresses the democratic ideal that everyone who wishes to participate in policy making ought to have opportunities for involvement at all important stages in the policy process.[7] The corresponding evaluative questions are: To what extent do all members of the community have access to a decision-making process? Do all members have the information they need to understand what is at stake in a decision, what alternatives are under consideration, and how they can participate? Are members encouraged to offer new alternatives not already on the public agenda? How realistic are the means offered for community involvement in terms of time and location of meetings, and so on? If breadth entails extensive opportunities for participation, depth requires that citizen involvement actually make a difference to the outcome of a decision process.[8] Questions to be addressed include: Are the views and preferences of all citizens given equal weight? Do final decisions reflect those views and preferences? Are policies that are decided in a participatory manner implemented effectively?

These are strict criteria for judging a decision process, and probably no political system could satisfy all of them all the time. I have no doubt that the best way to fulfill the requirements of strong citizen involvement is through institutional innovations such as those Berry, Portney, and Thomson found in Dayton, Birmingham, Portland, St. Paul, and San Antonio. But in the absence of participatory institutions, political contention is often the best alternative for citizens wishing to gain a strong voice in urban redevelopment projects.

Among the five cases of redevelopment considered in chapters 3 and 5, only the challengers in Highland Park (case 1) and Fifth and Forbes (case 5) overcame the initial disadvantages they faced against an urban growth coalition that controlled when and how projects were placed on the public agenda. Residents in Highland Park managed to stop the city from building a civic arena in their neighborhood. Opponents of Market Place at Fifth and Forbes participated in multiple face-to-face discussions about the future of downtown, and Mayor Murphy selected many of them for his Plan C Task Force after they helped to defeat his original redevelopment proposal.

The structure and processes of contention in Highland Park were more similar to the other three cases of the 1949–1960 period than they were to the Fifth and Forbes case. Based on the descriptions of mobilizing and political opportunity structures contained in chapters 2 and 4, it is clear that Highland Park residents faced much less favorable conditions for a successful protest than the challengers of Market Place at Fifth and Forbes. These basic structural conditions are depicted in figure 6.1, which suggests that Highland Park is a rather interesting anomaly since structural theories of social movements suggest that the protesters should have failed in their efforts. Instead, the protesters forced concessions from the city, even if they did not achieve the same breadth or depth of participation as their counterparts in Fifth and Forbes. In what follows, I apply the mechanism-based theory

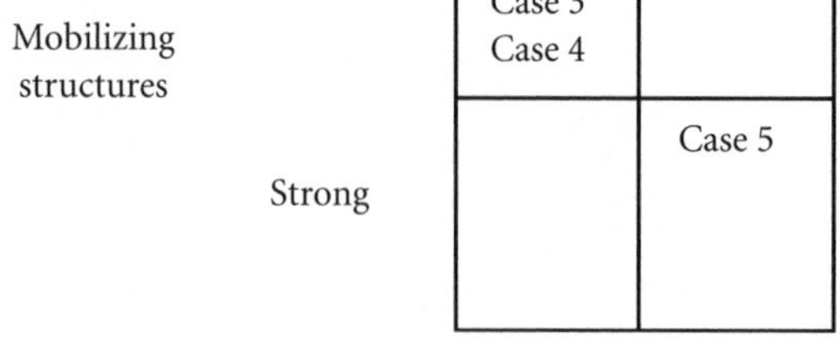

Structure of political
opportunities

		Closed	Open
Mobilizing structures	Weak	Case 1 Case 2 Case 3 Case 4	
	Strong		Case 5

Figure 6.1. Structures of urban contention in five cases

introduced in chapter 1 to explain the wide variation in the breadth and depth of participation opportunities that challengers encountered in each of the five cases. How did the pathways of political contention in Highland Park and Fifth and Forbes diverge from those in the other neighborhoods? Why did the pathway of Fifth and Forbes lead to strong democratic participation for challengers while the pathway in Highland Park did not?

Timing and Sequence

I begin by analyzing the timing and sequence of mechanisms in the five cases. The analysis of timing and sequence is based on the premise that a social event will have different consequences depending upon when it occurs in relation to other events.[9] Patterns of timing and sequence were fundamental to the failures of the challengers in cases 2–4 as well as to the successes of those in case 5. (The outcome of the anomalous case 1 was not affected significantly by timing and sequence.)

Category formation (CF) and social appropriation of resources (SAR) are primary mechanisms of contention in the sense that their presence can activate other important mechanisms. Without the formation of a collective identity and some basic efforts toward accessing and mobilizing resources through social connections, mechanisms such as certification (C), polarization (P), and object shift (OS) could not come into play in a contentious episode. One striking difference between cases 1–4 and case 5 is the timing of CF and SAR in relation to other events. Category formation and social appropriation of resources did not occur in cases 1–4 until city officials had already arrived at an advanced stage of redevelopment planning. Leaders in Highland Park and the Lower Triangle responded to the city's plans for their neighborhoods just a few weeks before City Council was scheduled to vote on them. Residents in St. Clair and Spring Hill–City View did not react until they received letters from the housing authority requesting conferences to discuss acquisition of their properties. Parishioners of St. Peter's waited until most of the neighborhood surrounding their church had been demolished before organizing their fight to save the church. The consequence in each case was that neighborhood redevelopment plans were nearly faits accompli by the time protest movements had formed to oppose them. Protesters were left in the unfortunate position of saying no to nearly completed projects that were meant to improve the quality of life and the economic status of the city as a whole. Because the neighborhoods were so late in laying the foundations for collective action, they had formulated no ideas of their own about how best to solve neighborhood problems and grow the local economy when redevelopment plans were on the public agenda. Having produced nothing for policy makers to say yes to, protesters were easily labeled as self-interested naysayers standing in the way of progress.

Given the lack of autonomous mobilizing structures available to neighborhood leaders in Highland Park, the Lower Triangle, St. Clair, Spring Hill–City View, and the Lower Hill, it is understandable why it took so long for them to create collective action categories and allocate resources for mobilization. There were no organizations in their multiorganizational fields with a dedicated capacity to monitor and, if necessary, dispute land-use initiatives openly before they were placed on the public agenda. It is unlikely that property owners, small businesses, or residents would have had the time or organizational resources required for this kind of activity.

Of the first four cases, only in Highland Park (case 1) were challengers able to overcome their disadvantages in timing to gain some control over the redevelopment process. Unlike the other challengers, residents of Highland Park benefited from temporary shifts in the structure of political opportunities brought about by processes of contention itself. Highland Park residents attributed political opportunity to divisions appearing within Mayor Lawrence's City Council. Destabilizing attacks on the corporatist growth agenda by disgruntled members of City Council encouraged residents to intensify their grassroots mobilization. The neighborhood group formed an alliance with the defectors from Lawrence's council to sponsor a resolution to accept Robert King's offer of land to the city on condition that

Highland Park properties not be condemned for the building of an amphitheater.

The events in Highland Park illustrate how resources identified in the process of contention itself (Robert King's estate) can be used to bargain for a stronger voice in urban decision making. Highland Park residents achieved greater depth of participation than their counterparts in the 1940s and 1950s inasmuch as their protests affected the outcome of the decision process. However, their participation fell short of satisfying breadth of participation norms. Nothing in the contingent sequence of events in Highland Park presented residents with opportunities to participate at various important stages of the redevelopment process. Participation was stronger than expected in view of the closed structure of political opportunities and weak mobilizing structures of the time, but was still less than ideal from the point of view of strong democracy.

Autonomous mobilizing structures had an important effect upon the timing and sequence of events in Fifth and Forbes and the overall strength of participation. Two autonomous organizations, the Pittsburgh History and Landmarks Foundation and Preservation Pittsburgh, started monitoring Fifth and Forbes planning as early as two years before the formal approval process began in October 1999. About a year before the official announcement of Market Place, preservationists shifted to a contentious strategy for gaining influence over the planning process. As a result of their mobilization a collective action category formed (CF), which created the foundation for a protest movement that achieved significantly greater momentum than the earlier cases by the time the public agenda was announced.

The movement gathered force through a sequence of four crucial mechanisms activated by CF: social appropriation of resources (SAR), attribution of political opportunity (APO), object shift (OS) and brokerage (B). In November, PHLF created a memorandum of agreement with Preservation Pittsburgh to organize a movement to challenge the "secretive" Market Place at Fifth and Forbes planning process (SAR). Preservationists then began attending the Historic Review Commission meetings in spring 1999 (APO and OS). Since Bernie Lynch and her group of business and property owners also attended (APO and OS), the meetings served as a site of brokerage (B) between the two groups, the creation of the Fifth/Forbes Planning Group, and the subsequent alternative planning processes.

The alternative planning process was getting underway in the summer and fall of 1999, just as polarization (P) was intensifying between the city and its opponents. As more and more previously inactive business owners in the Fifth and Forbes district, CDC leaders in other neighborhoods, and young professionals became outraged at the apparent secrecy of the dealings between the city and Urban Retail, they were drawn into the alternative planning process. The alternative plan sponsored by PHLF became an outlet for both the expression of dissatisfaction with the planning process for Market Place and for participation in a constructive dialogue about how to deal with the decline of the Fifth and Forbes retail corridor. It was the strongest episode of citizen participation in retail redevelopment up to that point.

In terms of breadth of participation, the alternative planning process was widely accessible and was publicized in newspapers, radio, television, letters to organizational leaders across the region, Web-based alerts, newsletters of preservation groups, and informally through networks of social activists. Communication about the alternative plan was informative, defining the various stakes involved in downtown redevelopment—the risks involved for existing businesses, the security of property rights, the fate of older buildings, the character of the neighborhood, and so on—and also described important features of Market Place at Fifth and Forbes, proposed that alternatives were possible, and invited everyone who wished to participate to attend the planning sessions led by architect Stan Eckstut. Communication was not perfect, however, since much of it was framed in oppositional terms biased against the Urban Retail plan. In this sense participation at the alternative planning stage did not fully meet the depth of participation norm of giving equal consideration and respect to each alternative on the agenda.

Additionally, citizens had opportunities to participate at all important stages in the alternative planning process. Developed in three pairs of meetings over a three-month period, the Ehrenkrantz, Eckstut, and Kuhn plan encouraged public input from the very beginning and created opportunities for further participation as the plan was developed. Yet the plan was not officially sanctioned, and this was its greatest limitation from the point of view of the depth of participation norm, which requires that citizen input actually make a difference in policy decisions.

If the alternative planning process did not itself facilitate an impressive depth of participation, it did trigger events that eventually deepened citizen engagement. The alternative plans created a crisis atmosphere that suggested that something was deeply wrong with the "secret" planning process between the city and Urban Retail. With the legitimacy of Market Place at Fifth and Forbes called into question, several community organizations began demanding a voice in the planning process. The PDP, PUMP, and Ground Zero each made public appeals for broader participation, but only after PHLF had initiated the alternative planning process. Both the Planning Commission and the Historic Review Commission agreed to delay their decisions in order to review the Ehrenkrantz, Eckstut, and Kuhn plan and to consider public comment upon it. The short-term result of this was negligible, since each agency conditionally approved Market Place at Fifth and Forbes. But intense opposition and anger expressed at public hearings convinced some City Council members to declare they would not vote until comprehensive input from the public and full review of alternatives were completed.

In the context of uncertainty in City Council, Councilman Sala Udin, the Pittsburgh Downtown Partnership (PDP), and the Allegheny Conference convened the Planning Collaborative to facilitate input from all interested members of the community that would lead to specific recommendations to the mayor's office and City Council. The collaborative was a practical accomplishment of contentious collective action. Given the mayor's strong urging for a speedy approval of Market Place and the prompt approval by the URA, the Planning Commission, and the Historic Review Commission, it is hard to imagine that the Pittsburgh Downtown Partnership and Allegheny Conference would have supported a protracted community planning process if not prompted to do so

by the crisis situation. The collaborative is analogous to the negotiations between Robert King and City Council in 1949. In both
instances, stakeholders used resources identified in the process of
contention itself (Robert King's offer in 1949 and the alternative
plans in 2000) to bargain for a stronger voice in urban decision
making. But unlike their midcentury counterparts, challengers of
Fifth and Forbes did not mobilize mainly for the purpose of saying no to the city's redevelopment agenda. They were serious
about showing that alternatives to the city's agenda were possible
and that the quality of any plan would be a function of the extent
of public participation going into it.

The Downtown Planning Collaborative was the first opportunity for all stakeholders to work face-to-face toward a consensus
on the agenda for downtown retail redevelopment. It was open to
anyone, and stakeholder group interaction occurred on a small
enough scale to enable members to directly influence specific
areas in which they had expertise or interest, whether merchandising, design, disruption mitigation, relocation, or financing and
redevelopment. Multiple meetings enabled direct participation in
various stages of the collaborative's process, a process that was officially sanctioned, which added depth to the participation effort.
Organizers of the Planning Collaborative sought a community
consensus on concrete recommendations to the mayor, the URA,
and City Council, giving participants some assurance that their
input would be taken seriously in any final policy decision. And
rules established at the beginning of the Planning Collaborative
allowed stakeholder groups to initiate dialogue with the city administration as needed. In terms of resources devoted to the participation effort, each stakeholder group was provided with a
stenographer, a recorder, a professional facilitator, and relevant
reports and analyses to ensure that the group could effectively
evaluate the plan and arrive at concrete recommendations.

The Downtown Planning Collaborative also called for concur-
rent town meetings held in each City Council district to introduce
Market Place at Fifth and Forbes, to describe the Downtown Planning Collaborative, and to get feedback and recommendations
from neighborhood residents not involved in the collaborative. In
connection with this neighborhood outreach effort, the collabo-

rative convened several special informational sessions, or "post-agenda" meetings that allowed the public to be present while City Council, representatives of stakeholder planning groups, the mayor's office, the URA, and developers exchanged ideas originating in the collaborative's process.

The comparison of sequences of CF, SAR, and agenda announcement mechanisms in cases 1–4 and case 5 suggests a proposition subject to testing and elaboration in future research. Urban contention will create more opportunities for strong participation the earlier CF and SAR are activated before an agenda is presented for public approval. Figure 6.2 illustrates the sequence pattern associated with strong democratic participation.

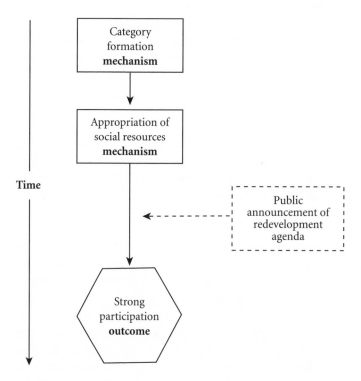

Figure 6.2. Mechanism sequence associated with strong participation outcome

Combinations of Mechanisms

The timing and sequence of mechanisms, as I have shown above, can determine the capacity of a movement to gather momentum sufficient to generate meaningful opportunities for citizen participation in a redevelopment process. Different combinations of mechanisms also affected the outcomes of the five cases. Mechanism-based theory holds that similar mechanisms can produce different outcomes when they occur in the presence of other mechanisms.[10] In what follows I show how the certification (C) mechanism had very different consequences in case 5 than in the other four cases because of how it combined with social appropriation of resources (SAR) and object shift (OS). As was the case with timing and sequence, the mechanism-based account illustrates how autonomous mobilizing structures actually produced a process and outcome in case 5 (strong democratic participation) that differed fundamentally from those in cases 1–4.

Certification of challengers' claims by legitimate authorities occurred in all five cases. In the 1940s and 1950s, however, attorneys with expertise in property law were the main agents certifying claims of challengers, whereas in the 1990s attorneys were joined by urban policy professionals, historic preservationists, and other staff of autonomous, nonprofit organizations. Protesters in Highland Park, the Lower Triangle, St. Clair, Spring Hill–City View, and the Lower Hill hired attorneys who then endorsed their claims that the use of eminent domain by the city would infringe the constitutional rights of property owners. The impact of the attorneys' certifying claims, however, was significantly diminished by their limited public exposure. Petition drives and City Council hearings received some media coverage, especially in the Highland Park protest, but attorneys in all cases took their battles to the courts rather than to the streets, the meeting halls, and the media. The recurring shift in the object of claims into the courts subjected those claims to evaluation by juridical rules, which were biased against property owners at the time, leading to the defeat of all but one movement in the early postwar era.

The certification process for Fifth and Forbes differed fundamentally from those of the earlier cases. Unlike cases 1–4, where expert discourse was confined largely within the walls of the courts, professional historic preservationists, policy experts, and public interest lawyers in case 5 made their claims in combination with efforts to allocate resources toward mobilization. In their role as leaders of nonprofit organizations, experts certified the claims of neighborhood protesters while at the same time appropriating resources to disseminate their claims across a wide variety of arenas of public discourse. Professional certification occurred at the sites where people were mobilized for collective claim making rather than behind the walls of the courts. The Pittsburgh History and Landmarks Foundation made certifying claims in their lecture series, on their Web site, in their newsletter, on television and radio, in testimonials at public hearings, in letters to regional leaders, and in the open meetings they held during the alternative planning process. Allegheny Institute made certifying claims in reports and news faxes, in testimonials at public hearings, and, along with the Institute for Justice, on billboards and through the bullhorn at street-level protests. Each of these crucial mobilizing structures both certified the claims of nonexpert challengers of the Fifth and Forbes plan and appropriated resources for the mobilization of those same challengers. The consequence was to keep the public controversy alive and to prevent it from shifting into and then dying in the courts, as occurred at midcentury.

Instead of shifting the controversy into the courts, experts critical of the Fifth and Forbes proposal enacted multiple object shifts that organized new forms of citizen engagement. The PHLF shifted the object from the mayor's office to the Historic Review Commission in spring 1999, providing the first opportunity for opponents to speak directly to a public authority about their concerns. They shifted the object again by making claims to the City Planning Commission, and then again by presenting arguments to state lawmakers considering new eminent domain legislation. Allegheny Institute shifted the object when they pleaded with County Council to repeal the TIF legislation for Fifth and Forbes and to adopt a countywide eminent domain code. Each object shift brought a new set of actors to bear upon the outcome of the controversy and served as a rallying point for social mobilization.

The comparison of combinations of mechanisms in the five cases suggests another proposition for testing and elaboration in future research. Urban contention creates more opportunities for strong participation as more experts certify claims in combination with efforts at social appropriation of resources. Figure 6.3 illustrates the combination pattern associated with the strong democratic outcome.

The two major propositions constructed from the case studies' evidence summarize how causal conditions produce their effects in contentious episodes. Although the propositions are stated in terms of sequences and combinations of mechanisms that propel contention, this is not to say that structural conditions were irrel-

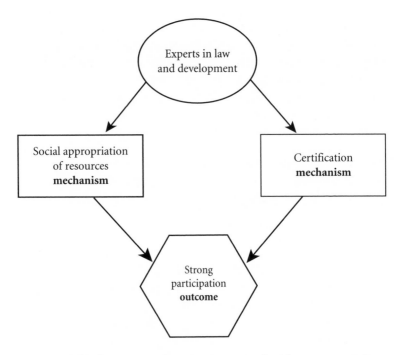

Figure 6.3. Mechanism combination associated with strong participation outcome

evant to the outcomes of the cases. To the contrary, the propositions identify processes that were generated under specific structural conditions. To be sure, mobilizing structures—autonomous, nonprofit organizations connected to broad social movements—effectively produced opportunities for citizen participation in case 5, but they did so by affecting the sequences and combinations of mechanisms that produce urban contention. Other cases of contentious urban redevelopment may confirm both the sequence proposition and the combination proposition; or, it may turn out that some successful cases hinge on timing and sequence, while others hinge on mechanism combination. These issues are subject to further research, along with the question of whether a favorable structure of political opportunity is required to yield such patterns.

Political Processes and Unintended Consequences

How does ideology shape the policy process? The Institute for Justice, the Allegheny Institute, and the Pittsburgh History and Landmarks Foundation all received financial support from the Scaife family trusts. Along with Bradley, Smith Richardson, Olin, Coors, and other conservative foundations, Scaife was an important financial force behind the powerful movement that dismantled the American "liberal consensus" in the last quarter of the twentieth century.[11] Thus, if the mobilizing structures financed by the Scaife trusts were autonomous from Pittsburgh's urban growth coalition, they were hardly free of political bias, which raises the question: Did participation in the Fifth and Forbes plan serve mainly to advance a particular ideological agenda?

There is little evidence to support such a belief. Mechanisms such as CF, SAR, and others activated by the interventions of PHLF, Allegheny Institute, and the Institute for Justice, helped to facilitate significant participation in Fifth and Forbes. But those same mechanisms concatenated into processes that took on a life of their own and were not under the control of these organizations. Nowhere is this more evident than in PHLF's alternative planning process. The preservationist group financed and organized a half dozen open planning sessions in order to "show that alternatives were possible" to Market Place. But the brokerage function of those meetings, and the creation of new organizations (the Golden Triangle CDC and Ground Zero) and alternative plans (the Main Street approach), were not intended. Such unintended consequences fundamentally changed the outcome of the Fifth and Forbes process.

Like the PHLF, Allegheny Institute and the Institute for Justice helped to unleash political processes they neither intended nor controlled. Each organization attacked eminent domain "abuse" through a variety of strategies, and their goal was to protect property rights, not to endorse one particular redevelopment plan over another. But the unintended consequence of their attacks was to certify the Main Street proposal. Advocates of Main Street were grassroots leaders who sought ways to revitalize downtown without displacing existing businesses. They believed that an incremental approach not reliant upon eminent domain was the most sensible way to achieve their objectives. Although these leaders were not themselves moved by ideological goals, because their plan did not rely upon eminent domain, they benefited from a campaign against eminent domain undertaken by nonprofits that were perhaps more ideologically motivated.

From the perspective of Robert Dahl's leadership-control view of democracy, effective leadership is at the heart of good governance. While autonomous mobilizing structures facilitate the direct involvement of citizens in government decisions, perhaps their most important function is to impose costs on urban growth leaders who attempt to assemble land-use projects without substantive public involvement. These structures make it rational for leaders to involve the community in early stages of policy planning since failing to do so ensures the loss of community support and the collapse of their proposals in the heat of controversy.

Appendix

Case Study Research Design

According to Robert Yin, the case study is a research strategy for exploring how a phenomenon is generated from within a historical context defined in terms of some theoretical framework.[1] For example, in *States and Social Revolutions,* Theda Skocpol used the case method to explain how three modern social revolutions occurred in the global context of uneven capitalist development and nation-state formation. In *The Contentious French,* Charles Tilly used the method to explore how the same historical context observed by Skocpol transformed the character of French popular contention over a period of four centuries. Yin would refer to these as historical works rather than case studies because they are of noncontemporary events, which limits the data collection and analysis available to the investigator. Otherwise, case studies and histories are indistinguishable. Both strategies give mechanism-based accounts of processes that clarify associations between variables. Both strive for complete explanations of how some class of phenomena "arise, how they persist and how they change."[2] Adopting a case study research design has allowed me to search for sequences and combinations of mechanisms that might agree or differ across multiple cases of roughly equivalent phenomena, namely, contentious urban redevelopment.

A case of contentious urban redevelopment refers to a collective event in which an urban growth coalition formulates a redevelopment agenda in private while outsiders in the community (for example, neighborhood leaders, small business owners, and preservationists) attempt to oppose or redefine the agenda in episodes of public and collective interaction. In this research I construct a total of five case studies, each of which is defined in relation to the structural context in which it originated, developed over time, and ended. In order to account for both context and case, the empirical chapters in this book alternate between context descriptions (chapters 2 and 4) and case descriptions (chapters 3 and 5). The methods I used for collecting data differ for each type of description.

Data Collection

I constructed the narratives for chapters 2 and 4 (the context for each case) using multiple primary and secondary sources. For chapter 2 (covering the first period, 1920–1947), I relied on a vast body of published research on the Pittsburgh renaissance, postwar machine politics, urban redevelopment, and public-private partnerships. I also drew heavily upon three dissertations, two from historians and one from a political scientist, which describe and analyze the politics of urban redevelopment in Pittsburgh in the immediate postwar period. In addition, I made use of published biographical material about Mayor David L. Lawrence.

In addition to the secondary literature, I drew upon multiple forms of primary data for chapter 2, including census data, organization reports, memoirs, interviews with public officials and civic leaders, and newspaper articles. All interviews pertinent to chapter 2 are available in the Stanton Balfour Oral History Collection, Archives of Industrial Society, or the State and Local Government Oral History Project, Twentieth Century Transition. Both collections are stored at the Archives of Industrial Society at the University of Pittsburgh, Pittsburgh, Pennsylvania.

I composed chapter 4 in a manner similar to chapter 2, with a couple of exceptions. First, I relied more on contemporary newspaper coverage and data presented on organization Web sites. Both sources were far more abundant for reconstructing events of the 1990s than of earlier periods. Second, I was able to draw upon detailed information about the context for contemporary redevelopment in Pittsburgh from the semistructured, open-ended interviews I conducted primarily for the construction of the case studies.

I followed an inductive procedure in constructing the five cases of contentious urban redevelopment. For the first four cases (see chapter 3), I identified the existence of contentious episodes by reading all the available scholarly literature on the postwar renaissance. After exhausting the secondary literature, I searched for primary data, mainly in the form of reports, archived and nonarchived organizational documents, municipal records, interviews, and newspaper articles that could help fill out the details of contentious episodes. Newspaper articles were essential to the task of following sequences of contentious events. My strategy was to search microfilms (available in the Pennsylvania Room at Carnegie Library, Pittsburgh, main branch) for issues of the *Pittsburgh Press* and the *Pittsburgh Post-Gazette* printed before, during, and after major redevelopment events identified in the other primary and secondary literature. For example, from historian Michael P. Weber's account in *Don't Call Me Boss* of the 1949 condemnation proceedings in Highland Park, I knew to look for newspaper articles in June, July, and August 1949 for journalistic coverage of the events.

I constructed case 5 (chapter 5) somewhat differently from the previous four, due to the fact that contentious events were unfolding in "real time" while my research was underway. I first learned casually of the controversy over Fifth and Forbes through newspaper coverage. In addition to reading and documenting events in articles in the *Pittsburgh Post-Gazette,* the *Pittsburgh Tribune-Review,* the *Pittsburgh Business Times,* and the *Pittsburgh City Paper,* I also conducted an archive search in the *Tribune-Review,* the region's second largest daily newspaper in total circulation. I searched for all articles containing the key words "Fifth *and* Forbes *and* retail" for the period January 1, 1998, to June 1, 2000. The search recovered 254 articles, all but a handful pertinent to the Fifth and Forbes retail redevelopment issue.

After reading the *Tribune-Review* articles, I came up with a list of twenty actors (including organizations and individuals) named repeatedly as prime movers in the Fifth and Forbes issue. With help from Morton Coleman, then director of the University of Pittsburgh Institute of Politics, I scheduled interviews with most members on the list. I was not able to interview every member because some had repeated scheduling difficulties. For example, members of Pittsburgh City Council were especially difficult to contact and I met with none of them. I also utilized a snowball method of sampling. After each interview I asked interviewees for names of others I should contact. In most cases interviewees helped to facilitate my meeting the new contacts.

I conducted all interviews using a semistructured, open-ended format that began with lead questions such as, "How did you get involved in the Fifth and Forbes issue?" and "What interests did you have in getting involved?" Inevitably, a conversation would unfold, replete with data with crucial details concerning the Fifth and Forbes controversy. The purpose of the interviews was to tie together sequences of events not covered in news reports or easily found in other primary sources. For example, the question of when downtown merchants and landowners began organizing to oppose Fifth and Forbes was not answered in news reports, so I asked about it in the interview with one of the main organizers of merchants and landowners. All interviews were tape-recorded and transcribed for further analysis. The name of each person interviewed is listed in the acknowledgments at the beginning of the book.

Perhaps the greatest advantage of the interviews was that they allowed me to gain access to other sources of nonarchived documents in the possession of the organizations or individuals I interviewed. With consent from the interviewees, I was able to access copies of internal memos, transcripts of testimonials at public hearings, saved e-mails, letters, reports, and promotional materials. I am indebted to the Pittsburgh History and Landmarks Foundation (PHLF) for providing me with the greatest data source of this type.

Content Analysis of Newspaper Articles

I have made selected use of document content analysis as a means of measuring the frequency of use of particular terms and phrases in news reporting on controversial redevelopment issues. Qualitative interpretation of news reporting is essential to understanding how the media frame issues. Media framing, in turn, influences the kinds of issues its consumers discuss (though it does not determine how they interpret issues).[3] Quantitative content analysis allows the investigator to identify patterns in media discourse not detectable through qualitative interpretation alone.[4]

I conducted two separate content analyses of newspaper articles. The first analysis was of a sample of N = 31 daily *Pittsburgh Press* newspapers, consecutive from July 1 to July 31, 1949, the month in which the first case of contentious redevelopment occurred (the Highland Park case). My purpose was to determine the prominence of the Highland Park controversy in the media, as stated in chapter 3. I located daily editions of the *Press* on microfilm; each of the 31 editions was coded for whether or not an article on the Highland Park controversy appeared on the front page. Relevant results are reported in the text and footnotes to the case study. Since the other three midcentury cases received only sporadic news coverage, a content analysis was not warranted.

The second content analysis was for the fifth case study (chapter 5) dealing with the Fifth and Forbes controversy. It consisted of a sample of N = 247 articles retrieved from the *Tribune-Review* archive search mentioned above. Each article was coded for a range of contents, which are described in the text and footnotes to chapter 5. The methodological justification for content analysis is evident in the context of its use throughout the case study.

Notes

Introduction

1. Tarrow, *Power in Movement*, 5.
2. Mansbridge, *Beyond Adversary Democracy*, 4–5.
3. Barber, *Strong Democracy*, 178.
4. Berry, Portney, and Thomson, *Rebirth of Urban Democracy*, 55.
5. Haeberle, *Planting the Grassroots*, ix–x.
6. See especially McAdam, Tarrow, and Tilly, *Dynamics of Contention*.
7. The phrase "structure of political opportunities" is from Eisinger, "Conditions of Protest Behavior," 11; the term "mobilizing structures" is from McAdam, McCarthy, and Zald, "Opportunities, Mobilizing Structures, and Framing Processes."
8. See Putnam, "Tuning In, Tuning Out," 665–66, "Bowling Alone," 71; Hall, "Vital Signs," 241–45; Skocpol, *Diminished Democracy*, 127–61.

Chapter 1: Contentious Urban Redevelopment

1. See Stone, "Study of the Politics of Urban Development," 3–22.
2. Hunter, *Community Power Structure*, 5–7.
3. Ibid., 94.
4. For a complete list and overview of studies, see Walton, "Systematic Survey," 443–64.
5. Polsby, *Community Power and Political Theory*, 115–17.
6. Banfield, *Political Influence;* Dahl, *Who Governs?*
7. Dahl, *Who Governs?* 128.
8. Ricci, *Community Power and Democratic Theory*, 125–43.
9. Dahl, *Who Governs?*, 138.
10. McFarland, "Social Movements and Theories," 7–12.
11. Olson, *Logic of Collective Action*, 2.
12. See Hunt, "Sacred and the French Revolution," 25–43; Tiryakian, "Durkheim to Managua," 44–65.
13. Tarrow, "Cycles of Collective Action," 89–116.
14. For a discussion of urban growth coalitions, see Mollenkopf, "Post-War Politics," 247–95; Molotch, "City as a Growth Machine," 309–32.

15. Whitt, "Arts Coalition," 144–56.
16. Eisinger, *The Rise of the Entrepreneurial State*, 9.
17. Peterson, *City Limits*, 17–37.
18. Ibid., 25.
19. Pagano and Bowman, *Cityscapes and Capital*, 3.
20. See Sassen, *Cities in a World Economy*; Fleischmann and Feagin, "Politics of Growth-Oriented Urban Alliances," 207–32; Logan and Swanstrom, *Beyond the City Limits*; DiGaetano and Klemanski, *Power and City Governance*; Savitch and Kantor, *Cities in the International Marketplace*.
21. Wilson, *When Work Disappears*, 3–24.
22. Dreier, Mollenkopf, and Swanstrom, *Place Matters*, 35.
23. Pagano and Bowman, *Cityscapes and Capital*, 44–51.
24. Historic preservationists, public interest law firms, "think tanks," and other stakeholders can also have a role in urban contention. The significance of these stakeholders has increased since the 1960s, and I shall say more about them in chapters 4 and 5.
25. Logan and Molotch, *Urban Fortunes*, 17–23.
26. Ibid., 19.
27. Elkin, "Cities without Power," 266. Stone, "Study of the Politics of Urban Development," 8–11; DiGaetano and Klemanski, *Power and City Governance*, 20–21.
28. Stone, *Regime Politics*, 6, 5.
29. Stone, "Preemptive Power," 82–104.
30. Logan and Molotch, *Urban Fortunes*, 111.
31. Lindblom, *Politics and Markets*, 170–88.
32. Stone, "Systemic Power," 978–90; also Emerson, "Power-Dependence Relations," 31–41.
33. McAdam, Tarrow, and Tilly, *Dynamics of Contention*; Tilly, "Mechanisms in Political Processes," 21–41; Giddens, *Constitution*, 172–74; McAdam, McCarthy, and Zald, "Opportunities, Mobilizing Structures, and Framing Processes," in *Comparative Perspectives on Social Movements*, 1–22.
34. Eisinger, "Conditions of Protest Behavior," 25.
35. McAdam, *Political Process*, 36–59.
36. McAdam, "Conceptual Origins," 29.
37. McCarthy and Zald, "Resource Mobilization and Social Movements," 1212–41; McCarthy, "Constraints and Opportunities," 142–47.
38. Klandermans, "Theoretical Framework," 5; Markoff, *Waves of Democracy*, 20–36.
39. Stoker, "Regime Theory and Urban Politics," 66.
40. For a philosophical treatment of mechanism-based theory, see Hedstrom and Swedberg, "Social Mechanisms: An Introductory Essay," in Hedstrom and Swedberg, *Social Mechanisms*, 1–31.
41. Tilly, "Mechanisms in Political Processes," 25; Merton, *Social Theory and Social Structure*, 421–39.
42. McAdam, Tarrow, and Tilly, *Dynamics of Contention*, 27.

43. Fararo and Skvoretz, "Institutions as Production Systems," 121.

44. There could just as well be eight, nine, or more mechanisms operating across the cases. The types and combinations observed depend to some extent on the problematic features of the case at hand. The mechanisms described here appear to be crucial for explaining the three outcomes at the heart of this study: concessions, collapse, and strong participation.　　·

45. Polletta and Jasper, "Collective Identity and Social Movements," 283–305; Snow and Benford, "Master Frames," 137; Snow et al., "Frame Alignment Processes."

46. Latour, *Pasteurization of France*, 85–110.

47. Cox, "Ideology and the Growth Coalition," 22.

48. Berry, Portney, and Thomson, *Rebirth of Urban Democracy*, 146.

49. Green, Guth, and Wilcox, "Less than Conquerors," 117–35.

50. Gans, *Urban Villagers*, 323–46.

51. Tarrow, "Very Excess of Democracy," 20–38; Dufour, "Mobilizing Gay Activists," 59–72.

52. McAdam, Tarrow, and Tilly, *Dynamics of Contention*, 158, 144.

53. Schattsneider, *Semi-Sovereign People*, 1–190; Cobb and Elder, *Participation in American Politics*, 14–16.

54. McAdam, Tarrow, and Tilly, *Dynamics of Contention*, 13.

Chapter 2: Urban Restructuring and the Formation of an Urban Growth Coalition

1. Houston, "Brief History," 37. My use of the term "region" in connection with Pittsburgh is equivalent to the four-county Pittsburgh Metropolitan Statistical Area (MSA) as described by the U.S. Census Bureau during the period covered in this chapter, including the Counties of Allegheny (location of Pittsburgh), Beaver, Washington, and Westmoreland. The terms "Pittsburgh," "city of Pittsburgh," or "the city" all refer to the municipal corporation the U.S. Census refers to as "Pittsburgh city."

2. Stevens, "Hearth of the Nation," 178.

3. Faires, "Immigrants and Industry," 10.

4. McLaughlin and Watkins, "Problem of Industrial Growth," 6–7.

5. See University of Virginia Geospatial and Statistical Data Center, United States Historical Census Data Browser, University of Virginia, 1998. Available at http://fisher.lib.virginia.edu/census/ (accessed September 22, 2004).

6. McLaughlin and Watkins, "Problem of Industrial Growth," 8–9.

7. Lorant, "Between Two Wars," 340.

8. Lowe, *Cities in a Race with Time*, 112.

9. Stevens, "Role of Nonprofit Corporations," 28.

10. See Econometric Institute, "The Long Range Outlook for the Pittsburgh Industrial Area," and "What We're Doing about Pittsburgh's Reputation." *Greater Pittsburgh*, December 1947, 20–21.

11. Gugliotta, "How, When, and for Whom," 111–12.

12. Grinder, "From Insurgency to Efficiency," 187–202.

13. Gugliotta, "How, When, and for Whom," 114.

14. "Reports of Chamber Divisions," 11.

15. See Lubove, *Twentieth-Century Pittsburgh*, 1:101–5.

16. Mershon, "Corporate Social Responsibility," 117.

17. Nichols, "Pittsburgh Looks Ahead," 2; also McLaughlin and Watkins, "Problem of Industrial Growth," 1–14.

18. See DiGaetano and Klemanski, *Power and City Governance*, 61–85.

19. Scott, *American City Planning since 1890*, 362–452.

20. Gelfland, *A Nation of Cities*, 86.

21. Ibid., 112–18.

22. During the war Pittsburgh Mayor Cornelius D. Scully initiated a "long-range program" for the postwar planning process and invited NRPB consultants to participate. See Buente, "Pittsburgh's Post-War Program," 42–43.

23. Funigiello, *Challenge of Urban Liberalism*, 174–86.

24. Mershon, "Corporate Social Responsibility," 134–35.

25. See Gelfland, *A Nation of Cities*, 112–26.

26. This paragraph is based on Mershon, "Corporate Social Responsibility," 149–52.

27. Scott, *American City Planning since 1890*, 425.

28. On the national political circumstances surrounding the Housing Act of 1949, see Mollenkopf, *Contested City*, 47–97; Teaford, "Urban Renewal and Its Aftermath," 443.

29. Lubove, *Twentieth-Century Pittsburgh*, 1:90–91.

30. Martin, "Pittsburgh Comprehensive Improvement Program," 885–86.

31. Quoted in Robin and Lorant, "Rebirth," 419.

32. Quoted in "Teamwork for Pittsburgh," 10.

33. "Comments by *Pittsburgh Post-Gazette*," 10.

34. Steinberg, "Pittsburgh, a New City," 129.

35. See "Pittsburgh's New Powers," 69–74, 76–77, 182, 184, 186; Hawkins, "Lawrence of Pittsburgh," 55–61.

36. Coleman, "Interest Intermediation"; Jezierski, "Neighborhoods and Public-Private Partnerships," 217–49; Ferman, *Challenging the Growth Machine*, 93–94; Schmitter, "Modes of Interest Intermediation," 7–38; Wilson, "Interest Groups and Politics," 105–23.

37. Muller, "Metropolis and Region," 194.

38. Robin and Lorant, "Rebirth," 386.

39. See Mershon, "Corporate Social Responsibility," 153–221.

40. Lubove, *Twentieth-Century Pittsburgh*, 1:109–10.

41. Quoted in "Pittsburgh's Thrilling Civic Renaissance," 131, 155.

42. Martin, "Narrative of the Allegheny Conference," 4.

43. Mershon, "Corporate Social Responsibility," 179; Martin, "Narrative of the Allegheny Conference," 8.

44. Doherty, "Pittsburgh of Tomorrow," 18.

45. Stewman and Tarr, "Public-Private Partnerships in Pittsburgh," 156–57.

46. Stave, *New Deal and the Last Hurrah*, 53–83.

47. Aldo Colautti, interview by Michael Snow, July 31, 1998, transcript, State and Local Government Oral History Program, Archives of Industrial Society, University of Pittsburgh.

48. Thomas, *Fortunes and Misfortunes;* Jezierski, "Neighborhoods and Public-Private Partnerships," 225.

49. Weber, *Don't Call Me Boss,* 232.

50. Ibid., 232; "Mellons Discover Pittsburgh," 30.

51. Urban Redevelopment Authority, *Gateway Center,* 4.

52. Jezierski, "Political Limits to Development," 173–89.

53. Thomas, "Invisible Governments."

54. For a study in the contrast between corporatist style decision making that prevailed in postwar Pittsburgh and the "political logic" prevailing in Chicago during the same period, see Ferman, *Challenging the Growth Machine.*

55. Jacobson, "Labor Mobility and Structural Change," 438–48.

56. Muller, "Historical Aspects of Regional Structural Change," 17–48.

57. Bigger, "Pittsburgh and the Pittsburgh Plan," 271–72; Tarr, "Infrastructure and City Building," 245–46.

58. See Bigger, "Obstacles," 814, 815; Bigger, "Anatomy of Pittsburgh," 172–73.

59. Mershon, "Corporate Social Responsibility," 86; Martin, "Narrative of the Allegheny Conference," 1; quotation from Lubove, *Twentieth-Century Pittsburgh,* 1:91.

60. Tarr, "Infrastructure and City Building," 247; Lubove, *Twentieth-Century Pittsburgh,* 1:92.

61. Quotation from Robin and Lorant, "Rebirth," 383. Richards was instrumental in the founding of the Conference. See Lubove, *Twentieth-Century Pittsburgh,* 1:381, 385. It was not Bigger's job at City Planning but his frequent quarrels with Wallace Richards and others at the PRPA that caused him to give up his consulting role. See Alberts, *The Shaping of the Point,* 70, 144; *Bulletin Index,* July 11, 1940, 6.

62. *Bulletin Index,* November 23, 1939, 6; Moses, "Arterial Plan for Pittsburgh."

63. Mayor Scully's 1940 Point Park Commission revived an earlier one he appointed in 1937, when a Chamber of Commerce official first discussed with the City Planning Commission the idea of a national park. See Alberts, *The Shaping of the Point,* 43–44, 55.

64. Alberts, *The Shaping of the Point,* 44–45; quotation on 47. See also

Bulletin Index, July 11, 1940, 6–7; "Pittsburgh Experts Resent $50,000 Outlay for Moses Survey," *Pittsburgh Sun-Telegraph*, December 10, 1939; "County Planners," *Pittsburgh Post-Gazette*, December 9, 1939.

65. Alberts, *The Shaping of the Point*, 70.

66. Ibid., 69.

67. Ibid., 76–77.

68. Martin, "Narrative of the Allegheny Conference," 13.

69. Mershon, "Corporate Social Responsibility," 402–4; quotation on 404.

Chapter 3: Contentious Politics of Neighborhood Redevelopment

1. Brignano, *Pittsburgh Civic Light Opera*, 58.

2. Mallet, "Redevelopment and Response," 182; Pittsburgh City Council, *Municipal Record* 24, June 20, 1949, 385–86.

3. Pittsburgh City Council, *Municipal Record* 26, July 5, 1949, 403.

4. "300 Protest Site for Light Operas," *Pittsburgh Press*, July 8, 1949; "Protests Stall Plans for Highland Park Light Opera Site," *Pittsburgh Press*, July 7, 1949; Burke quotation from "New Park Offered in Place of Opera," *Pittsburgh Press*, July 9, 1949.

5. *Municipal Record* 27, July 11, 1949; "Highland Park Likes Music but Not Six Nights a Week," *Pittsburgh Press*, July 6, 1949; Pittsburgh City Council, Committee on Hearings, July 8, 1949, 391–402; "Protests Stall Plans for Highland Park Light Opera Site," *Pittsburgh Press*, July 7, 1949; "300 Protest Site for Light Operas," *Pittsburgh Press*, July 8, 1949; "City Offered New Park," *Pittsburgh Press*, July 9, 1949.

6. "300 Protest Site for Light Operas"; "City Offered New Park."

7. Weber, *Don't Call Me Boss*, 269; Pittsburgh City Council, Committee on Hearings, July 8, 1949.

8. Weber, *Don't Call Me Boss*, 248–53; "'Politics' Charges Fly as Councilmen Ratify Park Site for Operas," *Pittsburgh Press*, July 13, 1949.

9. Leonard quote from "300 Protest Site"; McArdle quote and Leonard quote on Robin from "'Politics' Charges Fly."

10. Pittsburgh City Council, Committee on Hearings, July 8, 1949, 397; Pittsburgh City Council, *Municipal Record* 27, July 11, 1949, 423; "Highland Park Site Held Best for Opera: Approval Assured," *Pittsburgh Press*, July 12, 1949.

11. "Highland Park Opera Site Gets Secret Council OK," *Pittsburgh Press*, July 11, 1949.

12. *Municipal Record* 28, July 18, 1949, 435.

13. Ibid., 433.

14. "Highland Opera Site"; McArdle quote from Pittsburgh City Council, *Municipal Record* 28, July 18, 1949, 435.

15. All quantitative relationships reported on the content of newspapers

were computed through methods of content analysis summarized in the appendix.

16. The opinion letters are all quoted from the *Pittsburgh Press*.

17. Pittsburgh City Council, *Municipal Record* 33, August 22, 1949, 504–5.

18. Weber, *Don't Call Me Boss*, 269.

19. Mershon, "Corporate Social Responsibility," 408; City Investing Company, "Proposal for the Utilization of the Redevelopment Area Adjoining Point Park, Pittsburgh, Pennsylvania," prepared for the Equitable Life Assurance Society of the United States (undated).

20. Demmler, *The First Century of an Institution*, 166–67.

21. Alberts, *Shaping of the Point*, 101–7.

22. Gateway Center Records, Boxes 1 and 2, Library and Archives Division, Historical Society of Western Pennsylvania; also, "Point Building Plans Go to Council Monday," *Pittsburgh Post-Gazette*, November 26, 1949.

23. Mershon, "Corporate Social Responsibility," 411.

24. "Plan to Rebuild Triangle Gets New Impetus," *Pittsburgh Post-Gazette*, March 27, 1947; quote is from Alberts, *Shaping of the Point*, 101.

25. Pittsburgh City Council, *Municipal Record* 46, November 28, 1949, 680–81; "Point Building Plans to Council Monday," *Pittsburgh Post-Gazette*, November 26, 1949; "Group Will Fight Point Area Plans," *Pittsburgh Post-Gazette*, December 9, 1949.

26. "Lower Triangle Project to Go to High Court," *Pittsburgh Post-Gazette*, December 21, 1949; "Triangle Plan Wins Approval of High Court," *Pittsburgh Post-Gazette*, January 12, 1950.

27. "Lower Triangle Plan Faces Double Baptism of Fire During Week," *Pittsburgh Post-Gazette*, January 2, 1950; "Building Plan at Point Is Attacked," *Pittsburgh-Post Gazette*, January 4, 1950.

28. "Building Plan at Point Is Attacked."

29. Weber, *Don't Call Me Boss*, 80.

30. "Gateway Plan Facing New Legal Hurdle," *Pittsburgh Post-Gazette*, April 12, 1950; "Gateway Case Sent to Federal Judges," *Pittsburgh Post-Gazette*, April 13, 1950; "Gateway Rulings Speeded," editorial, *Pittsburgh Post-Gazette*, April 24, 1950; "New Suits Go Before U.S. Court," *Pittsburgh Post-Gazette*, April 24, 1950; "Gateway Plan Wins in U.S. Court Ruling," *Pittsburgh Post-Gazette*, April 26, 1950.

31. "High Court Approves Point Plan," *Pittsburgh Post-Gazette*, January 12, 1950; Pittsburgh City Council, *Municipal Record* 4, January 23, 1950; "Triangle Project Advances," *Pittsburgh Post-Gazette*, January 17, 1950.

32. Seven property owners did, however, file exceptions in common pleas court to the compensation offered for their properties by the URA. They asked the court to restrain the authority from taking their properties until they received what they felt was adequate compensation for the value

of their land. The court granted their exceptions. See "Legal Action May Hold Up Gateway Plan," *Pittsburgh Post-Gazette*, April 5, 1950, 1; "2 Gateway Titles Acquired," *Pittsburgh Post-Gazette*, April 7, 1950.

33. Colker, "Gaining Gateway Center," 140.

34. Gateway Center Records, "Equitable Life Assurance and Urban Redevelopment Personality Reports on First Set of Hearings," box 2, folder 4, 1950, Library and Archives Division, Historical Society of Western Pennsylvania.

35. "Here's a Pittsburgh Example of How You Can Throw a Going Business into the Street," *Pittsburgh Post-Gazette*, May 8, 1950. See also "Many Property Owners Not Protesting Development Plan in Lower Triangle," *Pittsburgh Post-Gazette*, May 9, 1950.

36. "Point Area Development Called Unjust," *Pittsburgh Post-Gazette*, May 10, 1950.

37. Alberts, *The Shaping of the Point*, 106.

38. "Gateway Start Set Despite Suit," *Pittsburgh Post-Gazette*, May 25, 1950.

39. Stevens, "Role of Nonprofit Corporations," 88.

40. "Showdown Near on Henger Hill Housing Project," *Pittsburgh Press*, September 10, 1950.

41. Mallet, "Redevelopment and Response," 182.

42. Weber, *Don't Call Me Boss*, 264.

43. Mershon, "Corporate Social Responsibility," 498.

44. Pittsburgh City Council, Committee on Hearings, November 10, 1949; Pittsburgh City Council, *Municipal Record* 45, November 21, 1949, 666.

45. Pittsburgh Department of City Planning, "The City Moves Forward."

46. The Pittsburgh Housing Authority is a municipal corporation created under the United States Housing Act of 1937. Its board is appointed by the mayor. In 1949 the authority applied for a $650,000 federal grant to begin planning five thousand new public housing units. See "Big Projects," *Pittsburgh Press*, September 24, 1950.

47. The authority began by purchasing a fourteen-acre farm for back taxes, which was located in the middle of St. Clair. It then moved to purchase ninety-three more surrounding acres required to convert the site into low-income housing.

48. Pittsburgh City Council, *Municipal Record* 32, August 28, 1950.

49. "City to Condemn Unfinished Homes to Make Room for Low-Cost Plan," *Pittsburgh Press*, September 3, 1950.

50. Ibid.

51. "North Siders Get 'Dutch Up' in Housing Plan Protest," *Pittsburgh Press*, September 21, 1950. See also "Favored Status of Low Rent Projects Heats Up Protests," *Pittsburgh Press*, September 25, 1950.

52. "Letter to the Editor," *Pittsburgh Press*, September 9, 1950.

53. Reporters covering the story stated that protesters "[opposed] the planned project on the grounds that it would disrupt a community developed and settled by ancestors a century ago." See "Housing Protest Meeting Tonight," *Pittsburgh Press,* September 11, 1950.

54. "St. Clair Group Fails to Halt Home Project," *Pittsburgh Press,* September 12, 1950.

55. "St. Clair Group Fails to Halt Home Project"; quotation from "Showdown Near on Henger Hill Housing Project," *Pittsburgh Press,* September 10, 1950.

56. "Protests Gain on North Side Housing Plans," *Pittsburgh Press,* September 17, 1950.

57. "Housing Plan Foes to Stage March," *Pittsburgh Press,* September 22, 1950.

58. Pittsburgh City Council, Committee on Hearings, September 27, 1950; "Objectors to Jam Housing Hearing," *Pittsburgh Press,* September 27, 1950; "Public Housing Foes Threaten to Bolt Party," *Pittsburgh Press,* September 28, 1950; "Council to Hear Housing Protests," *Pittsburgh Press,* September 26, 1950.

59. "Court Okays Housing Plan in City View," *Pittsburgh Post-Gazette,* November 23, 1954; see also Pittsburgh Neighborhood Alliance, *Pittsburgh Neighborhood Atlas: Northview Heights,* 1977, 2.

60. Mollenkopf, *Contested City,* 117.

61. Weiss, "Origins and Legacy of Urban Renewal."

62. Pittsburgh Neighborhood Alliance, *Atlas of the Hill,* 2; "Renaissance Dooms Landmarks, but Legends of 'Hill' Live On," *Pittsburgh Post-Gazette,* December 26, 1956.

63. "Action Demanded on Hill's Slums," *Pittsburgh Press,* November 13, 1946; quotation from Mallet, "Redevelopment and Response," 182.

64. Pittsburgh Chamber of Commerce, "Pittsburgh Center"; Mallet, "Redevelopment and Response," 182; Urban Redevelopment Authority, "Lower Hill Redevelopment Project," 1; Public Auditorium Authority of Pittsburgh and Allegheny County, "An All-Purpose Civic Auditorium."

65. Quoted in Mershon, "Corporate Social Responsibility," 516.

66. Pittsburgh Neighborhood Alliance, *Atlas of the Hill,* 2; "U.S. Funds Spur Hill Plan," *Pittsburgh Press,* September 13, 1955.

67. Data prepared by Robert Pease and presented in Weber, *Don't Call Me Boss,* appendix A.

68. Pittsburgh Department of City Planning, "Relocation Report," 23.

69. Glasco, "Civil Rights Movement in Pittsburgh," 6.

70. Morton Coleman, interview by Michael Snow, July 31, 1998, transcript, State and Local Government Oral History Program, Archives of Industrial Society, University of Pittsburgh.

71. Quoted in Timothy McNulty, "New Heights for the Hill," Pittsburgh *Post-Gazette,* July 9, 1999.

72. Erie, *Rainbow's End,* 165.
73. Lubove, "City Beautiful, City Banal," 33.
74. Charles Covert Arensberg, interview by Dodie Carpenter, August 19, 1974, transcript, Pittsburgh Renaissance Project, the Stanton Belfour Oral History Collection, Archives of Industrial Society, University of Pittsburgh.
75. "Bulldozers to Begin Clearing Lower Hill March 1," *Pittsburgh Post-Gazette,* January 9, 1957; Pittsburgh Department of City Planning, "Relocation Report," 24–40; Glasco, "Civil Rights Movement in Pittsburgh," 6–8.
76. "Plea Made to Save St. Peter's Church Here," *Pittsburgh Post-Gazette,* March 14, 1958.
77. "10,000 Battle to Save Church," *Pittsburgh Press,* undated news file, Carnegie Library, Pennsylvania Department.
78. "High Court Seals Fate of St. Peter's," *Pittsburgh Press,* December 4, 1958.
79. "Glasso Fails in Hill Church Plea to Pope," *Pittsburgh Post-Gazette,* July 16, 1960.
80. "Grandmother Sure Prayers Will Save St. Peter's," *Pittsburgh Post-Gazette,* July 13, 1960.
81. "St. Peter's Surrendered to Authority," *Pittsburgh Post-Gazette,* September 20, 1960; "Wreckers Start Demolition of St. Peter's," *Pittsburgh Post-Gazette,* October 29, 1960.

Chapter 4: Another Wave of Urban Restructuring

1. Dicken, *Global Shift,* 28.
2. Ibid., 28.
3. Castells, *Rise of the Network Society,* 253–54, 282–83.
4. Fitzgerald, "Pittsburgh, Pennsylvania," 238; Long, *Book on Pittsburgh,* 42–47.
5. Hoerr, *And the Wolf Finally Came,* 589.
6. Allegheny Conference on Community Development, "Toward a Shared Economic Vision," 8, 7.
7. "Out-Migration Steady in the Region," 1–2; DeFrancesco, "To Have and to Hold."
8. Brookings Institution Center on Urban and Metropolitan Affairs, "Back to Prosperity," 28–38.
9. Sustainable Pittsburgh, "Southwestern Pennsylvania," 6.
10. Mollenkopf, *Contested City,* 122–33.
11. Keating, "Federal Policy and Poor Urban Neighborhoods."
12. Nathan, "Federal Grants," 534.
13. Fosler and Berger, "Public-Private Partnership."
14. Clarke and Gaile, *The Work of Cities,* 45–46.
15. DiGaetano and Klemanski, *Power and City Governance,* 77.
16. Caraley, "Washington Abandons the Cities," 12.
17. Rich, "Riot and Reason," 115–34.

18. Clark and Gaile, *The Work of Cities*, 50.

19. Stevens, "Role of Nonprofit Corporations," 55–65.

20. Quoted in Thomas, "Fortunes and Misfortunes," 53.

21. Ferman, *Challenging the Growth Machine*, 86–88.

22. Quoted in Lorant, "Levelling Off," 526.

23. Pittsburgh History and Landmarks Foundation, "Five Year Report," vii.

24. Charles Covert Arensberg, interview by Dodie Carpenter.

25. Pittsburgh History and Landmarks Foundation, "Fifteen Year Report," 11.

26. Richter, "Pittsburgh's Innovative Renovation Record."

27. Ziegler, *Historic Preservation in Inner City Areas*.

28. Pittsburgh History and Landmarks Foundation, "A City's Living Memory," 1; Richter, "Pittsburgh's Innovative Renovation Record."

29. Bramhall, "Planners Advocate for Communities"; Ahlbrandt, "Public-Private Partnerships," 125; quote is from Lurcott and Downing, "Public-Private Support System," 461.

30. Sbragia, "Pittsburgh's 'Third Way,'" 53.

31. Quoted in Lorant, "Great Transformation in the Eighties," 612–14.

32. For example, one CEO responded, "When you look at my predecessors two or three back, they would have been able to devote their time to Pittsburgh on an 80:20 ratio. Today, I can hardly afford to give Pittsburgh 20:80. Although I have an interest in Pittsburgh, I have too many things elsewhere, so that I personally can't give it that kind of attention." Quoted in Ahlbrandt and Coleman, "Role of the Corporation," 19.

33. Weiss and Metzger, "Technology Development."

34. Lubove, *Twentieth-Century Pittsburgh*, 2:57–85. The convention center was conceived while Flaherty was mayor but completed in Caliguiri's administration.

35. Jezierski, "Neighborhoods and Public-Private Partnerships," 217–49; Weiss and Metzger, "Technology Development," 469–77.

36. Lurcott and Downing, "Public-Private Support System."

37. The Local Initiatives Support Corporation is a national organization funded by the Ford Foundation to give technical assistance to over four hundred CDCs in twenty-three cities.

38. Van Trump, "Station Square."

39. Quoted in Moe and Wilkie, *Changing Places*, 136.

40. Ibid., 137.

41. Allegheny Conference on Community Development, "Toward a Shared Economic Vision," 9; "Wage Levels in Pittsburgh," 1.

42. Allegheny Conference on Community Development, "Toward a Shared Economic Vision," 1.

43. Quote and mention of two hundred organizations from ibid., 5. Agency numbers in Mellon-Lawrence era from Jezierski, "Pittsburgh," 159–81.

44. Richard M. Scaife's newspaper, the *Pittsburgh Tribune-Review*, has been a voice of criticism against the Democratically controlled government and its downtown business partners in the Allegheny Conference. *Tribune-Review* editorial pages have regularly attacked the system of state subsidies to local businesses and the apparent implication of public service unions in the rising costs and inefficiencies of local government.

45. Cathy McCollom, interview by the author, May 7, 2002.

46. Haulk, "Message from the President."

47. Mellor, "Dozen Years Later"; Institute for Justice, *Financial Report;* Moser, "Training Advocates for Liberty"; Elgendy, "A Summer Well Spent."

48. Metzger, "Remaking the Growth Coalition"; Southwestern Pennsylvania Strategic Investment Partnership, "Investing in the Future"; Regional Marketing Coalition, "A Marketing Strategy and Action Plan to Accelerate Economic Growth in Southwestern Pennsylvania," McKinsey and Company, November 20, 1997.

49. See Lindeman, "City's Retail Strategy One of a Kind," *Pittsburgh Post-Gazette,* November 2, 1998; "Across the Region Retail Projects Break Ground," *Pittsburgh Post-Gazette,* June 17, 2003.

50. Metzger, "Reinventing Housing in Pittsburgh," 8.

51. Ibid., 8.

Chapter 5: Contentious Politics of Downtown Revitalization

1. Dan Fitzpatrick, "Developer Signs Fifth and Forbes Retail Deal," *Pittsburgh Business Times,* September 15, 1997.

2. A content analysis of *Pittsburgh Tribune-Review* articles, the region's second largest daily newspaper, reveals that comments referring to secrecy of the dealings between the city and Urban Retail were repeated in over 30 percent of articles between March 28, 1998, and May 28, 2000 (N = 247). See appendix for an explanation of my methodology of content analysis.

3. Michael Coleman, "Coming Attraction: A Downtown Cinema?" *Pittsburgh Tribune-Review,* March 28, 1998.

4. The downtown plan's approach to retail redevelopment was to attract "investment by national retail and entertainment developers," a goal that participants agreed would require a "coordinated strategy and effort." The plan also stated, however, that the development, management, and marketing of retail would, "unlike festival marketplaces or enclosed malls," be "focused on existing streets and users." The downtown plan expressed a set of general objectives for retail redevelopment agreed upon by stakeholder-participants, but not a proposal specifying ownership and management of properties in the redevelopment area or the role of government authority in establishing a particular mix of tenants. See Pittsburgh Department of City Planning, "Pittsburgh Downtown Plan."

5. Ziegler to director of development, letter, September 30, 1997, Fifth and Forbes documents, Pittsburgh History and Landmarks Foundation storage (photocopy). Ziegler's concern about the "significance" of buildings in

the area refers to local, state, and national categories of historic designation that provide varying levels of protection from destructive projects, especially those using federal or state money. Any visible, exterior alterations, including demolition, renovations or additions, to buildings or districts with city historic designation must be reviewed by the Historic Review Commission, whose members are appointed by the mayor of Pittsburgh.

6. Fitzpatrick, "Developer Signs Fifth and Forbes"; Cathy McCollom, interview by the author.

7. Arthur P. Ziegler to director of city planning, letter, June 4; Ziegler to deputy mayor, letters, June 10, July 9; all found in Fifth and Forbes documents, Pittsburgh History and Landmarks Foundation storage (photocopies).

8. Arthur P. Ziegler, letter to Pennsylvania Historical & Museum Commission, July 22, Fifth and Forbes documents, Pittsburgh History and Landmarks Foundation storage (photocopy).

9. Lowry, "Planning Ahead, Recalling the Past: Developers Inviting Local Groups' Input," *Pittsburgh Post-Gazette,* July 15, 1998.

10. As late as June 30, 1999, Ziegler wrote in a letter to the mayor, "We have developed a series of recommendations that we submitted to you and we have been trying to meet on this subject in accordance with [the deputy mayor's] original suggestion for nearly a year. The main problem here in getting to a solution is simply getting to a meeting" (Fifth and Forbes documents, Pittsburgh History and Landmarks Foundation storage [photocopy]).

11. Rich Lord, "Pittsburgh City Council Somewhat Cool on Mellon Bank Subsidies," *Pittsburgh Tribune-Review,* July 23, 1998.

12. Rich Lord, "Downtown Project Gets $10 Million," *Pittsburgh Tribune-Review,* July 29, 1998.

13. Rich Lord, "Rebuilt Downtown Retail Site Outlined," *Pittsburgh Tribune-Review,* July 31, 1998.

14. Dan Fitzpatrick, "A Tale of Reinventing Cities," *Pittsburgh Post-Gazette,* November 1, 1998; Fitzpatrick, "Market Place Is Odds-On Favorite with Mayor—But Will It Work?" *Pittsburgh Post-Gazette,* November 1, 1998.

15. Bernie Lynch, interview by the author, June 18, 2002.

16. Lynch, "IJ's Work Shows It Is Time."

17. Arthur P. Ziegler, letter to deputy mayor, July 24, 1998, Fifth and Forbes documents, Pittsburgh History and Landmarks Foundation storage (photocopy).

18. Patricia Lowry, "Urban Expert Decries Downtown Development Plan," *Pittsburgh Post-Gazette,* October 8, 1998.

19. Jeff Stacklin, "Urban Writer Scoffs at Plan for Corridor," *Pittsburgh Tribune-Review,* October 8, 1998.

20. Lowry, "Urban Expert Decries Downtown."

21. Jeff Stacklin, "Downtown Lands Lord and Taylor Store," *Pittsburgh Tribune-Review,* October 9, 1998.

22. Schmidlapp, "Great Space and Departed Hope," 6–7. Quote from Arthur P. Ziegler letter to mayor, June 30, 1999, Fifth and Forbes documents, Pittsburgh History and Landmarks Foundation storage (photocopy).

23. Pittsburgh History and Landmarks Foundation, memorandum of agreement with Preservation Pittsburgh, "Market Place at Fifth and Forbes," November 10, 1999, Fifth and Forbes documents, Pittsburgh History and Landmarks Foundation storage (photocopy); Arthur P. Ziegler, memo to staff, January 14, 1999, Fifth and Forbes documents, Pittsburgh History and Landmarks Foundation storage (photocopy).

24. Rich Lord, "History, Progress Clashing," *Pittsburgh Tribune-Review,* December 31, 1998; Patricia Lowry, "Merchants Sound Off on City Redevelopment Plan," *Pittsburgh Post-Gazette,* January 10, 1999.

25. Jeff Stacklin, "Chicago Firm Worries Pittsburgh," *Pittsburgh Tribune-Review,* January 9, 1999; "Developers Pledge Mix of Old and New," *Pittsburgh Tribune-Review,* March 6, 1999.

26. The City Planning Commission is a nine-member panel appointed by the mayor that reviews major development proposals. The Historic Review Commission, a seven-member panel of mayoral appointees, has jurisdiction to protect and maintain historically and architecturally significant buildings and neighborhoods in the city.

27. The listing was announced on Preservation Pennsylvania's Web site, in its quarterly newsletter, in a local press conference arranged by PHLF, and in a letter addressed to Mayor Murphy.

28. Included in the mailing were major charitable foundations, the local chapter of the American Institute of Architects, the Pittsburgh Cultural Trust, the Historic Review Commission, the City Planning Commission, TV and print media, the mayor's office, and City Council. This list is compiled from copies of letters written in August 1999 and located in Fifth and Forbes documents, PHLF storage.

29. Patricia Lowry, "A Landmark Dispute? History Foundation Issues Call to Arms against Proposed Downtown Development," *Pittsburgh Post-Gazette,* August 18, 1999.

30. Patricia Lowry and Tom Barnes, "Group Says Downtown Planning Is Closed: Charge City Is Shutting Public Out of Process," *Pittsburgh Post-Gazette,* September 17, 1999.

31. McCollom, interview by the author; Arthur P. Ziegler, letter to Eckstut, September 23, 1999, Fifth and Forbes documents, Pittsburgh History and Landmarks Foundation storage (photocopy).

32. Arthur P. Ziegler, memo to Arthur Lubetz and Bernie Lynch, September 17, 1999, Fifth and Forbes documents, Pittsburgh History and Landmarks Foundation storage (photocopy).

33. Patty Maloney, interview by the author, July 11, 2002; Jeff Stacklin, "Fifth-Forbes Details Emerge: Market Place Developer Fills in Vision for Shopping District," *Pittsburgh Tribune-Review,* June 6, 1999.

34. Maloney, interview by the author.

35. Lynch quoted in Stacklin, "Fifth-Forbes Details Emerge"; bookstore owner quoted in "Cityscapes Booked for Change," *Pittsburgh Tribune-Review*, July 18, 1999; restaurant owners quoted in Eric Heyl, "Forbes Reconstruction Draws Fire: Firstside Shop Owners Unhappy about Project," *Pittsburgh Tribune-Review*, June 28, 1999, and Jeff Stacklin, "Market Square's Popularity Growing," *Pittsburgh Tribune-Review*, July 5, 1999.

36. Stacklin, "Fifth and Forbes Funds Forthcoming," *Pittsburgh Tribune-Review*, September 10, 1999. The Redevelopment Assistance Capital Program grant had been submitted but not yet approved; see Christopher Keough, "Council OKs Fifth, Forbes Grant," *Pittsburgh Tribune-Review*, July 21, 1999.

37. Urban Redevelopment Authority, director of real estate, form letter, "Relocation Information: Fifth and Forbes Redevelopment Project," October 1999, Fifth and Forbes documents, Pittsburgh History and Landmarks Foundation storage (photocopy); Christopher Keough, "Merchants See Plan as Beginning of the End," *Pittsburgh Tribune-Review*, October 1, 1999. See also David R. Eltz, "Pittsburgh Mayor Unveils Blueprint: Marketplace's Prosperity Uncertain," *Pittsburgh Tribune-Review*, October 5, 1999.

38. Maloney, interview by the author.

39. The following comment by a Murphy spokesman in March 1999 is characteristic: "We're still in the planning stage. . . . When we're in the development stage, everybody will know"; quoted in Jeff Stacklin, "City Wants Developer to Agree to Design Guidelines," *Pittsburgh Tribune-Review*, March 4, 1999. The executive director of the URA made a similar statement in May 1999: "We have to finalize our deal with Urban [Retail Properties] before we go public"; quoted in Jeff Stacklin, "Marketplace Project Would Topple Buildings: Historic Facades Might Be Spared Wrecking Ball," *Pittsburgh Tribune-Review*, May 13, 1999.

40. On the day of the announcement the mayor urged the authorizing agencies to move swiftly through the approval process, as he was hoping to secure final approval from City Council before Christmas. See Christopher Keough, "Council Asks for Input on Marketplace: Some Critical of Hasty Approval," *Pittsburgh Tribune-Review*, October 22, 1999; Keough, "Fifth-Forbes Feedback: Public Rates Downtown Development," *Pittsburgh Tribune-Review*, October 22, 1999.

41. Urban Redevelopment Authority of Pittsburgh, director of development, e-mail to Pittsburgh Urban Magnet Project, January 27, 2000, Fifth and Forbes documents, Pittsburgh History and Landmarks Foundation storage (photocopy).

42. Lynch, interview by the author; Maloney, interview by the author; Jake Haulk, interview by the author, May 16, 2002; Pat Clark, interview by the author, May 30, 2002. The "usual suspects" phrase was used by Ehrenkrantz, Eckstut, and Kuhn, "Fifth and Forbes Development Plan."

43. Maloney, interview by the author.

44. The newspapers began citing $100 million as the projected public investment, a number estimated by the executive director of the URA in a June interview. See Rich Lord, "Forbes-Fifth Rehab Could Be Signature Piece of Cox's Career," *Pittsburgh Tribune-Review,* July 4, 1999.

45. Clark, interview by the author.

46. Philip B. Hallen, memorandum to staff, Pittsburgh History and Landmarks Foundation, "Follow up Meeting on Fifth-Forbes Plan," November 11, 1999, Fifth and Forbes documents, Pittsburgh History and Landmarks Foundation storage (photocopy); Christopher Keough, "Fifth-Forbes Corridor Plan Counters Mayor's," *Pittsburgh Tribune-Review,* November 20, 1999.

47. The commission's decision was based on the belief that it was "unlikely that the conditions of blight [in the redevelopment area] can be remedied by private enterprise without additional incentives offered by public participation." See Pittsburgh Department of City Planning, "Fifth and Forbes Redevelopment."

48. Quoted in Anthony Todd Carlisle, "Project Decision Delayed: Opposition, Lack of Specifics Prompt Panel to Postpone Fifth and Forbes Vote," *Pittsburgh Tribune-Review,* December 11, 1999. The commission expected to take action after just one hearing, but delayed because "there were so many people who came to speak, it ended up taking three meetings. They just couldn't push it through"; see Maloney, interview by the author.

49. Quoted in Anthony Todd Carlisle, "Market Place Garners Approval: Historic Commission OKs Mayor's Plan," *Pittsburgh Tribune-Review,* January 8, 2000.

50. McCollom, interview by the author.

51. Pittsburgh Downtown Partnership, "Downtown Planning Collaborative."

52. Bob O'Connor, letter to mayor of Pittsburgh, March 29, 2000, Fifth and Forbes documents, Pittsburgh History and Landmarks Foundation storage (photocopy); "Resolution Establishing the Pittsburgh Main Street Task Force," March 28, 2000.

53. Clark, interview by the author, May 30, 2002. Under the rubric of "young professional," the group included "architects, designers, tech types, artists, urban planners, creative types, writers, cultural directors, policy makers, marketing types, journalists." See Ground Zero, "Ground Zero Declaration."

54. Clark, interview by the author.

55. Ground Zero Action Network, "Regarding Fifth and Forbes," July 2000.

56. McAdam, Tarrow, and Tilly, *Dynamics of Contention,* 8.

57. Jeff Stacklin, "New Lazarus Nears Opening: Department Store Cor-

nerstone in Redevelopment of Downtown," *Pittsburgh Tribune-Review,* October 23, 1998; Haulk, interview by the author.

58. Allegheny Institute, "Will Lazarus Resurrect Downtown?" The news fax was sent by e-mail free of charge to everyone who subscribed.

59. Allegheny Institute, "TIF'd Off," "Cost $57 Million," "Roddey Stiffens TIF Administrative Requirements," "Lazarus"; Haulk and Montarti, "Primer."

60. Tom Barnes, "Fifth-Forbes Foes Shift to County: Council Urged to Kill Key Funding Point for Downtown," *Pittsburgh Post-Gazette,* June 7, 2000.

61. Quoted in Jeffrey Cohan, "Allegheny County Council Set to Take on County Code, Fifth-Forbes," *Pittsburgh Post-Gazette,* June 3, 2000. The institute also mounted a campaign for a citywide referendum asking voters to prohibit public money from aiding the downtown makeover. The battles to rescind government financing of Market Place continued but were not resolved during the Fifth and Forbes debate.

62. Quoted in Jason Togyer, "Justice Group Fights Property Seizures," *Pittsburgh Tribune-Review,* October 27, 1999.

63. Reed, "Eminent Domain Code for Allegheny County."

64. Haulk, interview by the author; also McNulty, "Downtown Renewal Foes Seek Referendum."

65. Haulk, interview by the author.

66. Ibid.

67. Argall, memo to Urban Affairs Committee, May 1, 2000 (photocopy); Lynch, e-mail distribution, May 26, 2000 (photocopy).

68. Pittsburgh Downtown Partnership, *Downtown Planning Collaborative,* appendix XII, 1–25.

69. Earlier, PHLF took its own plan off the table and had begun working closely with the Main Street people. Main Street had become the sole competitor of Market Place at Fifth and Forbes.

70. Nordstrom Inc., "Nordstrom Issues Statement," media release, November 22, 2000.

71. City of Pittsburgh, Mayor's Office, "Murphy Outlines 'Plan C,'" November 22, 2000.

72. Suzanne Elliott, "Murphy Debuts Plan 'C' for Market Place," *Pittsburgh Business Times,* November 22, 2000.

Chapter 6: Contentious Urban Redevelopment and Strong Democracy

1. Schumpeter, *Capitalism, Socialism, and Democracy,* 269. For a detailed account of Schumpeter's influence on democratic theory, see Pateman, *Participation and Democratic Theory,* 3–21.

2. Dahl, *A Preface to Democratic Theory.*

3. Barber, *Strong Democracy,* 145, 240.

4. Ibid., 240. Quote is from Mansbridge, *Beyond Adversary Democracy,* 4–5.

5. Peterson, *City Limits*, 143.

6. Elkin, *City and Regime*, 137.

7. Berry, Portney, and Thomson, *The Rebirth of Urban Democracy*, 57–63.

8. Ibid., 63–70.

9. Pierson, *Politics in Time*, 54–78.

10. Elster, "A Plea for Mechanisms," 47–52.

11. Covington, "Right Thinking, Big Grants"; Lapham, "Tentacles of Rage"; Bai, "Wiring the Vast Left-Wing Conspiracy."

Appendix

1. Yin, *Case Study Research*, 13.

2. Fararo, *Social Action Systems*, 16.

3. McCarthy, Smith, and Zald, "Accessing Public," 291–311.

4. Neumann, *Social Research Methods*, 31–32.

Bibliography

Ahlbrandt, Roger S. "Public-Private Partnerships for Neighborhood Renewal." *Annals of the American Academy of Political and Social Science* 488 (November 1986): 120–34.

Ahlbrandt, Roger S., and Morton Coleman. "The Role of the Corporation in Community Development as Viewed by 21 Corporate Executives". University Center for Social and Urban Research, University of Pittsburgh, 1987.

Alberts, Robert C. *The Shaping of the Point: Pittsburgh's Renaissance Park.* Pittsburgh, PA: University of Pittsburgh Press, 1980.

Allegheny Conference on Community Development. "Toward a Shared Economic Vision for Pittsburgh and Southwestern Pennsylvania." November 1993. Report.

Allegheny Institute for Public Policy. "Mission." http://www.allegheny institute.org/mission.php (accessed November 20, 2002).

———. "Cost $57 Million, Assessed at Only $17 Million—Why? County Records Tell an Interesting Tale." *Behind the Headlines Newsfax* 5 (December 15, 1999). Photocopy.

———. "Lazarus: Promises and Reality, Speculation about Poor Performance Confirmed." *Behind the Headlines Newsfax* 5 (April 12, 2000).

———. "Roddy Stiffens TIF Administrative Requirements." *Behind the Headlines Newsfax* 5 (January 9, 2000). Photocopy.

———. "TIF'd Off: County Should Stop Subsidizing Downtown Retail." *Behind the Headlines Newsfax* 5 (October 15, 1999). Photocopy.

———. "Will Lazarus Resurrect Downtown? The Center Triangle Project is a Poorly Conceived TIF Plan." *Behind the Headlines Newsfax* 5 (May 1999). Photocopy.

Bai, Matt. "Wiring the Vast Left-Wing Conspiracy." *New York Times Magazine,* July 25, 2004. http://www.nytimes.com/2004/07/25/magazine/25DEMOCRATS.html (accessed November 3, 2004).

Banfield, Edward. *Political Influence: A New Theory of Urban Politics.* New York: The Free Press, 1961.

Barber, Benjamin. *Strong Democracy: Participatory Democracy for a New Age.*

Berkeley and Los Angeles: University of California Press, 2003.

Berry, Jeffrey M., Kent E. Portney, and Ken Thomson. *The Rebirth of Urban Democracy*. Washington, DC: The Brookings Institution, 1993.

Bigger, Frederick. "The Anatomy of Pittsburgh—And Its Challenge to the Planner." *American Architect and Architecture* 151 (December 1937): 52–54. Reprinted in *Pittsburgh,* edited by Roy Lubove, 170–76. New York: New Viewpoints, 1976.

———. "Obstacles to the Development of a Recreation System." *The American City* 36 (June 1927): 813–15.

———. "Pittsburgh and the Pittsburgh Plan." *Art and Archaeology* 14 (November–December 1922): 271–72.

Bramhall, Billie. "Planners Advocate for Communities within Planning Department." *Planners Notebook* 4 (1974): 1–8.

Brignano, Mary. *Pittsburgh Civic Light Opera: How the Dreams Came True.* Sewickley, PA: White Oak Publishing, 1996.

Brookings Institution Center on Urban and Metropolitan Affairs. "Back to Prosperity: A Competitive Agenda for Renewing Pennsylvania." December 2003. Report.

Buente, Williard H. "Pittsburgh's Post-War Program." *The American City* 63 (March 1943): 42–43.

Cairns, Robert. "A City's Living Memory." Reprint from *The Orange Disc,* magazine of the Gulf Oil Corporation. In *The Stones of Pittsburgh,* no. 9. Pittsburgh: Pittsburgh History and Landmarks Foundation. Booklet.

Caraley, Demetrios. "Washington Abandons the Cities." *Political Science Quarterly* 107, no. 1 (1992): 1–30.

Castells, Manuel. *The Rise of the Network Society.* Malden, MA: Blackwell, 1996.

City of Pittsburgh, Mayor's Office. "Murphy Outlines 'Plan C,'" November 22, 2000. http://www.city.pittsburgh.pa.us/mayor/html/city_press_releases.html (accessed January 10, 2001).

Clarke, Susan E., and Gary L. Gaile. *The Work of Cities.* Minneapolis: University of Minnesota Press, 1998.

Cobb, Roger W., and Charles D. Elder. *Participation in American Politics: The Dynamics of Agenda Building.* Baltimore: Johns Hopkins University Press, 1983.

Coleman, Morton. "Interest Intermediation and Local Urban Development." PhD diss., Department of Political Science, University of Pittsburgh, 1983.

Colker, Rachel Balliet. "Gaining Gateway Center: Eminent Domain, Redevelopment, and Resistance." *Pittsburgh History* 78, no. 3 (1995): 134–44.

"Comments by *Pittsburgh Post-Gazette.*" *Greater Pittsburgh,* February 1946, 10.

Covington, Sally. "Right Thinking, Big Grants, and Long-Term Strategy: How Conservative Philanthropies and Think Tanks Transform U.S. Policy." *Covert Action Quarterly* 63 (Winter 1998): 6–16.

Cox, Kevin. "Ideology and the Growth Coalition." In *The Urban Growth Ma-*

chine: Critical Perspectives Two Decades Later, edited by Andrew E. G. Jonas and David Wilson, 21–36. Albany, NY: State University of New York Press, 1999.

Dahl, Robert. *A Preface to Democratic Theory.* Chicago: University of Chicago Press, 1956.

———. *Who Governs? Democracy and Power in an American City.* New Haven, CT: Yale University Press, 1961.

DeFrancesco, Joyce. "To Have and to Hold: Pittsburgh Strives to Attract and Retain Young People." *Pittsburgh Magazine,* August 2001 (online version). http://www.wqed.org/mag/features/0801_young.shtml (accessed November 4, 2004).

Demmler, Ralph. *The First Century of an Institution: Reed Smith Shaw & Mc-Clay.* Pittsburgh: self-published, 1977.

Dicken, Peter. *Global Shift: Transforming the World Economy.* 3rd edition. New York: Guilford Publications, 1998.

DiGaetano, Alan, and John S. Klemanski. *Power and City Governance: Comparative Perspectives on Urban Development.* Minneapolis: University of Minnesota Press, 1999.

Doherty, Robert. "The Pittsburgh of Tomorrow." *Greater Pittsburgh,* March 1947, 18–19.

Dreier, Peter, John Mollenkopf, and Todd Swanstrom. *Place Matters: Metropolitics for the Twenty-First Century.* Lawrence: University Press of Kansas, 2001.

Dufour, Claude. "Mobilizing Gay Activists." In *Social Movements and American Political Institutions,* edited by Anne N. Costain and Andrew S. McFarland, 59–72. New York: Rowman & Littlefield, 1998.

The Econometric Institute. "The Long Range Outlook for the Pittsburgh Industrial Area." Prepared for the Pittsburgh Chamber of Commerce, the Allegheny Conference on Community Development, and the Pittsburgh Civic-Business Council, 1946.

Ehrenkrantz, Eckstut, and Kuhn. "Fifth and Forbes Development Plan, Prepared for Pittsburgh History and Landmarks Foundation." February 2000. Booklet.

Eisinger, Peter K. "The Conditions of Protest Behavior in American Cities." *American Political Science Review* 67 (1973): 11–28.

———. *The Rise of the Entrepreneurial State.* Madison: University of Wisconsin Press, 1988.

Elgendy. Rick. "A Summer Well Spent." *Liberty and Law* 12 (October 2003). http://www.ij.org/publications/index.html (accessed August 9, 2004).

Elkin, Stephen L. "Cities without Power: The Transformation of American Urban Regimes." In *National Resources and Urban Policy,* edited by Douglas E. Ashford, 265–93. New York: Methuen, 1980.

———. *City and Regime in the American Republic.* Chicago: University of Chicago Press, 1987.

Elster, Jon. "A Plea for Mechanisms." In *Social Mechanisms: An Analytical Approach to Social Theory,* 47–52. New York: Cambridge University Press, 1998.

Emerson, Richard M. "Power-Dependence Relations." *American Sociological Review* 27: 31–41.

Erie, Steven P. *Rainbow's End: Irish Americans and the Dilemmas of Urban Machine Politics, 1840–1985.* Berkeley and Los Angeles: University of California Press, 1988.

Faires, Nora. "Immigrants and Industry: Peopling the 'Iron City.'" In *City at the Point: Essays on the Social History of Pittsburgh,* edited by Samuel P. Hays, 3–32. Pittsburgh: University of Pittsburgh Press, 1989.

Fararo, Thomas J. *Social Action Systems: Foundations and Synthesis in Sociological Theory.* Westport, CT: Praeger Press, 2001.

Fararo, Thomas J., and John Skvoretz. "Institutions as Production Systems." *Journal of Mathematical Sociology* 10 (1984): 117–81.

Ferman, Barbara. *Challenging the Growth Machine: Neighborhood Politics in Chicago and Pittsburgh.* Lawrence: University Press of Kansas, 1996.

Fitzgerald, Joan. "Pittsburgh, Pennsylvania: From Steel Town to Advanced Technology Center." In *Economic Restructuring of the American Midwest,* edited by Richard D. Bingham and Randall W. Eberts, 237–54. Boston: Klewer Publishers, 1988.

Fleischmann, Arnold, and Joe R. Feagin. "The Politics of Growth-Oriented Urban Alliances: Comparing Old Industrial and New Sunbelt Cities." *Urban Affairs Quarterly* 23 (December 1987): 207–32.

Fosler, R. Scott, and Renee A. Berger. "Public-Private Partnership: An Overview." In *Public-Private Partnership in American Cities,* edited by R. Scott Fosler and Renee Berger, 1–15. Lexington, MA: Lexington Books, 1984.

Funigiello, Philip J. *The Challenge of Urban Liberalism: Federal-City Relations during World War II.* Knoxville: University of Tennessee Press, 1978.

Gans, Herbert. *The Urban Villagers: Group and Class in the Life of Italian Americans.* New York: Free Press, 1962.

Gateway Center Records. Boxes 1 and 2, Library and Archives Division, Historical Society of Western Pennsylvania.

———. "Equitable Life Assurance and Urban Redevelopment Personality Reports on First Set of Hearings." Box 2, folder 4, 1950. Library and Archives Division, Historical Society of Western Pennsylvania.

Gelfand, Mark I. *A Nation of Cities: The Federal Government and Urban America, 1933–1965.* New York: Oxford University Press, 1975.

Giddens, Anthony. *The Constitution of Society: Outline of the Theory of Structuration.* Berkeley and Los Angeles: University of California Press, 1984.

Glasco, Laurence. "The Civil Rights Movement in Pittsburgh: To Make This City 'Some Place Special.'" Freedom Corner dedication program, Urban League of Pittsburgh. http//www.org/downloads/glasgo.pdf. (accessed March 12, 2003).

Gratz, Roberta. *Cities Back from the Edge.* New York: John Wiley and Sons, 1998.

Green, John C., James L. Guth, and Clyde Wilcox. "Less than Conquerors: The Christian Right in State Republican Parties." In *Social Movements and American Political Institutions,* edited by Anne N. Costain and Andrew S. McFarland, 117–35. New York: Rowman & Littlefield, 1998.

Grinder, Robert Dale. "'From Insurgency to Efficiency': The Smoke Abatement Campaign in Pittsburgh before World War I." *Western Pennsylvania Historical Magazine* 61 (1978): 187–202.

Ground Zero Action Network. "Ground Zero Declaration." Undated booklet.

Gugliotta, Angela. "How, When, and for Whom Was Smoke a Problem in Pittsburgh." In *Devastation and Renewal: An Environmental History of Pittsburgh and Its Region,* edited by Joel A. Tarr, 110–25. Pittsburgh: University of Pittsburgh Press, 2003.

Haeberle, Steven H. *Planting the Grassroots: Structuring Citizen Participation.* Westport, CT: Praeger Press, 1989.

Hall, Peter Dobkin. "Vital Signs: Organizational Population Trends and Civic Engagement in New Haven, Connecticut, 1950–1998." In *Civic Engagement in American Democracy,* edited by Theda Skocpol and Morris P. Fiorina, 211–48. Washington DC: Brookings Institution Press, 1999.

Haulk, Jake. "Message from the President." *Allegheny Institute Policy Brief* 1 (March 2001). http://www.alleghenyinstitute.org/briefs/vol1no1.pdf (accessed August 23, 2002).

Haulk, Jake, and Eric Montarti. "A Primer on Tax Increment Financing in Pittsburgh." *Allegheny Institute Report* 99–6 (June 1999).

Hawkins, Frank. "Lawrence of Pittsburgh: Boss of the Mellon Patch." *Harper's Magazine* 213 (August 1956): 55–61.

Hedstrom, Peter, and Richard Swedberg, eds. *Social Mechanisms: An Analytical Approach to Social Theory.* Cambridge: Cambridge University Press, 1998.

Hoerr, John P. *And the Wolf Finally Came: The Decline of the American Steel Industry.* Pittsburgh: University of Pittsburgh Press, 1988.

Houston, David. "A Brief History of the Process of Capital Accumulation in Pittsburgh: A Marxist Interpretation." In *Pittsburgh-Sheffield: Sister Cities,* edited by Joel Tarr, 29–70. Pittsburgh: Carnegie Mellon University College of Fine Arts, 1986.

Hunt, Lynn. "The Sacred and the French Revolution." In *Durkheimian Sociology: Cultural Studies,* edited by Jeffrey C. Alexander, 25–43. Cambridge: Cambridge University Press, 1988.

Hunter, Floyd. *Community Power Structure.* Garden City, NY: Anchor Books, 1963.

Institute for Justice. "Financial Report." http://www.ij.org/profile/index.html (accessed December 19, 2004).

————. "Regarding Fifth and Forbes," July 2000. Flyer.

Jacobsen, Louis. "Labor Mobility and Structural Change in Pittsburgh." *Journal of the American Planners Association* 53 (1987): 438–48.

Jezierski, Louise. "Political Limits to Development in Two Declining Cities: Cleveland and Pittsburgh." In *Research in Politics and Society,* vol. 3, edited by M. Wallace and J. Rothschild, 173–89. Greenwich, CT: Jai Press, 1988.

————. "Neighborhoods and Public-Private Partnerships in Pittsburgh." *Urban Affairs Quarterly* 26 (December 1990): 217–49.

————. "Pittsburgh: Partnerships in a Regional City." In *Regional Politics: America in a Post-City Age,* edited by H. V. Savitch and Ronald K. Vogel, 159–81. Newbury Park, CA: Sage, 1996.

Judd, Dennis, and Michael Parkinson, eds. *Leadership and Urban Regeneration: Cities in North America and Europe.* Newbury Park, CA: Sage, 1990.

Keating, W. Dennis. "Federal Policy and Poor Urban Neighborhoods." In *Rebuilding Urban Neighborhoods: Achievements, Opportunities, and Limits,* edited by W. Dennis Keating and Norman Krumholz, 14–32. Thousand Oaks, CA: Sage, 1999.

Klandermans, Bert. "A Theoretical Framework for Comparison of Social Movement Participation." *Sociological Forum* 8 (September 1993): 383–402.

Lapham, Lewis. "Tentacles of Rage: The Republican Propaganda Mill, a Brief History." *Harper's Magazine,* September 2004, 31–41.

Latour, Bruno. *The Pasteurization of France.* Cambridge, MA: Harvard University Press, 1988.

Lindblom, Charles. *Politics and Markets.* New York: Basic Books, 1977.

Logan, John R., and Harvey Molotch. *Urban Fortunes: The Political Economy of Place.* Berkeley and Los Angeles: University of California Press, 1987.

Logan, John R., and Todd Swanstrom. *Beyond the City Limits: Urban Policy and Economic Restructuring in Comparative Perspective.* Philadelphia: Temple University Press, 1990.

Long, Philip D. *The Book on Pittsburgh: The Other Side of the Story.* Pittsburgh: DMS/East Liberty Lutheran Church, 1985.

Lorant, Stefan. "Between Two Wars." In *Pittsburgh: The Story of an American City,* 5th ed., updated and enlarged, ed. Stefan Lorant, 321–72. Pittsburgh: Esselmont Books, 1999.

————. "The Great Transformation in the Eighties." In *Pittsburgh: The Story of an American City,* 5th ed., updated and enlarged, ed. Stefan Lorant, 593–640. Pittsburgh: Esselmont Books, 1999.

————. "Levelling Off." In *Pittsburgh: The Story of an American City,* 5th ed., updated and enlarged, ed. Stefan Lorant, 439–536. Pittsburgh: Esselmont Books, 1999.

Lowe, Jeanne R. *Cities in a Race with Time.* New York: Random House, 1967.

Lubove, Roy. "City Beautiful, City Banal: Design Advocacy and Historic Preservation in Pittsburgh." *Pittsburgh History* (Spring 1992): 26–36.

———. *Twentieth-Century Pittsburgh*. New York: John Wiley and Sons, 1969.

———. *Twentieth-Century Pittsburgh*. Vol. 2, *The Post Steel Era*. Pittsburgh: University of Pittsburgh Press, 1996.

Lurcott, Robert H., and Jane A. Downing. "A Public-Private Support System for Community-Based Organizations in Pittsburgh." *Journal of the American Planning Association* 53 (Summer 1987): 459–68.

Lynch, Bernie. "IJ's Work Shows It Is Time to Respect Private Property Rights." *Liberty and Law* 10 (January 2001). http://www.ij.org/publications/liberty/2001/10_1_01_i.asp (accessed May 6, 2003).

Mallet, William J. "Redevelopment and Response: The Lower Hill Renewal and Pittsburgh's Original Cultural District." *Pittsburgh History* (Winter 1992): 176–90.

Mansbridge, Jane J. *Beyond Adversary Democracy*. Chicago: University of Chicago Press, 1980.

Markoff, John. *Waves of Democracy: Social Movements and Political Change*. Thousand Oaks, CA: Pine Forge Press, 1996.

Martin, Park H. "Narrative of the Allegheny Conference on Community Development and the Pittsburgh Renaissance, 1943–1958." Stanton Balfour Oral History Collection, Archives of the Industrial Society, University of Pittsburgh, 1964. Photocopy.

———. "Pittsburgh Comprehensive Improvement Program." American Society of Civil Engineers. *Transactions* 121 (1956): 885–92.

McAdam, Doug. *Political Process and the Development of Black Insurgency 1930–1970*. Chicago: University of Chicago Press, 1982.

McAdam, Doug, John D. McCarthy, and Mayer N. Zald. "Opportunities, Mobilizing Structures, and Framing Processes: Toward a Synthetic, Comparative Perspective on Social Movements." In *Comparative Perspectives on Social Movements,* edited by Doug McAdam, John D. McCarthy, and Mayer N. Zald, 1-22. Cambridge: Cambridge University Press, 1996.

McAdam, Doug, John D. McCarthy, and Mayer N. Zald, eds. *Comparative Perspectives on Social Movements*. Cambridge: Cambridge University Press, 1996.

McAdam, Doug, Sidney Tarrow, and Charles Tilly. *Dynamics of Contention*. Cambridge: Cambridge University Press, 2001.

McCarthy, John D. "Constraints and Opportunities in Adopting, Adapting, and Inventing." In *Comparative Perspectives on Social Movements,* edited by Doug McAdam, John D. McCarthy, and Mayer N. Zald, 141–51. Cambridge: Cambridge University Press, 1996.

McCarthy, John D., and Mayer N. Zald. "Resource Mobilization and Social Movements: A Partial Theory." *American Journal of Sociology* 82 (May 1977): 1212–41.

McCarthy, John D., Jackie Smith, and Mayer Zald. "Accessing Public, Media,

Electoral, and Governmental Agendas." In *Comparative Perspectives on Social Movements*, edited by Doug McAdam, John D. McCarthy, and Mayer N. Zald, 291–311. Cambridge: Cambridge University Press, 1996.

McFarland, Andrew S. "Social Movements and Theories of American Politics." In *Social Movements and American Political Institutions*, edited by Anne N. Costain and Andrew S. McFarland, 7–19. New York: Rowman & Littlefield, 1998.

McLaughlin, Glenn E., and Ralph J. Watkins. "The Problem of Industrial Growth in a Mature Economy." *American Economic Review* 29 (March 1939): 1–14.

"The Mellons Discover Pittsburgh." *Greater Pittsburgh*, December 1947, 30–31.

Mellor, Chip. "A Dozen Years Later Investment in IJ Pays Off." *Liberty and Law* 12 (December 2003). http://www.ij.org/publications/index.html (accessed August 9, 2004).

Mershon, Sheri. "Corporate Social Responsibility and Urban Revitalization: The Allegheny Conference on Community Development, 1943–1968." PhD diss., Department of History, Carnegie Mellon University, 2000.

Merton, Robert K. *Social Theory and Social Structure*. Rev. ed. New York: The Free Press, 1968.

Metzger, John T. "Reinventing Housing in Pittsburgh: A Former CDC Director Becomes Mayor." *Shelterforce Online*, March/April 1996. http://www.nhi.org/online/issues/86/reinvpitt.html (accessed April 12, 2001).

———. "Remaking the Growth Coalition: The Pittsburgh Partnership for Neighborhood Development." *Economic Development Quarterly* 12 (February 1998): 12–30.

Moe, Richard, and Carter Wilkie. *Changing Places: Rebuilding Community in the Age of Sprawl*. New York: Henry Holt and Company, 1997.

Mollenkopf, John. *The Contested City*. Princeton, NJ: Princeton University Press, 1983.

———. "The Post-War Politics of Urban Development." *Politics and Society* 5, no. 3 (1975): 247–95.

Molotch, Harvey. "The City as a Growth Machine: Toward a Political Economy of Place." *American Journal of Sociology* 82 (September 1976): 309–32.

Moser, Elizabeth. "Training Advocates for Liberty." *Liberty and Law* 12 (October 2003). http://www.ij.org/publications/index.html (accessed August 9, 2004).

Moses, Robert. "An Arterial Plan for Pittsburgh." Pittsburgh: Pittsburgh Regional Planning Association, 1939.

Muller, Edward. "Historical Aspects of Regional Structural Change in the Pittsburgh Region." In *Regional Structural Change and Industrial Policy in International Perspective: United States, Great Britain, France, Federal Republic of Germany,* edited by Joachim Jens Hesse, 17–48. Baden-Baden: Nomos Verlagsgesellschaft, 1988.

———. "Metropolis and Region: A Framework for Enquiry into Western Pennsylvania." In *City at the Point: Essays on the Social History of Pittsburgh,* edited by Samuel P. Hays, 181–211. Pittsburgh: University of Pittsburgh Press, 1989.

Nathan, Richard. "Federal Grants: How Are They Working?" In *Cities under Stress: The Fiscal Crises of Urban America,* edited by Robert W. Burchell and David Listokin, 529–39. New Brunswick: Rutgers Center for Urban Policy Research, 1980.

Neumann, Lawrence, W. *Social Research Methods: Qualitative and Quantitative Approaches.* 3rd ed. Boston: Allyn and Bacon, 1997.

Nichols, Bervard. "Pittsburgh Looks Ahead." *Pittsburgh Business Review,* July 30, 1942, 1–3.

Nordstrom Inc. "Nordstrom Issues Statement on Proposed Pittsburgh Store," media release, November 22, 2000. "Fifth and Forbes" documents, Pittsburgh History and Landmarks Foundation storage.

Olson, Mancur, Jr. *The Logic of Collective Action: Public Goods and the Theory of Groups.* Cambridge, MA: Harvard University Press, 1971.

"Out-Migration Steady in the Region." *Pittsburgh Economic Quarterly* 1 (September 2000): 1–2.

Pagano, Michael A., and Ann O'M. Bowman. *Cityscapes and Capital: The Politics of Urban Development.* Baltimore: Johns Hopkins University Press, 1995.

Pateman, Carole. *Participation and Democratic Theory.* New York: Cambridge University Press, 1970.

Peterson, Paul. E. *City Limits.* Chicago: University of Chicago Press, 1981.

Pierson, Paul. *Politics in Time: History, Institutions, and Social Analysis.* Princeton, NJ: Princeton University Press, 2004.

Pittsburgh Chamber of Commerce. "The Pittsburgh Center," October 1947. Carnegie Library of Pittsburgh, Pennsylvania Department. Prospectus.

Pittsburgh City Council. Committee on Hearings, Minutes, August 21, 1946–April 11, 1951.

———. *Municipal Record,* Minutes, 1949–1960.

Pittsburgh Department of City Planning. Community Development Division. "The City Moves Forward: A Progress Report on Urban Renewal and Redevelopment Areas." January 1, 1961.

———. Community Renewal Program. "Relocation Report: Social Aspects." 1963.

———. "Fifth and Forbes Redevelopment Proposal and Plan: Zoning Report." November 23, 1999.

———. "The Pittsburgh Downtown Plan." 1998.

Pittsburgh Downtown Partnership. http://www.downtownpittsburgh.com/07pdp.html (accessed April 3, 2004).

Pittsburgh Downtown Partnership. "Downtown Planning Collaborative, Final Report and Coordinating Committee Executive Summary." December 2000.

Pittsburgh History and Landmarks Foundation. "A City's Living Memory." *Stones of Pittsburgh* 9, undated booklet.

————. "Fifteen Year Report, Five Year Master Plan." 1981.

————. "Five Year Report to our Members and to the Community, 1964–1969." Booklet.

Pittsburgh Neighborhood Alliance. "An Atlas of the Hill Neighborhood of Pittsburgh." 1977.

————. *Pittsburgh Neighborhood Atlas: Northview Heights.* 1977.

"Pittsburgh State and Nation." *The Bulletin Index: Pittsburgh's Weekly Newsmagazine,* November 23, 1939, 6.

"Pittsburgh's New Powers." *Fortune,* February 1947, 69–74, 76–77, 182, 184, 186.

"Pittsburgh's Thrilling Civic Renaissance." *The American City* 65 (July 1950): 131, 155.

Polletta, Francesca, and James M. Jasper. "Collective Identity and Social Movements." *Annual Review of Sociology* 27 (2001): 283–305.

Polsby, Nelson W. *Community Power and Political Theory: A Further Look at Problems of Evidence and Inference.* New Haven, CT: Yale University Press, 1980.

Public Auditorium Authority of Pittsburgh and Allegheny County. "An All-Purpose Civic Auditorium for the New Pittsburgh and Allegheny County." Undated pamphlet.

Putnam, Robert D. "Bowling Alone: America's Declining Social Capital." *Journal of Democracy* 6, no. 1 (1995): 65–78.

————. *Making Democracy Work: Civic Traditions in Modern Italy.* Princeton, NJ: Princeton University Press, 1993.

————. "Tuning In, Tuning Out: The Strange Disappearance of Social Capital in America." *PS: Political Science and Politics* 28, no. 4 (1995): 664–83.

"Reports of Chamber Divisions: Golden Triangle Division." *Greater Pittsburgh,* February 1940, 11.

Ragin, Charles. *The Comparative Method: Moving Beyond Qualitative and Quantitative Strategies.* Berkeley and Los Angeles: University of California Press, 1987.

Reed, Doug. "Eminent Domain Code for Allegheny County." Allegheny Institute Report 98-14. November 1999.

Ricci, David. *Community Power and Democratic Theory: The Logic of Political Analysis.* New York: Random House, 1971.

Rich, Michael J. "Riot and Reason: Crafting an Urban Policy Response." *Publius* 23 (1993): 115–34.

Richter, Nora. "Pittsburgh's Innovative Renovation Record." Pittsburgh History and Landmarks Foundation, 1978. Photocopy.

Robin, John P., and Stefan Lorant. "Rebirth." In *Pittsburgh: The Story of an American City,* 5th ed., updated and enlarged, ed. Stefan Lorant, 373–448. Pittsburgh: Esselmont Books.

Sassen, Saskia. *Cities in a World Economy.* 2nd ed. Thousand Oaks, CA: Pine Forge Press, 2000.

Savitch, H. V., and Paul Kantor. *Cities in the International Marketplace: The Political Economy of Urban Development in North America and Western Europe.* Princeton, NJ: Princeton University Press, 2002.

Sbragia, Alberta. "Pittsburgh's 'Third Way': The Non-Profit Sector as a Key to Urban Regeneration." In *Urban Affairs Annual Review* 37, edited by D. Judd and M. Parkinson, 51–68. Newbury Park: Sage, 1990.

Schattsneider, E. E. *The Semi-Sovereign People: A Realist's View of Democracy.* New York: Holt, Rinehart & Winston, 1960.

Schmidlapp, Ellis. "A Great Space and Departed Hope." *PHLF News* 155 (August 1999).

Schmitter, Phillipe. "Modes of Interest Intermediation and Models of Societal Change in Western Europe." *Comparative Political Studies* 10 (1977): 7–38.

Schumpeter, Joseph. *Capitalism, Socialism, and Democracy.* New York: Harper and Row, 1962.

Scott, Mel. *American City Planning since 1890.* Berkeley and Los Angeles: University of California Press, 1969.

Skocpol, Theda. *Diminished Democracy: From Membership to Management in American Civic Life.* Norman: University of Oklahoma Press, 2003.

———. *States and Social Revolutions: A Comparative Analysis of France, Russia, & China.* New York: Cambridge University Press, 1979.

Snow, David A., and Robert D. Benford. "Master Frames and Cycles of Protest." In *Frontiers in Social Movement Theory,* edited by Aldon Morris and Carol McClurg Mueller, 135–55. New Haven, CT: Yale University Press, 1992.

Snow, David A., E. Burke Rochford Jr., Steven K. Worden, and Robert D. Benford. "Frame Alignment Processes, Micromobilization, and Movement Participation." *American Sociological Review* 51 (August 1986): 464–81.

Southwestern Pennsylvania Strategic Investment Partnership. "Investing in the Future: Strategies for Strengthening Southwestern Pennsylvania's Regional Core and Restoring Its Manufacturing Base." November 1995.

Stave, Bruce. *The New Deal and the Last Hurrah.* Pittsburgh: University of Pittsburgh Press, 1970.

Steinberg, Alfred. "Pittsburgh, a New City." *National Municipal Review* 44 (March 1955): 126–31.

Stevens, Donald, Jr. "The Role of Nonprofit Corporations in Urban Development: A Case Study of ACTION-Housing, Inc., Pittsburgh." PhD diss., Department of History, Carnegie-Mellon University, 1987.

Stevens, Sylvester K. "The Hearth of the Nation." In *Pittsburgh: The Story of an American City*, 5th ed., updated and enlarged, ed. Stefan Lorant, 177–208. Pittsburgh: Esselmont Books.

Stewman, Shelby, and Joel A. Tarr. "Four Decades of Public-Private Partnership in Pittsburgh." In *Public-Private Partnership in American Cities*, edited by R. Scott Fosler and Renee Berger, 59–123. Lexington, MA: Lexington Books, 1984.

————. "Public-Private Partnerships in Pittsburgh: An Approach to Governance." In *Pittsburgh-Sheffield: Sister Cities*, edited by Joel A. Tarr, 141–82. Pittsburgh: Carnegie Mellon University Press, 1981.

Stoker, Gerry. "Regime Theory and Urban Politics." In *Theories of Urban Politics*, edited by David Judge, Gerry Stoker, and Harry Wolman, 54–71. London: Sage, 1995.

Stone, Clarence, N. "Preemptive Power: Floyd Hunter's 'Community Power Structure' Reconsidered." *American Journal of Political Science* 32 (February 1988): 82–104.

————. *Regime Politics: Governing Atlanta, 1946–1988*. Lawrence: University Press of Kansas, 1989.

————. "The Study of the Politics of Urban Development." In *The Politics of Urban Development*, edited by Clarence N. Stone and Heywood T. Sanders, 3–22. Lawrence: University Press of Kansas, 1987.

————. "Systemic Power in Community Decision Making." *American Political Science Review* 74 (December 1980): 978–90.

Sustainable Pittsburgh. "Southwestern Pennsylvania Citizens' Vision for Smart Growth." 2003.

Tarr, Joel A. "Infrastructure and City Building in the Nineteenth and Twentieth Centuries." In *City at the Point: Essays on the Social History of Pittsburgh*, edited by Samuel P. Hays, 213–64. Pittsburgh: University of Pittsburgh Press, 1989.

Tarrow, Sidney. "Cycles of Collective Action: Between Moments of Madness and the Repertoire of Contention." In *Repertoires and Cycles of Collective Action*, edited by Marc Traugott, 89–116. Durham, NC: Duke University Press, 1995.

————. *Power in Movement: Social Movements and Contentious Politics*. 2nd ed. Cambridge: Cambridge University Press, 1998.

————. "'The Very Excess of Democracy': State Building and Contentious Politics in America." In *Social Movements and American Political Institutions*, edited by Anne N. Costain and Andrew S. McFarland, 20–38. New York: Rowman & Littlefield, 1998.

Teaford, Jon C. "Urban Renewal and Its Aftermath." *Housing Policy Debate* 11, no. 2 (2000): 443–65.

"Teamwork for Pittsburgh." *Greater Pittsburgh*, February 1946, 10–11.

Thomas, Clarke M. "Fortunes and Misfortunes: Pittsburgh and Allegheny

County Politics, 1930–95." *Issues,* University of Pittsburgh, Institute for Politics. Undated booklet.

———. "Invisible Governments: Pennsylvania's Municipal Authorities." *Issues,* University of Pittsburgh, Institute for Politics. Undated booklet.

Tilly, Charles. *The Contentious French.* Cambridge: Belknap Press, 1986.

———. "Mechanisms in Political Processes." *Annual Review of Political Science* 4 (2001): 21–41.

Tiryakian, Edward A. "From Durkheim to Managua: Revolutions as Religious Revivals." In *Durkheimian Sociology: Cultural Studies,* edited by Jeffrey C. Alexander, 44–65. Cambridge: Cambridge University Press, 1988.

Urban Redevelopment Authority, Pittsburgh, Pennsylvania. "Fifth and Forbes Proposal for Redevelopment Activities." October 1999. Booklet.

———. "Gateway Center, Pittsburgh, Pennsylvania." January 1966. Brochure.

———. "Lower Hill Redevelopment Project." Pennsylvania Department, Carnegie Library of Pittsburgh. Undated booklet.

Van Trump, James D. "Station Square: A Golden Age Revived." Pittsburgh History and Landmarks Foundation, 1978. Booklet.

"Wage Levels in Pittsburgh." *Pittsburgh Economic Quarterly* (Fall 2001): 1, 4–5.

Walton, John. "A Systematic Survey of Community Power Research." In *The Structure of Community Power,* edited by Michael Aiken and Paul E. Mott, 443–464. New York: Random House, 1970.

Warren, Mark R. *Dry Bones Rattling: Community Building to Revitalize American Democracy.* Princeton, NJ: Princeton University Press, 2001.

Weber, Michael P. *Don't Call Me Boss: David L. Lawrence, Pittsburgh's Renaissance Mayor.* Pittsburgh: University of Pittsburgh Press, 1988.

Weiss, Marc. "The Origins and Legacy of Urban Renewal." In *Federal Housing Policy and Programs: Past and Present,* edited by J. Paul Mitchell, 253–76. New Brunswick, NJ: Center for Urban Policy Research, 1985.

Weiss, Marc, and John T. Metzger. "Technology Development, Neighborhood Planning, and Negotiated Partnerships." *Journal of the American Planning Association* 53 (1987): 469–77.

"What We're Doing about Pittsburgh's Reputation." *Greater Pittsburgh,* December 1947, 20–21.

Whitt, J. Allen. "The Arts Coalition in Strategies of Urban Development." In *The Politics of Urban Development,* edited by Clarence N. Stone and Heywood T. Sanders, 144–56. Lawrence: University Press of Kansas, 1987.

Wilson, Frank. "Interest Groups and Politics in Western Europe: The Neo-Corporatist Approach." *Comparative Politics* 16 (1983): 105–23.

Wilson, William Julius. *When Work Disappears: The World of the New Urban Poor.* New York: Vintage Books, 1996.

Yin, Robert K. *Case Study Research: Design and Methods.* 2nd ed. Thousand
  Oaks, CA: Sage, 1994.

Zald, Mayer N., and John D. McCarthy, eds. *The Dynamics of Social Movements.* Cambridge, MA: Winthrop Publishers, 1979.

Ziegler, Arthur P., Jr. *Historic Preservation in Inner City Areas: A Manual of
  Practice.* Pittsburgh: Ober Park Associates, 1975.

Index

"Action for Cities: A Guide for Community Planning" (NRPB), 39–40
African Americans: as Lower Hill residents, 82, 86; in Manchester neighborhood, 99–100
Ahlbrandt, Roger, 102
Allegheny Conference on Community Development: and ACTION-Housing, 97–98; Civic Light Opera arena and, 59–61, 83; criticisms of, 174n44; on downtown office space, 67–68; on eminent domain, 69–70; influence of, 49, 62, 72, 99; limiting participation in planning, 50–51, 56; Martin's narrative of, 46–47; other organizations and, 103, 130, 149–50; Point Park and, 55–56; research by, 47–48, 105; support for redevelopment, 50, 58, 82, 86
Allegheny Council to Improve Our Neighborhoods (ACTION-Housing, Inc.), 97–98
Allegheny County, 135, 165n1; industrialization in, 31–33; population of, 33–34, 104–5
Allegheny Foundation, 104
Allegheny Institute for Public Policy, 107, 155–56; challenges to corporatism by, 110; Market Place opposition and, 132–38, 153
annexations, of municipalities adjoining Pittsburgh, 32, 76, 78
An Approach to Federal Urban Policy (CED), 95
appropriation. See social appropriation of resources, as mechanism of social action
architecture, 99–100. See also historic preservation movement

attribution of political opportunity. See political opportunity, attribution of

Bally Design Co., 139
Banfield, Edward, 10–11
banks, downtown, 45, 109
Barber, Benjamin, 141
Barr, Joseph, 98
Beaver County, 165n1
Berry, Jeffrey, 2
Bigger, Frederick, 51–52, 167n61
Bolick, Clint, 136
bonds, URA selling, 67
Braun, A. E., 52
brokerage, as mechanism of social action, 26–27; in opposition to Market Place, 123, 128, 147–48; in opposition to St. Clair public housing, 78–79
Brown, Homer, 86
Bullock, Scott, 138
Burke, Vincent J., 61–62, 64
Bush, George H. W., 95–97
business: bankruptcies of, 34; city government and, 49, 98–99, 119; cooperation with government in redevelopment, 11, 18–19, 38, 44–45, 50, 55, 95, 97; downtown, 35, 43, 67, 82; federal funds for urban renewal and, 42, 81; lack of time for civic affairs, 102, 173n32; as leader in public-private partnerships, 9–10, 40–41; local vs. national, 1, 112, 118, 125–26; looking for investment locations, 14, 42; moving out of downtown, 16, 34; participation in planning, 51, 123; power of, 45–46, 50–51, 56, 102, 111; relations with government, 18, 42–43,

51–52; as stakeholders in land-use decisions, 13, 42; supporting downtown improvements and maintenance, 53, 105; in urban empowerment zones, 97. *See also* retail businesses

business district, Pittsburgh. *See* downtown; Golden Triangle; retail district

business owners: in opposition to Gateway Center, 69, 71–72; on plans for Market Place and alternatives, 125–27, 148

Caliguiri, Richard, 101–4
Caraley, Demetrios, 96
Carnegie Mellon University, 102
Carnegie Steel, 31
Carter, Jimmy, 95
category formation, as mechanism of social action, 24–26; in contention over residential neighborhoods, 89; in opposition to Civic Light Opera amphitheater, 60; in opposition to Gateway Center, 69, 72; in opposition to Market Place, 118–20, 122, 147; in opposition to St. Clair public housing, 76–78; timing and sequence of, 145–47, 151
certification of actors, as mechanism of social action, 28; by Allegheny Institute and Institute for Justice, 137; on behalf of preserving St. Peter's Church, 88; in combination with other mechanisms, 152, 154; in contention over residential neighborhoods, 80, 89; of criticisms of Market Place plan, 133, 135–37, 152–53; in opposition to Civic Light Opera arena, 61; in opposition to Gateway Center, 70, 72
Chamber of Commerce, Pittsburgh, 45, 47; and cultural center in Lower Hill, 82–83; in redevelopment of Golden Triangle, 42–43. *See also* Golden Triangle Chamber of Commerce
Chapin, William, 54
citizen action committees, 10
citizen participation, 12, 87; breadth and depth of, 2, 143–44, 147–50;

combinations of mechanisms leading to, 28–29; in downtown planning, 113, 149–51; factors encouraging, 100–101, 141, 145, 155; in Fifth/Forbes Planning Group's alternative plan, 123–24, 126; in Highland Park opposition to arena, 144, 147; historic preservation movement's belief in, 99–100, 121–22, 124; in Market Place alternatives planning, 148–49, 176n28; in Market Place planning, 114, 128, 130–31; Market Place planning lacking, 118, 120, 125–28, 177n39; reasons to solicit or exclude, 18–19, 100, 114, 142–43, 156; techniques to control opposition in, 25–26, 118–19. *See also* contentious politics
Citizens' Committee on City Plan, 51–52
Citizens for Pennsylvania's Future, 106
City Council, Pittsburgh, 75, 86; at-large *vs.* district electoral system of, 20–21, 49, 104; on Civic Light Opera arena, 60–61, 63–64, 150; Democratic influence on, 48–49; divisiveness on, 62, 146; Downtown Planning Collaborative and, 150; on Gateway Center plans, 69–70; influences on, 49, 137; on legality of eminent domain, 70–71; on Main Street concept, 130–31; on Market Place, 123, 129–31, 149; relations with mayors, 62, 98–99, 110–11; secret meetings by, 49, 63; special use of St. Peter's Church appealed to, 87–88; support for redevelopment, 50, 114
city planning: business leaders advocating, 51–52; as experimental, 39–40; inadequate, 68
City Planning, Department of, 99, 103
City Planning Commission, Pittsburgh, 45, 102; approval of Market Place plan needed, 123, 129, 153; approving Market Place plan, 137, 149, 178n47; on Gateway Center plans, 69; in Highland Park controversy, 65–66; makeup of, 176n26; on national historical park, 54

City View neighborhood. *See* Spring
Hill–City View neighborhood
Civic Light Opera amphitheater, 83;
Highland Park's opposition to, 7,
60–65; Highland Park's success in
opposing, 89, 146–47; need for,
59–60; site selection for, 60–61,
65–66
Clark, Pat, 128, 131
Coleman, Morton, 84–86, 102
collapse, as outcome of contention, 8,
28–29, 72, 165n44
collective action groups: amalgam of
interests in, 128–29; Ground Zero
Action Network as, 131–32; resources of, 22–23, 26–27. *See also*
community groups
commercial public interest, 142–43
Committee for Economic Development (CED), 40–41, 44, 95–96
common interest: searching for, in redevelopment, 141–42; urban
growth coalitions manufacturing,
25. *See also* public benefit
communism, land acquisition measures compared to, 64–65, 77
community development block grants
(CDBGs), 94–96, 101
Community Development Corporations (CDCs), 5, 103, 105; Golden
Triangle CDC, 130; Market Place
development and, 122, 148
community development movement,
104–6; historic preservation movement's ties to, 99–100
community groups, 146; involvement
in planning, 22, 97, 149; Market
Place planning and, 122, 124. *See
also* collective action groups
Community Planning Program (CPP),
100–101, 103
community power, research on, 12,
22–23
Community Technical Assistance Center, 103
Comprehensive Program, postwar, 45
concessions, in outcomes of contention, 8, 28–29, 59, 165n44
condemnation of property. *See also* eminent domain: for Civic Light Opera

amphitheater, 60–61, 63–66, 147;
for residential redevelopment, 58
Congress of Clubs, 68, 70
contentious politics: definitions of, 12;
factors in success of, 3–4, 20–23, 90,
110–11, 144, 154–55; marginaliza-
tion/exclusion leading to, 8, 13, 17;
mechanisms of, 23–29, 145–55; motivations for, 12–13, 147, 155; over
redevelopment in neighborhoods,
58, 80, 89; transgressive, 132
convention center. *See* David L.
Lawrence Convention Center
corporatism, 98; challenges to, 106–7,
110, 146; goals in redevelopment,
66; limiting participation in development process, 56, 59, 86; Pittsburgh urban governing coalition
called, 45, 50
Crawford Square, 110
cultural center, hopelessness about opposing, 84–86
cultural organizations: opposition to
seizing property for, 60–61; proposed cultural center in Lower Hill,
82–86; as stakeholders in land-use
decisions, 13–14

Dahl, Robert, 10–11; on exclusion
from redevelopment planning,
17–18; on Schumpeter's definition
of democracy, 140–41
David L. Lawrence Convention Center, 109, 173n34
Dearden, Bishop, 88
Delano, Frederic A., 39
democracy: adversary *vs.* unitary, 2;
definitions of, 140–41. *See also*
strong democracy
Democrats, 80, 86, 95, 174n44; cooperation by, 44, 54–55; limiting participation in planning, 50, 56;
mayors as, 48–49, 98
Depression: effects of, 34, 41, 52; rehabilitating neighborhoods during,
39–40
development agencies, quasi-independent, 42
Doherty, Robert H., 47–48
Downing, Jane, 101

downtown, Pittsburgh, 99, 105; danger of single management company controlling, 119–20; effects of decentralization on, 16, 33–35, 93–94; housing in, 83, 131; increasing office space in, 66–67; revitalizing, 108, 119–20, 156. *See also* Golden Triangle; retail district

Downtown Planning Collaborative, 130–31, 138, 149–51

downtowns: effects of decentralization on, 16; incremental revitalization of, 124

Duquesne University, 102

East Busway, 102

East End, 76, *82. See also* Highland Park neighborhood

Eckstut, Stan, 124, 148; plan for alternative to Market Place by, 127, 129, 132

Economic Development, Department of, 102

economic environment: Pittsburgh, 32–34; role of growth in politics, 15–16, 19; taxes' effect on, 14

economy: criticisms of Market Place as nonviable, 133, 135; diversification of, 45, 47, 101, 111; effects of loss of manufacturing jobs, 91–93, 96; government role in, 40–41, 51, 94–97; Pittsburgh and region's declining, 91–94, 97, 104–5; Pittsburgh's, 37, 45, 101; planning for return to peacetime, 37, 40–41; region's, 47, 105; U.S., 90–91, 94

Ehrenkrantz, Eckstut, and Kuhn architects, plan for alternative to Market Place by, 124, 127, 129, 132, 149

Eisenger, Peter, 20–22

elected officials, 100, 104; in leadership/process of urban redevelopment, 10; limiting participation in redevelopment planning, 18, 59; Market Place and, 127–28; motivations for redevelopment, 14, 16–17, 34, 53; need to form coalitions for urban projects, 94, 97; relations with business, 18–19, 38, 44–45, 50–52, 55; responsiveness to neighborhoods, 20–21, 59, 62–64, 77–78, 101; and urban growth coalitions, 14, 41–43. *See also* City Council; Caliguiri, Richard; Flaherty, Pete; Lawrence, David; Murphy, Tom

elections, importance of, 141

electoral systems: at-large representation, 20–21, 49; district representation, 104, 111

elites: commitment to civic action, 37–38, 43, 46; contentious politics challenging, 12–13; lack of time for civic action, 102, 111, 173n32; relations among, 43–45

Elkin, Stephen, 142

eminent domain: court decisions on, 27, 65–66, 69–71; injustices in use of, 25, 61; legislation on, 70–71, 137–38, 153; legitimacy of uses for, 61–63, 65–67; Market Place plan seen as abuse of, 127, 133, 135–38; opposition to, 25, 55, 107–8, 152; process for, 58, 68–69, 129

entertainment: in downtown plan for retail development, 108, 112, 117, 174n4; as illegitimate use of eminent domain, 61–62, 64

environmental degradation: as deterrent to downtown businesses, 35–36; growth of suburbs and, 93–94; improvement of, 36, 106

Equitable Life Assurance Society, 69–70, 72. *See also* Gateway Center

Federal Housing Act of 1949, 42, 73, 75–76

Ferlo, Jim, 130, 131

Fifth and Forbes: decline of retail corridor at, 148. *See also* Market Place at Fifth and Forbes

Fifth and Forbes Preservation Working Group, 122

Fifth/Forbes Planning Group, 123–24, 126–28

Flaherty, Pete, 173n34; Community Planning Program of, 100–101; mayoral nonintervention by, 110–11; relations with business, 98–99

flooding, as deterrent to downtown businesses, 35, 37

Ford Foundation, 103

foreclosures, on homes, 35
Fort Dearborn, 11
Fort Pitt, reconstruction in Point Park,
  53–54
foundations, funding downtown redevelopment, 109

Gamble, Andrew, 71
Gans, Herbert, 27
Gateway Center, 72; acquiring land
  for, 67–69, 71; demolition for, 72,
  71; opposition to, 8, 69, 71–72,
  145. *See also* Lower Triangle
Glasco, Laurence, 84
Golden Triangle, 32, 72; decreasing
  desirability of, 35, 51, 82; improvements in, 53, 105; redevelopment
  in, 42–43, 51–52, 99; relation to regional economy, 47. *See also* downtown; Lower Triangle
Golden Triangle Chamber of Commerce, 36, 38, 53
Golden Triangle Community Development Corporation, 130, 132
government, 45, 156; capacity for, 18,
  21–22, 55–56; city, 49–50, 86, 98;
  coalitions of, 18–19, 21; deliberative, 142; federal, 15, 101 (*see also*
  redevelopment funding); federal
  urban policy, 94–97, 110; levels of,
  27, 38–39, 54–55, 94, 136; local,
  15, 95; organizations to defend individuals from, 107–8; role in economy, 40–41, 51; role in
  redevelopment, 14–17, 40–43, 94,
  102, 109. *See also* City Council; elected officials; electoral systems
Gratz, Roberta, 119–20
Griswold, Ralph E., 54
Ground Zero Action Network,
  131–32, 139, 149
Group Against Smog and Pollution
  (GASP), 106
Gugliotta, Angela, 36

Hatley, Albert, 139
Haulk, Jake, 134, 137
Hazlett, Theodore, 74
Heinz, Howard, 52
Heinz Foundation, 130
Hertzberg, Alan, 131

Highland Park neighborhood: Civic
  Light Opera arena proposed in,
  60–64; opposition to arena in, 7,
  60–62, 64–66, 145; public sympathy
  for, 64–65; success in opposing
  arena, 65–66, 89, 143–44
high technology, 101–3, 108, 111
Hill District, 82–83
historic preservation movement, 109,
  174n5; alliances of, 99–100, 123;
  belief in citizen participation,
  99–100, 113; excluded from Urban
  Retail planning, 117, 121; on rebirth *vs.* rebuilding of downtowns,
  119; St. Peter's Church and, 86–89.
  See also Pittsburgh History and
  Landmarks Foundation (PHLF)
Historic Review Commission of Pittsburgh: approval of Market Place
  plan needed, 123, 129; approving
  Market Place plan, 137, 149,
  178n48; makeup of, 176n26; Market Place opposition appealing to,
  122–23, 125, 147, 153; task of,
  174n5
Home and Housing Finance Agency
  (HHFA), 73–76, 83
housing: clearing for redevelopment,
  58, 75; for displaced residents,
  74–75, 77, 80–81, 83, 87; federal
  urban renewal funds for, 42, 74–75,
  81, 101; Market Place plan lacking,
  131; in Pittsburgh renaissance,
  75–76; redevelopment to provide,
  84, 97–98, 110; trying to appeal to
  young professionals, 110
Housing and Community Development Act (1974), 94–95
Housing and Public Works, Department of, 102
Housing Authority, Pittsburgh, 80,
  170n46; project in St. Clair and,
  77–78, 170n47; using FHA funds,
  75–76
Howard Heinz Endowment, 103
Hunter, Floyd, 9–10

identity formation. *See* category formation, as mechanism of social action
ideology, effects of, 155–56
image building, 17, 106

immigrants, 32, 35
industry, 36; in Allegheny County,
31–34; decline of, 33–35; jobs in,
31–33, 51; loss of jobs in, 34,
91–92, 96, 104; in Pittsburgh, 37;
U.S., 90–92
injustice: of eminent domain use, 25,
69–70, 119, 133; PHLF's preservation "alerts" on, 122; to taxpayers,
133, 135
Institute for Justice, 155–56; on Market Place as abuse of eminent domain, 135–38; Market Place
opposition and, 119, 153; supporting property owners, 107–8, 138
investment: in bonds for redevelopment, 67; business criteria for, 14;
in downtown redevelopment, 67,
174n4; PHLF blending preservation
with, 104; politicians seeking, 15,
19, 66; public-private partnerships
in, 41; during WWII, 37. See also
business

Jezierski, Louise, 50
jobs, 75; construction, 39; failure to
create, 93, 135; loss of manufacturing, 31–34, 91–92, 96, 104; percentage in manufacturing, 51, 91–92;
unemployment during Depression,
34–35
Jones & Laughlin Steel Corporation,
67, 75, 91
Joseph Horne Company, 67

Kane, John J., 55
Kaufmann, Edgar J., 53, 59–60
Kaufmann's department store, 133
Kilgallen, Thomas, 49, 63–64
King, Robert B., 60; City Council ne-
gotiating with, 150; land bequest of,
63–64, 66, 89, 146
Klein, Bonnie, 139
Kramer, Harry, 98

labor unions, 13, 45, 75
land use: common interests in,
141–42; controllable factor for local
government, 15–16; inefficient,
93–94; obsolete, 41; in redevelopment project decisions, 3–4

land-use stakeholders, 13–14. See also
citizen participation; redevelopment
participants
Lawrence, David, 4–5, 59, 75; Allegheny Conference and, 47, 51; cooper-
ating with business, 46, 56; death,
98; Gateway Center and, 69; in
Highland Park controversy, 59,
65–66, 89; influence among Democrats, 48–49, 62; influence of,
62, 70, 88; participants in planning
under, 44–45, 86, 105; Point Park
development and, 54–55; roles of,
55, 69, 98; Urban Redevelopment
Authority and, 50, 69
Lazarus department store, 109, *116*,
133–34
Leonard, Edward, 62–63, 77
Local Initiatives Support Corporation,
103, 173n37
Logan, John, 17
"logic of collective action," 12
Lord & Taylor department store,
120–21, 133
Lower Hill District, *81*, 82, *82;* as
biggest neighborhood rebuilding
project, 80–81, 83–84; blight in, 35,
84; Crawford Square project in,
110; cultural center proposed for,
82–86; demolition of, 83, *85;* demolition of St. Peter's Church in, 8,
86–89; displacement from, 75–76,
83–84; redevelopment plans in, 83,
84, 85; response to redevelopment
in, 8, 83–84, 87
Lower Triangle: eminent domain
threats in, 66. See also Gateway Center
Lubove, Roy, 86–87
Lurcott, Robert, 101
Lynch, Bernie: and Main Street Plan
as alternative to Market Place, 130,
138; Market Square Association
and, 118–19; in Plan C Task Force,
139; rallying business owners, 123,
125
Lyon, Madeline, 78

Main Street concept, 138, 156; as alternative to Market Place plan, 130,
179n69; support for, 131

Making Cities Work lecture series, 119
Maloney, Patty, 126–27, 138–39
Manchester Citizens Corporation (MCC), 100
Manchester neighborhood, 99–100
Mansbridge, Jane, 1–2
marginalization: contentious politics resulting from, 8, 13, 17; by governing coalitions, 19, 22
Market Place at Fifth and Forbes: acquisition of property for, 117, 126–27, 133, 135–36; alternatives to, 127, 139; criticisms of, 119, 131–33, 135–38; funding for, 114, 117, 126–27, 133, 135, 178n44, 179n61; lack of citizen participation in, 114, 118–20, 125–28; Main Street concept as alternative to, 130, 179n69; marketing of, 117–18, 125; opposition to, 1–3, 5–6, 90, 127–29, 143–44; planning process for alternatives to, 148, 155–56, 176n28; preservationists and, 113–14, 120–23, 129; seen as abuse of eminent domain, 127, 133, 135–38; success of opposition to, 139, 143–44; tactics of opposition to, 119, 129–30, 145–51, 147; unveiling of plans for, 1, 117, 125. *See also* Urban Retail Properties
Market Square Association, 118
Market Square historic district, 113, *115;* business owners' anger at plans for, 125–26; Historic Review Commission of Pittsburgh protecting, 122–23
Marshall, Ira, 70
Martin, Edward, 41, 44, 54, 56
Martin, Park, 46–47, 54–55
Mayor's Development Council (MDC), 102
McAdam, Doug, 27, 132
McArdle, Joseph, 62–64, 70, 77
McCollom, Cathy, 113, 130
McFarland, Andrew S., 12
mechanisms, of social action, 23–29; combinations of, 24, 26, 28, 152–55; in contentious politics over neighborhood redevelopment, 89; numbers of, 165n44; timing and sequence of, 25–26, 28, 72, 145–51.

See also brokerage; category formation; certification of actors; object shift; polarization; political opportunity, attribution of; social appropriation of resources
media, 84, 132, 174n44; as broker, 78–80; coverage of Market Place plan and alternatives, 124–25, 134, 148; coverage of opposition to redevelopment projects, 64, 71–72, 77, 88, 171n53; on misuse of tax increment financing, 134–35; as stakeholder in land-use decisions, 13; on Urban Retail Properties, 112–13, 174n2
Mellon, Richard King, 4–5, 36; death, 98; influence of, 21, 45–46, 55–56; leadership in redevelopment, 37–38, 52; limiting participation in development process, 56, 105; Point Park development and, 53, 55; roles of, 46, 52
Mellon, William Larimer, 52
Mellon Bank, 45–46, 67, 91
Mellon Bank building, 120–21
Mellon Bank Foundation, 103
Mellon family financial holdings, 36; influence of, 50–51; in redevelopment efforts, 44–45
Merriam, Charles E., 39
Merton, Robert K., 24
mobilizing structures, 144; autonomous, 22–23, 59, 132, 147, 155–56; and citizen participation, 155–56; of Market Place opposition, 90, 132–38, 147, 153; neighborhoods' lack of, 59, 86, 146–47; use of, 26
Moe, Richard, 104
Molotch, Harvey, 17
Morecroft, G. E., 72
Moses, Robert, 52–54
Muller, Edward, 45
Municipal Planning Association, 52
Murphy, Tom, 1, 108–10; Market Place plan and, 117, 123, 126, 149, 177n40; Market Place planning process and, 113, 175n10, 177n39; opposition to Market Place and,

1–2, 125–26, 130; rethinking downtown development, 2, 131, 139,
144, 150

Nathan, Richard, 95
National Association of Real Estate
Boards (NAREB), 39–41
national historic park, at Point Park,
53–54, 167n63
national preservation movement, 107
National Recovery Act, 39
National Resources Planning Board
(NRPB), 38–40, 166n22
National Trust for Historic Preservation, 107, 129–30
neighborhoods, 75; condition of, 35,
101; elected officials' responsiveness
to, 20–21; identity formation
around, 24–25; lack of resources of,
38, 45; map of, 30; opposition to redevelopment in, 17, 38, 58–59, 89;
participation in redevelopment
planning, 5, 17–18, 97–98,
100–103, 150–51; political participation by, 2; redevelopment in, 39,
74–75, 99. See also Highland Park
neighborhood; Lower Hill District;
Manchester neighborhood; Oakland
neighborhood; "special-use values"
of place; Spring Hill–City View
neighborhood; St. Clair neighborhood
New Federalism, under Nixon, 94
Nichols, Bervard, 37
Nixon, Richard, 94–95
nonprofit organizations: challenges to
urban growth coalitions by, 110,
132; in community development
movement, 106; as stakeholders in
land-use decisions, 13–14, 41
Nordstrom department store, 120,
133, 138
North Side, 76; Manchester neighborhood, 99–100. See also Spring Hill–
City View neighborhood
North Side Protest Committee
(NSPC), 79–80

Oakland neighborhood, 83
Oakland Planning and Development
Corporation (OPDC), 103

object shift, as mechanism of social action, 27–28; on behalf of preserving
St. Peter's Church, 88; in combination with other mechanisms,
152–55; in contention over neighborhoods, 80, 89; by opposition to
Civic Light Opera arena, 62; by opposition to Gateway Center, 71–72;
by opposition to Market Place plan,
123, 135, 147–48, 151, 153–55; timing and sequence of, 145–51
O'Connor, Bob, 131
office space, downtown, 102; demand
for, 34, 66–67. See also Gateway Center
Olson, Mancur, 12
Omnibus Budget Reconciliation Act of
1981 (OBRA), 96

parking authority, 102
Penn Avenue Place, 109
Pennsylvania, state of: changing eminent domain legislation, 137–38,
153; funding for Pittsburgh redevelopment, 54–55, 117, 126
Pennsylvania Economy League (PEL),
Western Division, 47–49
Pennsylvania Post-War Planning Commission (PPWPC), 41–42
Pennsylvania Railroad (PRR), 55, 67
Pennsylvania Turnpike, 53
Peterson, Paul, 14–16, 141–42
Pittsburgh, city of: annexations by, 32,
76, 78; donating land for Point Park
development, 55; growth of, 31–33,
37; loss of federal aid to, 96–97;
map of, 30; population of, 92–93,
96–97, 105–6, 108, 110; region
and, 101–2, 104–5, 165n1; subur-
banization of, 16, 33–35, 93, 112;
suit filed against on behalf of St.
Peter's Church, 88; use of eminent
domain law, 60–61, 64–65. See also
City Council; elected officials
Pittsburgh Area Transit, 102
Pittsburgh Development Fund (PDF),
108–9, 126
Pittsburgh Downtown Partnership
(PDP), 105, 130, 149–50
Pittsburgh Downtown Plan, 113
Pittsburgh History and Landmarks

Foundation (PHLF), 99; commercial redevelopment by, 103–4; concerns of, 113, 121; funding for, 106, 155; goals of, 100, 109–10; leadership in opposing Market Place plan, 122, 132, 138, 147, 153; Making Cities Work lecture series, 119; methods of, 100, 121–22, 124; in planning alternatives to Market Place, 130, 148, 155–56, 179n69
Pittsburgh Housing Development Corporation (PHDC), 110
Pittsburgh Main Street Task Force, 131
"Pittsburgh Package," 47–48, 86
Pittsburgh Partnership for Neighborhood Development, 103
Pittsburgh Plate Glass Company, 67
Pittsburgh Regional Planning Association (PRPA), 60; Allegheny Conference and, 47–48; organization of, 46, 52–53; in Point Park development, 54–56; trying to diversify Pittsburgh's economy, 45
Pittsburgh renaissance, 38, 90, 94; environmental agenda in, 63, 66; housing in, 75–76, 89; response to, 1, 65
Pittsburgh Survey, 86
Pittsburgh Urban Magnet Project (PUMP), 105–6, 127, 149
Plan C Task Force, to rethink downtown development, 139, 144
pluralist theory, 12, 111
Point Park, 56, 74; acquiring property for, 65–67; differing visions for, 44, 52–54
Point Park Commission, 54, 167n63
Point Park Committee, 55
Point Redevelopment Committee, 66, 68, 72
Point State Park, 54–55
polarization, as mechanism of social action, 27–28, 89; in Highland Park opposition, 63, 66; in opposition to Market Place, 126, 148; timing and sequence of, 145–51
political capital: expending for redevelopment, 11; reasons for politicians to risk, 13, 16–17

political opportunity: closed structure of, 50–51, 56–57, 147; making use of, 79, 131, 146; open structure of, 90, 110; structure of, 20–22, 144–45, 155, 163n7
political opportunity, attribution of, as mechanism of social action, 26; in contention over residential neighborhoods, 89; in Highland Park opposition, 62, 146–47; in opposition to Market Place, 123, 147–48
political participation. *See* citizen participation; contentious politics
politics: Allegheny Conference's control of, 62; effects of community development block grants in, 95; electoral systems in, 20–21, 49, 104, 111; importance of competition and elections, 141; importance of land use in, 15–16; interfering in city planning, 51–52; "logic of collective action" in, 12; preservation "alerts" trying to influence, 121–22, 124; role of economic growth in, 15–17, 19; strong mayor system of, 49–50; and structure of political opportunities, 20–22. *See also* contentious politics
Polsby, Nelson, 10
power: identifying holders of, 9–11; preemptive, 18, 21–22, 72, 102, 111; residents' response to, 84–86
Preservation Pennsylvania, 123–24
Preservation Pittsburgh, 114, 122–24, 147
property owners: disputing compensation, 169n32; Institute for Justice supporting, 107–8, 135–36, 138
Property Owners and Tenants Protective Committee (POTPC), 71
property rights, 27. *See also* eminent domain
property values: declining residential, 34–35; in Golden Triangle, 34, 36–37, 43, 82; influences on, 61, 63, 94; special-use *vs.* commercial, 71–72; as tax base, 16, 34, 43. *See also* "special-use values" of place
public authorities, in strong mayor system, 50

public benefit: and commercial public
interest, 142–43; redevelopment
needing to provide, 68–69, 141–42.
See also common interest
public hearings: about Civic Light
Opera amphitheater, 60–61; about
Gateway Center, 69; about Market
Place plan, 123, 149; expert testimony at, 137
Public Housing Authority, Pittsburgh,
170n46; St. Clair project by, 76–78
public housing projects, 77, 170n46;
for displaced residents, 75–76, 83;
funding for, 73–74; opposition to, 8,
78–80, 87

Reagan, Ronald, 95–97
The Rebirth of Urban Democracy (Berry),
2
redevelopment: African Americans'
support for, 86; after WWII, 1, 4–5,
38–40, 84–86 (*see also* Pittsburgh
renaissance); agenda setting *vs.* implementation of, 11; commercial,
103–4, 108, 112–13, 117, 120–21,
138–39, 148; criticisms of, 84–88,
99, 109; displacement of residents
as obstacle to, 74–77, 80–81; ease
of, 57, 100; goals of, 66, 105, 119;
government role in, 14–17, 41–42,
94, 109; incremental, 101, 104,
124, 130, 156; large-scale, 101–2,
109; leadership in, 9–10, 53, 100;
needing to prove public benefit
from, 68–69, 141–42; opposition to,
7–8, 17–18, 25–26; research on, 7,
9–11, 47–48; searching for common
interests in, 141–42. *See also specific
projects*
Redevelopment Assistance Capital Program (state), 126
redevelopment authority. *See* Urban
Redevelopment Authority of Pittsburgh (URA)
redevelopment funding: criticism of
public money for, 128, 179n61; for
downtown retail district, 109, 126,
133–35, 153; federal, 81, 83, 96–97,
99–100, 114; innovations in,
99–100; for Market Place, 120–21,

126–27, 178n44, 179n61; tax increment financing plans, 114, 117,
126, 134–35, 153
redevelopment participants: community organizations as, 52, 100–101,
149; control and selection of, 4,
17–19, 40, 45, 50, 56; desire to be
included, 97–98, 149; in downtown
development, 120, 130–31, 139;
government as, 14–17, 40–43, 94,
102, 109; identifying, 9–11, 40;
land-use stakeholders as, 3–4,
13–14; in Market Place development, 117–18, 120–21, 132–33,
135; number of, 52, 105, 108,
164n24; odd coalitions of, 122–23,
128–29; postwar, 50; preservationists as, 122–23; professional organizations countering urban growth
coalitions, 132–33, 135. *See also* citizen participation
Reed, Doug, 135
Reed Smith Shaw & McClay, 67–68
Regional Industrial Development Corporation, 102
Republicans, 95, 98; cooperation with
Democrats on redevelopment, 44,
54–55
Reserve Township, annexation proposal for, 78
resources: of collective action groups,
22–23, 26–27, 72, 76–77, 126, 153;
collective action groups discovering
during struggle, 59, 66, 147, 150;
determining participation in planning, 45; effectiveness of use of, 26,
153; increasing access to, 26–27; of
urban growth coalitions, 19, 53,
126. *See also* social appropriation of
resources, as mechanism of social
action
retail businesses: downtown, 112–13;
national chains favored over local,
118; trying to lure downtown,
133–34
retail district: change of strategy for,
138–39; corridor at Fifth and
Forbes, 118; downtown, 112–13,
134. *See also* Market Place at Fifth
and Forbes

retail redevelopment district, 112–13, 117, 120–21, 174n4
revenue sharing (State and Local Fiscal Assistance Act), 94, 96
Richards, Wallace, 46, 52, 54, 167n61
Richardson, H. H., 87
Ridge, Tom, 117
Robin, John, 62, 74–75, 102
Roney, Francis, 71
Roosevelt, Franklin Delano, 38–39

Saint Patrick's Day Flood of 1936, 35
Saks Fifth Avenue department store, 133
Sarah Mellon Scaife Foundation, 99–100
Scaife, Richard M., 174n44
Scaife family trusts, 104, 106–7, 155
Schenck, Albert, 70
Schumpeter, Joseph, 140
Scott, Mel, 38
Scully, Cornelius D., 53, 166n22, 167n63
secrecy: of City Council meetings, 49, 63; about Market Place development, 112–14, 118–19, 132, 147–49; in process of urban redevelopment, 10–11, 63; of URA functioning, 62
Sierra Club, 106
Sloan, Al, 77
slums. *See* urban blight
smoke, as deterrent to downtown businesses, 35–36, 37
social appropriation of resources, as mechanism of social action, 26, 89; in combination with other mechanisms, 152, 154; in opposition to Gateway Center, 69, 72; in opposition to Market Place, 122, 147, 151–53; timing and sequence of, 145–46
social identities, 24–25
social movements: against coal smoke, 36; factors in success of, 140; research on mobilizing structures, 20, 22–29; research on structure of political opportunities, 20–22. *See also* collective action groups; community groups

South Side, 75
"special-use values" of place, 17; in commercial public interest, 142; of downtown, 119; identity formation around, 24–25, 60–62; in St. Clair, 76–78; of St. Peter's Church, 87; *vs.* commercial value of, 71–72
Spring Hill–City View neighborhood, 79; opposition to public housing project in, 8, 78–80, 87, 145
St. Clair neighborhood, 76; opposition to public housing project in, 8, 76–80, 87, 145, 171n53; targeted for public housing project, 76–78, 170n47
St. Joseph's Church, in St. Clair, 76–77
St. Peter's Church, opposition to demolition of, 8, 86–89, 145–46
Stacklin, Jeff, 134
State and Local Fiscal Assistance Act (1972) (general revenue sharing), 94, 96
Station Square, 103–4
steel industry, 36; decline of, 34, 91; influence of, 21, 31, 50–51
Stewart, William, 61
Stoker, Gerry, 23
Stone, Clarence, 18
Stotz, Charles, 54
Strategic Investment Fund (SIF), 108–9, 126
strong democracy, 2, 6; combinations of mechanisms leading to, 28–29, 155; contentious urban redevelopment in, 3–4; factors influencing participation in, 140, 145, 151; as result of contentious politics, 8, 28–29, 132
suburbs, Pittsburgh, 102; development of, 33–35, 93; effects on city, 16, 112
Supreme Court, Pennsylvania: eminent domain suits in, 69–71; suit against Pittsburgh Housing Authority in, 80
Supreme Court, U.S., suit against URA in, 71–72

Tarrow, Sidney, 27, 132
taxes: effects of new investment on,

15, 108–9; effects on economic environment, 14; increasing, 96, 108–9; making up for lost federal funds, 96–97; Market Place criticized as waste of, 133, 135; real estate value as base for, 16, 34, 43; uses of, 107, 133–35
tax increment financing (TIF) plans, 114, 117; funding downtown retail district, 126, 134–35, 153
10,000 Friends of Pennsylvania, 106
theaters, 112–13, 117
Tilly, Charles, 23–24, 27, 132
Title I, of Federal Housing Act of 1949, 42
traffic/parking: in Golden Triangle, 36, 51–54; from growth of suburbs, 93–94; opposition to Civic Light Opera arena on, 60–62; Point Park and, 52–54
transgressive contention, 132
transportation: improving, 36–37, 83, 102; public, 131; in and through Pittsburgh, 31–33. *See also* traffic/parking

Udin, Sala, 120, 130, 149
United Smoke Council, 47
universities, 102
University of Pittsburgh, 102
Upper Hill District, 83
urban blight: certifying to start eminent domain proceedings, 68–69, 129; definitions of, 71, 134–36; in Golden Triangle, 51, 53; increasing during Depression, 35, 41; in Lower Hill, 82, 84; mobilizing government against, 39–40, 74–75; public-private partnerships against, 37–38, 41–42; reversing, 51, 53, 74–75
Urban Development Action Grant (UDAG) program, 95–96
urban empowerment zones, 97
urban governing coalition, 44–45, 50, 105–6
urban growth coalitions, 17; under Caliguiri, 102–3; challenges to urban growth regime, 62, 65; participation in and exclusion from, 13–14, 18–19 (*see also* redevelop-

ment participants); postwar formation of, 42–50; to rebuild Golden Triangle, 52–53; stability of, 21–22; success in overcoming, 143–44; techniques to control opposition, 25–26, 118–19
Urban Redevelopment Authority of Pittsburgh (URA), 75, 100; acquisition of property by, 58, 68–69, 71, 108–9; approval of Market Place plan, 123, 126, 149; city government and, 99, 102; Civic Light Opera arena and, 61–62, 83; creation of, 50; funding for redevelopment and, 67, 83, 114, 134–35; in Market Place planning, 117, 127, 177n39; and other organizations, 103, 110, 150; preemptive power of, 72; property owners *vs.*, 71, 135–36, 169n32; St. Peter's Church and, 87–89; use of eminent domain by, 58, 66–67, 69–70
Urban Redevelopment Law (state), 42, 49–50, 68, 70
urban regime theory, 18–19, 22–23, 45
urban renewal. *See* redevelopment
Urban Retail Properties: directed to respond to critics, 130; Pittsburgh's contract with, 112–14, 139. *See also* Market Place at Fifth and Forbes
U.S. Steel, 91
utility companies, 13

Van Buskirk, Arthur, 55, 67

Wabash Terminal, 66
wages: in Depression, 34–35; in Pittsburgh, 32, 105
Warner Centre, *116*
War Production Board, 37
Washington County, 165n1
Weber, Michael P., 49, 65
Weir, Ernest T., 52
Weitlein, Edward, 59–60
Western Division of the Pennsylvania Economy League (PEL), 47–49
Westinghouse Airbrake Company, 67
Westinghouse Electric Corporation, 67
Westmoreland County, 165n1

Wilkie, Carter, 104
Wolk, A. I., 60–61
World War II: Pittsburgh growth during, 37; planning during for postwar urban development, 38–39, 41, 166n22; urban redevelopment after, 1, 4–5 (*see also* Pittsburgh renaissance); U.S. dominance in industry after, 90–91

young professionals, 131, 148, 178n53; importance of, 105–6, 110; loss of, 92–93, 104–5

Ziegler, Arthur, 104, 174n5; concern about Urban Retail plan, 113–14, 117, 121, 129, 175n10; in planning for Market Place alternatives, 124, 139